Key Concepts in
Sport Management

Key Concepts in
Sport Management

TERRI BYERS, TREVOR SLACK AND MILENA M. PARENT

Los Angeles | London | New Delhi
Singapore | Washington DC

Los Angeles | London | New Delhi
Singapore | Washington DC

SAGE Publications Ltd
1 Oliver's Yard
55 City Road
London EC1Y 1SP

SAGE Publications Inc.
2455 Teller Road
Thousand Oaks, California 91320

SAGE Publications India Pvt Ltd
B 1/I 1 Mohan Cooperative Industrial Area
Mathura Road
New Delhi 110 044

SAGE Publications Asia-Pacific Pte Ltd
3 Church Street
#10-04 Samsung Hub
Singapore 049483

Editor: Chris Rojek
Editorial assistant: Martine Jonsrud
Production editor: Katherine Haw
Copyeditor: Audrey Scriven
Marketing manager: Alison Borg
Cover design: Wendy Scott
Typeset by: C&M Digitals (P) Ltd, Chennai, India
Printed by: CPI Group (UK) Ltd, Croydon, CR0 4YY

Library of Congress Control Number: 2012933328

British Library Cataloguing in Publication data

A catalogue record for this book is available from the British Library

ISBN 978-1-4129-2841-0
ISBN 978-1-4129-2842-7 (pbk)

contents

key concepts in
sport management

vi

about the authors

Terri Byers is a Principal Lecturer in Sport Management at Coventry Business School and provides strategic leadership on Applied Research. Terri has published a variety of book chapters and journal articles, presented at conferences in the USA, Scotland, England and other European countries, and possesses over fifteen years' experience consulting for sport organizations and federations. She has been an external reviewer for the European Science Foundation, the *International Journal of Sport Management and Marketing*, *Journal of Sport Management* and the *European Sport Management Quarterly*. She has a particular interest in voluntary sport organizations and the use of Critical Realism in Sport Management research.

Trevor Slack is a Professor in the faculty of Physical Education and Recreation at the University of Alberta, Canada. He has also taught organizational theory in that university's business school to MBA students and has held a position as a Canada Research Chair in sport and leisure management. In addition Trevor has previously held positions at De Montfort University in Bedford, England, where he was head of the School of Physical Education, Recreation and Sport, and also a position at Warwick Business School, England, where he was Visiting Fellow in the Centre for Corporate Strategy and Change. He has received awards for his work on sport organizations from the North American Society of Sport Management, the European Association of Sport Management, the Canadian Administrative Sciences Association, and the Academy of Management.

Milena M. Parent is an Associate Professor in the School of Human Kinetics, University of Ottawa, Canada. She is also an invited professor at the Norwegian School of Sport Sciences, holds a Government of Ontario Early Researcher Award, and is a Research Fellow of the North American Society of Sport Management. Her main research interests fall under organization theory and strategic management as they apply to major sports events.

acknowledgements

We would like to thank the staff at Sage for their assistance and encouragement throughout the writing of this book. In particular our special thanks must go to Jai Seaman and Chris Rojek as well as Martine Jonsrud and Katherine Haw. We would also like to thank colleagues both in academia and in industry for their helpful comments and suggestions about the concepts: our gratitude goes to Ian Blackshaw, Bill Gerrard, Jean Harvey, Samantha Gorse, Eric MacIntosh, Mike Provance, Vassil Girginov, Steffan Goeringer, David Rowe and Alex Thurston. Finally, we must say thank you to the anonymous reviewers who provided very useful feedback on the manuscript. *(Terri, Trevor and Milena)*

My special thanks go to Trevor, who has always encouraged me in my writing and whose experience and contribution to this book have been invaluable. Thanks also to both my co-authors, Milena and Trevor, who brought considerable effort and expertise to the project. I would also like to thank my husband Andrew for his support of my work and career. *(Terri Byers)*

I would like to acknowledge Terri Byers for initiating and coordinating this project and also for asking me to be involved. I would also like to acknowledge Amy Brock and Erano 'Ernie' Lim for their welcome help with typing. And finally, without the help, love and support that I receive from my wife Janet, I would not have been able to do any of the things I have been able to accomplish. *(Trevor Slack)*

My thanks must go to Terri and Trevor for inviting me to contribute to this work. *(Milena M. Parent)*

USING THIS BOOK

This book is a quick and useful reference guide to some of the key concepts in sport management and is particularly useful for those studying the management of sport in order to identify appropriate research topics and to understand how past research is important for developing any current research focus. By examining past and current research we can start to build a rational and clear focus for our research enquiries and avoid unnecessary/repetitive studies which will add little to our field's knowledge base and/or will not contribute to the wider field of management. As the reader will notice, some of the past research to be considered includes sport-industry-specific research and more generic management and organization research rather than just focusing on the sport-specific research that has been conducted.

Many of the concepts included here are from a knowledge base known as Organization Theory (OT) and this book will help the reader to understand the power of OT in identifying appropriate research questions/problems and demonstrate to students especially how OT can be useful in understanding the management of sport. However, other concepts included in the book are broader in nature and refer to a larger discipline of study, such as media/broadcasting, sport law, sport funding and volunteers. These concepts are examined in order to provide the reader with

key concepts in sport management

a comprehensive (though not conclusive) array of concepts which have been and/or are currently being investigated by researchers interested in the management of sport.

Practitioners can also benefit from this reference guide as the concepts have very real and practical implications for those working in the industry and facing problems and challenges in the management of sport. The book identifies concepts which can be useful in meeting those challenges and managing sport successfully. It also identifies a multitude of resources, research articles and theories that are focused on the management of sport which may offer some helpful advice or solutions to the problems faced by sport practitioners.

It may also prove useful in bridging the gap between academia/students and industry. As each concept is discussed, it becomes apparent how students/academics and practitioners have common interests in, for example, sponsorship, conflict, governance and change. For academics/students to perform their research, access to the industry is often required, yet sometimes this is difficult to obtain. For practitioners who may be busy with the day-to-day or strategic aims of their business, but who also require knowledge and information to help them make decisions, student researchers or interns can be invaluable. The concepts presented in this book are relevant both to students/academics and practitioners and are therefore examples of where collaborations between research and industry in the management of sport would produce fruitful results.

For academic staff teaching research methods or supervising dissertations and research projects this text can be used as a starting point for discussions around forming a research question and rationale for a research project. The content of each concept should raise many questions that can be discussed by staff with students. Some challenges for students include the following:

- Taking a concept of your own choosing, find one article published in the last three months which is relevant to the research on that concept. Discuss the content and source of this article and suggest how it fits with what is mentioned in the book.
- Lots of relationships between concepts are discussed within this book – choose two concepts that are of interest and find one journal article that looks at these. Then suggest a possible research question you may pursue.
- Write a research question for a concept of your own choosing and discuss why this question is important. Then consider who may benefit from the answer to your question.
- The literature mentioned in each concept is not fully elaborated upon – choose an article mentioned in this book and access it via your library. Read the article and make a note of how you may build this into a full literature review or theoretical framework for a concept/research question.
- Taking a concept of your own choosing, identify the research methods usually adopted by researchers and discuss how you may utilize different methods and for what reasons.
- Make a more comprehensive chronological list of definitions adopted by researchers for a concept of your own choosing. Discuss how these different definitions would influence how you measure/recognize the concept in a research project.

introduction

The purpose of this book is to highlight what we believe to be the key concepts which relate to the management of sport. Many of the concepts come from a field of study known as 'organization theory' which is increasingly being used in research on the management of sport. Some of the concepts are much broader than those found in organization theory, such as the disciplinary areas of marketing/sponsorship, funding/finance, and sports law. We have set out to produce a book of key concepts which relates to the management of sport and is aimed primarily at students and academics. Undergraduate or postgraduate students can use this introductory text to gain an overview of concepts that have been and are currently being investigated by researchers and to begin to understand some of the research which has already been conducted. Practitioners in the management of sport may also be interested in this text as it identifies key issues in the management of sport that have very practical implications as well as giving a history of research and academic interest.

The concepts we present in this book as 'key' in the field of sport management are, as we have said above, primarily derived from organization theory. We have done this for several reasons. First, there has been a growing amount of research conducted using organization theory to understand the management of sport and so any person interested in studying sport management should be aware of this current knowledge base. Second, the area of organization theory covers a significant range of concepts and theoretical perspectives, which have been influential in developing current knowledge of the management of sport. And finally, it is organization theory which is our area of interest and expertise and thus we feel able to provide the reader with a thorough introduction to the numerous interesting concepts which have emerged in this area of study. However, before we begin exploring the key concepts it will be worthwhile to furnish the reader with some further details about organization theory and its significance both to sport management and conducting research in this field.

ORGANIZATIONAL THEORY

Organizational theory is an area within the field of business/management studies, concerned with the structure, processes, and design of organizations and their subunits. It is relevant to our understanding of sport organizations because we know little about the structural arrangement of these organizations and the influence that that structure may have on various organizational processes. Researchers who work in this field look to identify commonly occurring patterns and regularities in organizations or their subunits. Research, which examines issues related to organizational size, change, effectiveness, environment, structure and design, decision making, technology, power and politics, conflict and culture, encompasses all these organizational theory topics.

Researchers may use a variety of theoretical perspectives, which will include but are not limited to resource dependence, institutional theory, contingency theory, population ecology, and the life-cycle approach. Unfortunately it is beyond the scope of this book to explore all of these different perspectives for the various concepts introduced. For a thorough introduction to these issues in relation to the management of sport organizations, the reader is referred to Slack and Parent (2006).

While researchers who use organizational theory are concerned with issues of theory (that is to say, with pushing back the frontiers of knowledge about organizations), those who study the management of sport should not be concerned that the subject area has no practical application. On the contrary, scholars in this area frequently work with practising managers; the central focus of a large percentage of the research they undertake will be to discover ways to help managers in their jobs. For those who study the management of sport, organizational theory can provide a better understanding of how sports organizations are structured and designed, how they operate, and why some are effective and efficient while others are not.

Understanding sport organizations from an organization theory perspective can help those who study sport to analyze the problems they face and in turn prepare them to respond with appropriate solutions. Much of the work that is undertaken about the management of sport is not organizational theory based, rather it is more concerned with the actions of individuals within the organization (e.g., studies covering motivation, job satisfaction, and organizational commitment), which is an organizational behaviour approach. Researchers should not think that these two approaches are contradictory: they are instead complementary. Students who are interested in organizational theory approaches should investigate work by Slack and colleagues who have examined a wide variety of important issues in the management of sport, including change, decision making and strategy. For a contemporary view of the history of studying organizations, the reader is referred to March (2007), and for some thoughts on the future of organizational theory, see Czarniawska (2007).

Organization theory and behaviour offer key insights into the management of sport from a structural and interpersonal perspective. Yet other broader areas of research have also contributed to our understanding of the management of sport, such as economics, operations, law, ethics and marketing. So as to provide the reader with a sufficiently focused view of research on the management of sport and still be inclusive of the growing diversity of this field, we shall include concepts from these wider knowledge bases.

STRUCTURE OF THE BOOK

The concepts presented in this book are those that appear mainly in the journals which are relevant to the management of sport organizations, including sport-specific (such as the *Journal of Sport Management* and the *European Sport Management Quarterly*) and general management/business/economics periodicals (such as *Organization Studies* and *Administrative Science Quarterly*). While some of the concepts covered have received extensive attention from the research community, it is beyond the scope of this text to provide comprehensive and critical literature reviews for all the concepts that are of relevance to the management of sport. Instead we define each concept before going on to introduce some of the research which has been conducted, and where appropriate, we suggest some criticisms of the work and where future research may focus. By doing this we demonstrate how 'gaps' in the literature can indicate where a lack of knowledge exists. For each concept, a basic definition is provided within a text box and the general business and management literature is usually relayed before demonstrating how the concept has been explored by sport management scholars. In some instances, where appropriate (e.g., sport sponsorship) and owing to the specific nature of the concept in relation to sport, we address only literature from the management of sport.

We include 'mainstream' literature and sport-specific literature where possible to demonstrate to the reader that when conducting research into the management of sport it is necessary to recognize literature in the general field of management and organizations as well, rather than make assumptions that sport organizations are dissimilar to other organizations. This is particularly important for those researchers thinking of publishing their work, as it encourages them to think about the relevance of their research to both the management of sport and the management of organizations more generally, thereby increasing the audience and sources of publication for their research. For broader concepts, outside of the organization theory field, we illustrate some of the key concepts which have been identified in the literature and which are contemporary to the practising sport manager. As indicated above, owing to the very broad nature of some concepts we are restricted to identifying a few relevant concepts but would not suggest that we have by any means provided an exhaustive account of all the research conducted.

All of the concepts in this book are interrelated and in order to understand one concept it will often be necessary to refer to several others as well: as a result we highlight these interrelationships by placing concepts that appear elsewhere in the book in **bold** and then reiterate these at the end of each concept. Also, at the end of each entry the reader will find a short list of suggested reading. These may cover key references used in the preceding discussion of the concept, or be in addition to those references already provided. However, we would encourage the reader to explore the full list of references for each concept provided at the end of each entry and to seek additional reading by using the section on 'Keeping Up To Date' where we provide a short discussion of how the reader may keep abreast of current research on the management of sport by identifying appropriate journals, trade magazines and other publications where work and practice are reported. This is done in order to acknowledge the constantly changing nature and development of research on the management of sport, as well as to encourage students or academics to use the contents of this book as a starting point and the recommended publications as sources which will provide access to the most current and up-to-date research being conducted on the concepts presented. Finally, each reference list is organized in order to enable the reader to have a clear idea of those readings that are particularly relevant to every concept in the book.

A NOTE ABOUT CONTENT

It is important for the reader to recognize that the content of this book does not represent 'literature reviews' for each concept, as this is beyond the scope of the *Key Concept Series*. We have provided an indication of some of the research which has been done on each concept and would acknowledge that for those interested in a particular concept, some further reading and searching for literature would be required in order to develop a fuller understanding and begin more systematic critiques of the themes, theories and perspectives found within this literature. For illustrative purposes, we provide some criticisms of the current research and where appropriate make suggestions for how research may be advanced with future studies. We have therefore provided an introduction to the research on each concept rather than an exhaustive or systematic critical review of each of these.

REFERENCES

Czarniawska, B. (2007) Has organization theory a tomorrow? *Organization Studies*, 28(1): 27–29.

March, J.G. (2007) The study of organizations and organizing since 1945. *Organization Studies*, 28(1): 9–19.

Slack, T. and Parent, M.M. (2006) *Understanding Sport Organizations*. Leeds: Human Kinetics Europe.

introduction

> *Change is the process of becoming different and can refer to people, structures, technologies or organizational processes. Change can be planned and deliberate or reactive in response to some environmental pressure.*

Change is one of the most 'unchanging' aspects of all organizations. In spite of its frequency and importance, change is paradoxical. On the one hand, managers prefer organizations that are stable, i.e., that do not change a lot, but on the other hand, managers must respond to changes that affect their organization. Change may occur in a number of areas. For instance, it can take place in the people who work for the organization, in the technology it uses, in the products or services it offers, or in its structure and systems. The dynamic nature of change means that when a change occurs in one area (**structures**/systems, people, **technology** or products/ services), the remaining areas are also affected and likely to experience or require some change. The figure below is adapted from Slack and Parent (2006) and illustrates the dynamic and interrelated components of change in organizations. This model is limited in its explanation of change in that it identifies the components but also presents the change process as occurring within organizations and does not mention the impact of the external environment on internal processes, people, technology or systems. The nature of the change process is not indicated by the model and so there is no indication if change is thought to be linear, chaotic or otherwise. The model also assumes change to be the same regardless of **context**.

For a number of years change was seen as a logical series of steps where managers identified a problem and then proposed a solution: this solution would involve identifying the steps that needed to be taken to alleviate the problem. In other

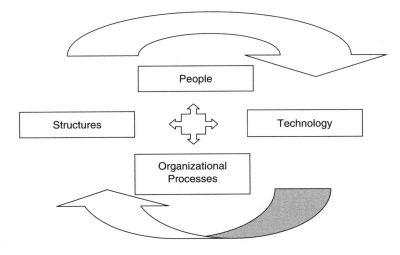

Figure 1 The Dynamics of Change Components

words, change was essentially seen as a linear, sequential process. Much emphasis was placed on the role of individuals acting as change 'agents'. However, this is now considered a 'rational' view of change and does not take into consideration different organizational **contexts** or different types of change.

In the past fifty years we have seen considerable movement in the political and economic situation of many countries. Consequently, new ways of looking at change have emerged. One of the approaches used in the general management literature is termed the contextualist approach. This emanates from the work of Andrew Pettigrew (1985) and his staff at the Centre for Corporate Strategy and Change at the University of Warwick Business School. Pettigrew's contextualist approach is best exemplified in his book about Imperial Chemical Industries, *The Awakening Giant*. Pettigrew is critical of much of the existing work on change. He suggests that it is ahistorical, aprocessual, and acontextual. Much of it, he suggests, views change as being a single event. To counteract his concerns, Pettigrew calls for a multilevel analysis and suggests that we should study changes over the period of the change process. He suggests three areas of change that we should look at, and indicates these areas as the corners of a triangle which he calls one context that he says consists of both an inner and outer context. He also suggests we need to look at the content and processes of change and goes on to look at the interaction among these three areas.

The contextualist approach uses detailed case studies of the change process in order to study change. Girginov and Sandanski (2008) employed the contextualist approach in his study of change in three Bulgarian national sport organizations. The study examined change in conceptual orientation, structures, resources, capabilities and outcomes over a twenty-five-year period from 1980 to 2004. The author suggested that the contextualist approach was useful in that it enabled an in-depth appreciation of the historical, contextual and processual factors that contributed to the changes observed as well as how these influenced the management of the sport organizations.

In contrast to this approach is the one termed 'population ecology', which has its roots in biology and particularly the idea of the survival of the fittest. It is mathematically underpinned and as the name suggests is concerned with the populations of organizations and how these will change to meet the demands placed on them. It also looks at a long change period rather than discrete change events.

Population ecologists see change as a number of phases. In the first phase of the process there is variation in the population of organizations (e.g., variation in **structure**, size, **effectiveness**, etc.). This occurs because managers will have to respond to the various contingency factors that their organization faces (e.g., competition, consumer **demand**, economic conditions, etc.). A number of these organizations will respond more appropriately to these factors. As such, those that change and respond to the contingency factors will survive while those that do not do so will, to use the language of population ecology, be selected out – that is to say, they will fail. This response to the various contingency factors is how organizations change in the population ecology approach.

Cunningham (2002) used the population ecology approach combined with institutional theory, strategic choice and resource dependence theories to examine radical organizational change in physical education and sport programmes. Resource dependence has been a popular theory among scholars, the fundamentals of which can be found in Pfeffer and Salancik's (1978) book *The External Control of*

Organizations. In resource dependence theory, the argument is made that organizations are dependent on their environment for the resources they need to operate. Resource dependence theory is not just about the dependency of organizations on their environment but also about the actions that are engaged in by organization members to ensure the continual flow of vital resources which are needed for that organization's operations. Because the environment of an organization will change, managers will have to engage in activities that will ensure this continued flow of resources. The activities that a manager may engage in are numerous, but the most important are changes in **strategy** such as merges, diversification and joint ventures.

Armstrong-Doherty (1995) used the resource dependency approach to look at the funding of Canadian intercollegiate athletics. Her work focused on the way athletic departments obtained funds. It does not however look at the techniques used by athletic departments to obtain funding. Another approach to understand organizational change is termed 'the life cycle'. As with population ecology, the life-cycle approach to understanding organizational change uses biology as its basis. In contrast to the idea of population ecology this approach looks at single organizations or small groups of organizations. It has been criticized for being too linear and deterministic. Essentially the life-cycle approach sees organizations as going through stages just as humans or animals do. These stages are referred to by various names but may include birth, maturity and death.

The life-cycle approach was developed by John Kimberly (1980) and can help to understand change. It sees this as developing from the birth of an organization, through growth, to maturity and possibly even death. Of course, organizations do not necessarily follow this life cycle in the same manner and some will be born, will grow and mature, and then through some innovation or change, will begin another period of growth. Likewise, death need not be a stage in every organization's life cycle. Kimberly (1987) referred to this method of understanding organizational change as the biographical approach. There are few studies that have substantially applied the life-cycle approach to sport organizations in order to understand the management of change. There are, however, numerous writings on organizations (e.g., Prouty's (1988) work on the US Cycling Federation, and Wolfe's (1989) work on the Dallas Cowboys) which if combined with either the life cycle or contextualist theoretical approaches could help us understand the change process using these theories.

Another approach that is currently popular is termed 'institutional theory'. In this, organizations will change because they are trying to imitate other successful organizations. Because of its emphasis on societal expectations, in the institutional approach the belief is that organizations should be studied from a sociological perspective. It has become the dominant perspective to study both sport organizations (cf. Berrett and Slack, 1999; Southall et al., 2008; Steen-Johnsen, 2008) and other types of organizations (cf. Greenwood et al., 2008; Washington and Ventresca, 2004).

The patterning of organizational elements is another approach which is used in the general management literature and it is one of the more contemporary views on organizational change. It is also the approach that has been utilized to undertake the most advanced work on sport organizations. Several studies have shown that organizations show patterns in the elements by which they are constituted. This patterning is variously referred to as archetypes, design archetypes, configurations, or *gestalts*. With the exception of archetypes this patterning looks only at the structural elements of organizations. Archetypes also look at the values and beliefs that under-pin the structure. The reader should note that there have been criticisms of arche-type theory (Kirkpatrick and Ackroyd, 2003) and its application in certain organizational **contexts** such as public service organizations. Kirkpatrick and Ackroyd (2003) provided a detailed analysis of the problematic elements of arche-type theory and offered an alternative approach which attempted to resolve the deficiencies in the theory that they had identified.

Greenwood and Hinings (1993) have noted that developments in organizational theory over the past several years have emphasized the importance of considering **structure** (i.e., the system of roles and responsibilities) and values (i.e., statements about what kinds of behaviours or end-states are preferable to others) in relationship to each other in order to understand organizational change. An organizational archetype in this sense is a particular composition of ideas, beliefs, and values connected with structural and systemic attributes. Change occurs because there is a lack of consistency between structures and values. They are, in Hinings and Greenwood's (1988) view, 'schizoid'.

Archetypes are institutionally specific. Kikulis et al. (1989), using a group of Canadian national sport organizations, identified three kinds of organization that they termed a 'kitchen table', an 'executive office' and a 'boardroom' design. The kitchen table design is relatively unstructured, with a low hierarchy of author-ity and attendant values that favour a volunteer-controlled organization where membership preferences and quality service are seen to produce an effective organization. In the boardroom design there is more structuring, with an emphasis still remaining on volunteers who are assisted by professionals. In the executive office design there is a structured organization where decisions are made by pro-fessionals who operate at the mid-levels of the organization. These professionals are assisted by volunteers; for more of an explanation of the three designs see the original Kikulis et al. (1989) article or the work by Slack and Parent (2006).

Hinings et al. (1996), in studying national sport organizations, found that those in an archetypical status showed consensus in the organization's values. They also found that when organizations were in an archetype there was consensus as regards the val-ues of the elite and when organizations were outside an archetype there was no value consensus. Amis et al. (2004), with the same sample of Canadian national sport organizations, used the concept of archetypes. They found that contrary to popular belief wide-scale rapid change was not a determining factor in whether or not an organization reached archetypal status. They also found that an early change in specific high impact systems was important if organizations were to achieve an archetypal change. They suggested that change was not necessarily linear in nature. The notion of archetypes is important for understanding organizational change and the reader can access Greenwood and Hinings (1988) work for more information on this concept.

We may well ask 'Why do organizations change?' The answer to this question will depend upon the approach from which changed is viewed. The table below summarizes the approaches discussed previously and briefly highlights their view of organizational change.

From the information it gives, it is apparent that the reason why a sport organi-zation (or any organization) will change may come about because of shifts in that

Table 1 Approaches to Studying Organizational Change

Contextualist	Change that occurs over an extended period of time should not be seen as a single event; the content, context and process of change need to be studied to fully understand the concept.
Population Ecology	Change occurs within organizations as a result of pressures in the external environment and it is the impact of this environment on whole groups of organizations that should be studied in order to understand how change occurs.
Resource Dependence	Organizations are wholly dependent upon resources in their external environment, and change occurs in response to the availability of resources. The steps the organization takes in order to secure the necessary resources are an important factor in how the organization may change.
Life Cycle	Change is akin to the biological process of life in that organizations are born, develop, and decline, and finally cease to exist.
Institutional Theory	Organizations change according to pressures from their institutional environment which indicates the appropriate structures and systems to adopt for their successful and legitimate operation.
Archetype Theory	Change occurs within archetypal forms and is specific to institutional environments. Archetypes represent consistency in values and change from one archetype to another indicates a significant shift in values.

organization's external environment, or alternatively this may arise from within the organization itself (from what are known as change agents). Those who study organizations from the population ecology or institutional perspective stress the role of the external environment in the change process. Those who study organizational change from the resource dependence or contextualist approaches stress the role of internal factors and their interaction with external factors in the change process. **Sport organizations**, like other organizations, do not like to change. Change may be resisted because the culture of the organization may work against the shifts that are proposed. Organizations do not change because they may have sunk costs into the way they currently operate. Members of organizations will not want to change if they perceive that change may result in them having less power. Alternatively those who perceive that change will bring them more **power** will favour the change.

As a result of power relations, managing change often involves managing **conflict** between individuals or groups. However, managing change and managing conflict have primarily been treated separately by researchers and so we shall refrain from examining conflict here and include it as a separate concept to be examined later.

To understand change more fully the reader may refer to the concepts of **structure**, **technology**, **context**, **power**, **sport organizations**, **conflict** and **strategy** that can be found elsewhere in this book.

FURTHER READING

For some further reading on this concept, we would recommend the following:

Burke, W.W., Lake, D.G. and Paine, J.W. (eds) (2009) *Organization Change: A Comprehensive Reader*. San Francisco, CA: Wiley.

change

5

Girginov, V. and Sandanski, I. (2008) Understanding the changing nature of sports organisations in transforming societies. *Sport Management Review*, 11(1): 21–50.

Steen-Johnsen, K. and Hanstad, D.V. (2008) Change and power in complex democratic organizations: the case of Norwegian elite sports. *European Sport Management Quarterly*, 8(2): 123–143.

Washington, M. and Patterson, K.D.W. (2011) Hostile takeover or joint venture? Connections between institutional theory and sport management research. *Sport Management Review*, 14(1): 1–12.

BIBLIOGRAPHY

Amis, J., Slack, T. and Hinings, C.R. (2004) The pace, sequence and linearity of radical change. *Academy of Management Journal*, 47: 15–39.

Armstrong-Doherty, A. (1995) The structure of funding in Canadian interuniversity athletics. *Journal of Sport Management*, 9: 59–69.

Berrett, T. and Slack, T. (1999) An analysis of the influence of competitive and institutional pressure on corporate sponsorship decisions. *Journal of Sport Management*, 13: 114–138.

Cunningham, G. (2002) Removing the blinders: toward an integrative model of organizational change in sport and physical activity. *Quest*, 54: 276–291.

Girginov, V. And Sandanski, I. (2008) Understanding the changing nature of sports organisations in transforming societies. *Sport Management Review*, 11(1): 21–50.

Greenwood, R. and Hinings, C.R. (1988) Organizational design types, tracks, and the dynamics of strategic change. *Organization Sudies*, 9: 293–316

Greenwood, R. and Hinings, C.R. (1993) Understanding strategic change: the contribution of archetypes. *Academy of Management Journal*, 36: 1052–1081.

Greenwood, R., Oliver, C., Sahlin, K. and Suddaby, R. (eds) (2008) *The SAGE Handbook of Organizational Institutionalism*. London: Sage.

Hinings, C.R. and Greenwood, R. (1988) *The Dynamics of Strategic Change*. Oxford: Basil Blackwell.

Hinings, C.R., Thibault, L., Slack, T. and Kikulis, L.M. (1996) Values and organization structure. *Human Relations*, 49: 129–50.

Kikulis, L., Slack, T. and Hinings, C.R. (1989) A structural taxonomy of amateur sport organizations. *Journal of Sport Management*, 3(2): 129–150.

Kimberly, J.R. (1980) The life cycle analogy and the study of organizations: introduction. In J.R. Kimberly and R.H. Miles (eds), *The Organizational Life Cycle*. San Francisco, CA: Jossey-Bass.

Kimberly, J.R. (1987) The study of organizations: toward a biographical perspective. In J.W. Lorsch (ed.), *Handbook of Organizational Behavior*. Englewood Cliffs, NJ: Prentice Hall.

Kirkpatrick, I. and Ackroyd, S. (2003) Archetype theory and the changing professional organization: a critique and alternative. *Organization*, 10(4): 731–750.

Pettigrew, A.M. (1985) *The Awakening Giant*. Oxford: Basil Blackwell.

Pfeffer, J. and Salancik, G. (1978) *The External Control of Organizations: A Resource-Dependence Perspective*. New York: Harper and Row.

Prouty, D.F. (1988) *In Spite of Us: My Education in the Big and Little Games of Amateur and Olympic Sports in the U.S. Velo-news Corp*. Brattleboro, VT: Vitesse Press.

Slack, T. and Parent, M. (2006) *Understanding Sport Organizations* (2nd edn). Champaign, IL: Human Kinetics.

Southall, R.M., Nagel, M.S., Amis, J. and Southall, C. (2008) A method to march madness? Institutional logics and the 2006 National Collegiate Athletic Association Division I men's basketball tournament. *Journal of Sport Management*, 22: 677–700.

Steen-Johnsen, K. (2008) Network and organization of identity: the case of Norwegian snowboarding. *European Sport Management Quarterly*, 8: 337–358.

Washington, M. and Ventresca, M.J. (2004) How organizations change: the role of institutional support mechanisms in the incorporation of higher education visibility strategies, 1874–1995. *Organization Science*, 15: 82–97.

Weed, M. (2005) Research synthesis in sport management: dealing with 'chaos in the brickyard'. *European Sport Management Quarterly*, 5(1): 77–90.

Wolfe, J. (1989) *The Murchisons: The Rise and Fall of a Texas Dynasty*. New York: St. Martin's Press.

Commercialization

> *Commercialization is the process used to involve something such as a product or service in commerce (the exchange of something for economic value).*

Commercialization generally describes the process whereby a product or service is evaluated in terms of its potential to secure some economic value from a defined target market. Many examples of research that investigates the process of commercialization in various contexts can be found. One area of research that has received increased attention recently is the commercialization of new technologies (Price et al., 2008). Thistoll and Pauleen (2010) explored the role of social **networks** and relationship management in commercializing high-technology innovations internationally. Specifically they focused on how individuals establish and manage network relationships. Their findings suggested that a variety of **stakeholders** established and managed relationships in different ways; they emphasized that the practical implications of their research suggested caution to managers and highlighted the need to be aware of different stakeholders' interpretations of risks and benefits. This is an interesting notion that the process of commercialization (including managing networks) may not be a standard generic one, but a process that is dependent upon various **contextual** factors.

There is also some research that examines **ethical** issues associated with the process of commercialization. Haddow and colleagues (2007) highlighted the ethical concerns held by members of the public over commercializing genetics-based research and the creation of databases related to such information. They presented a sociologically informed model that questioned the exclusivity of commercial interests in favour of a more pragmatic solution that would take into account public concerns. Other ethical concerns with commercialization have been examined in relation to marketing practices (Martin and Smith, 2008), highlighting how marketers and public policy makers should manage the ethical implications associated with this form of marketing.

As sport has become more visible and popular so has it become more commercialized. Sport clothing for example has become fashionable (see Key Note, 2009, 2010). With increased commercialization large corporations now manufacture several lines of sport clothing and will put their name or logo on the items they produce. Athletic footwear is also a rapidly expanding industry (cf. Sage, 2004; Strasser and Becklund, 1991) with athletic shoes by firms such as Nike, Reebok and Adidas appearing to be *de rigueur* in the wardrobe of any teenager. And as it has become more popular and visible, sport, like other social phenomena, has been subject to the pressures of **globalization**. In an attempt to secure more viewers, sponsors and advertisers teams are no longer subject to recruiting their athletes from the local area or a particular nation-state. Teams which play sports such as soccer and basketball will recruit their athletes from all over the world. Traditionally soccer has looked to Western Europe and basketball has looked to the United States for its athletes. Today, however, athletes come from all over the world to participate in particular sports as this increases the international commercial potential of sporting activity. Slack and Amis (2004) noted that Pau Gasol, a Spaniard playing for the Memphis Grizzlies, increased the amount of NBA basketball that was shown on Spanish TV (and no doubt the amount of money that advertisers spent on basketball in Spain).

Public–private partnerships are frequently seen in the delivery of sport services. Local governments involved in the delivery of sport services have traditionally partnered with other public sector agencies and non-profit organizations in order to provide sport services as an aspect of social welfare and where the market has failed. As Thibault et al. (2004) note, 'More recently, however, sport and leisure departments have developed partnerships and **strategic alliances** with organizations in the commercial sector as a means of providing programmes, facilities, equipment and/or resources.' Quoting Crompton (1989) they argue that this development is a strategic shift involving the adoption of an entrepreneurial mindset that has led to increased interest in cooperating with commercial enterprises. One factor which has had considerable influence on the commercialization process is the relationship of sport to television. Berrett and Slack (2001) found that those national sport organizations which appeared on television frequently were most likely to be the beneficiaries of commercial support. Rupert Murdoch, for example, used the commercial potential of sport to promote his television stations (see Robertson, 2004). Whereas sport was previously used to 'fill space' in broadcasters' schedules, channels now focus exclusively on sport and some of these are dedicated to specific sports.

Gerrard (2004) identified three stages in the relationship between sport and television on the road to commercialization (see the figure below). The first stage he termed 'regulated professionalism', which covers the period from the mid-nineteenth century to the 1950s when television emerged as a mass medium. Here, due to increases in income and available leisure time, sport became available to the masses and was no longer the sole domain of an elite class. It also became a commodity and was no longer played on village greens but in enclosed areas where spectators had to pay to watch. Thus in this respect sport became a business which in turn created a gap between those who owned the teams and the players: this represented the first step in the commercialization process.

Regulated Professionalism	Deregulated Professionalism	Technological Change
Mid-19th century to 1950s	1950s-	1990s-
Sport available to the masses, spectators paid to watch	Growth of television coverage, edited highlights	Digital TV, satellite, internet, mobile phone delivery of sport product

Figure 2 Stages of Commercialization: Sport

The second stage is referred to as 'deregulated professionalism'. This began in the 1950s and coincided with the growth of television. Spectators no longer had to travel to games and were instead able to watch them and edited highlights on TV. Professional sport was no longer a highly regulated commodity but a free market commodity in which players were not subjected to restrictions on the amount they could earn or the money they were able to obtain from image rights. Those people who played sport for a living started to realize the value of their skills. As a result the gap between owners and players became wider. Free agency, arbitration, the abolition of the maximum wage, and the reformation of the 'retain and transfer' policy all led to professional athletes demanding higher salaries. This had the effect of favouring the bigger teams and therefore **competitive balance** was hindered. This era of deregulated professionalism represented the second step in the commercialization process.

The third stage of the process was characterized by technological changes in the telecommunications and **media** industries. Digital TV, satellite broadcasting, the internet, and mobile phones are all examples of the way sport is now delivered. These new forms of media have meant that sport teams on both sides of the Atlantic are seen as profit-making vehicles rather than entities that win games. As Gerrard (2004: 255) notes, 'commercial sports teams are profit-led businesses seeking to increase shareholder value'. Gerrard (2004) wrote that in the future, sport teams will be owned by media groups. Quoting a 2000 survey, Gerrard noted that 29 sport teams in the USA were owned by media groups and that in Britain ten media groups had stakes in Premiership soccer teams and one Scottish Premiership team. Media groups also had interests in soccer teams in France, Italy, Greece and Switzerland. It is argued that media groups owning professional sport teams is an example of vertical integration. Gerrard suggested two reasons for this: the strategic importance of media groups owning sport broadcasting rights and extreme uncertainty. Specifically, he stated that 'sports broadcasting rights are absolutely vital to the commercial development of new media distribution networks'. Without ownership of major sports events, media groups are unable to attract new viewers and consequently advertisers to endorse their products. By owning teams, media groups are able to ensure that they can access broadcasting rights as they control their own programming and are thus able to televise the games which their teams play: 'Uncertainty comes from the internal dynamic generated by the conflict over income shares between teams, players and governing authorities but also the environmental uncertainty created by the rapid rate of technological change, particularly the convergence of television and the Internet' (Gerrard, 2004).

In addition to those organizations mentioned above, the process of commercialization has affected a number of other **sport organizations**. Staurowsky (2004) showed how American college sport had become more commercialized and how students' educational goals were being subverted towards the commercial activities of their college or university. Kikulis et al. (1995) also explained how amateur sport organizations had become more commercialized, and specifically more professional and bureaucratic, as it was held that this organizational design was more likely to win medals at major competitions. They suggested that such commercialized organizations showed a greater specialization of tasks, that there was more standardization of procedures, and that decisions were more likely to be made by professional staff and not the volunteers who provided the backbone for such organizations.

Research focusing on the commercialization of sport has largely centred on how it has been commercialized through the development of sport as a business, media technologies and increasing consumer demand. This has served to increase the focus on educating sport managers to commercialize sport products and services, but future research should perhaps also look more critically at the negative implications of the commercialization process on sport such as **corruption**, decreasing voluntarism, the increased use of performance-enhancing drugs, and changes in the amateur values associated with sport participation.

To understand commercialization more fully, the reader may refer to the concepts of **networks**, **stakeholders**, **context**, **ethics**, **strategic alliances**, **media**, **competitive balance**, **globalization** and **sport organizations** that can be found elsewhere in the book.

FURTHER READING

For some further reading on this concept, we would recommend the following:

Enjolras, B. (2002) Does the commercialization of voluntary organizations 'crowd out' voluntary work? *Annals Of Public And Cooperative Economics*, 73 (3): 375–398.
O'Brien, D. and Slack, T. (2004) The emergence of a professional logic in English rugby union: the role of isomorphic and diffusion processes. *Journal of Sport Management*, 18(7): 13–39.
Slack, T. (ed.) (2004) *The Commercialization of Sport*. Abingdon: Routledge.

BIBLIOGRAPHY

Berrett, T. and Slack, T. (2001) A framework for the analysis of strategic approaches employed by non-profit sport organizations in seeking corporate sponsorship. *Sport Management Review*, 4: 21–45.
Crompton, J.L. (1989) A taxonomy of public-commercial joint ventures. *Loisir et société* [*Society and Leisure*], 12: 107–121.
Gerrard, W. (2004) Media ownership of teams: the latest stage in the commercialization of team sports: 247–266. In T. Slack (ed.), *The Commercialization of Sport*. Abingdon: Routledge.
Haddow, G., Laurie, G., Cunningham-Burley, S. and Hunter, K.G. (2007) Tackling community concerns about commercialisation and genetic research: a modest interdisciplinary proposal. *Social Science and Medicine*, 64(2): 272–282.
Key Note (2009) *Sports Clothing and Footwear 2009*. Teddington: Key Note.
Key Note (2010) *Sports Market*. Teddington: Key Note.
Kikulis, L., Slack, T. and Hinings, C.R. (1995) Sector-specific patterns of organizational design change. *Journal of Management Studies*, 32: 67–100.
Martin, K.D. and Smith, N.C. (2008) Commercializing social interaction: the ethics of stealth marketing. *Journal of Public Policy and Marketing*, 27(1): 45–56.
Price, C., Huston, R. and Meyers, A.D. (2008) A new approach to improve technology commercialization in university medical schools. *Journal of Commercial Biotechnology*, 14(2): 96–102.
Robertson, C. (2004) A sporting gesture? BSkyB, Manchester United, global media and television. *New Media*, 5(4): 4291–4314.

Sage, G. (2004) The sporting goods industry: from struggling entrepreneurs to national businesses to transnational corporations: 29–52. In T. Slack (ed.), *The Commercialization of Sport*. Abingdon: Routledge.

Slack, T. and Amis, J. (2004) Money for nothing and your cheques for free? A critical perspective on sport sponsorship: 269–286. In T. Slack (ed.), *The Commercialization of Sport*. Abingdon: Routledge.

Staurowsky, E. (2004) Piercing the veil of amateurism? Commercialization, corruption and US college sports: 143–163. In T. Slack (ed.), *The Commercialization of Sport*. Abingdon: Routledge.

Strasser, J.B. and Becklund, L. (1991) *The Unauthorized Story of Nike and the Men Who Played There*. Orlando, FL: Harcourt Brace Jovanovich.

Thibault, L., Kikulis, L. and Frisby, W. (2004) Partnerships between local government sport and leisure departments and the commercial sector: changes, complexities and consequences: 119–140. In T. Slack (ed.), *The Commercialization of Sport*. Abingdon: Routledge.

Thistoll, T. and Pauleen, D. (2010) Commercializing innovation internationally: a case study of social network and relationship management. *Journal of International Entrepreneurship*, 8(1): 36–54

Competitive Balance

> *Competitive balance occurs when there is equality in playing talent among individual opponents or teams in a sporting contest, ensuring that the match has a high degree of uncertainty with regard to the probable outcome of the competition.*

The term 'competitive balance' (CB) can be traced back to Rottenburg (1956) who suggested that this was necessary in a sporting contest to encourage the uncertainty of the outcome and thereby ensure that consumers would be willing to pay for tickets to a game or event. The reader may refer to Fort and Quirk (1995) for a review of the early theoretical development of the concept, including the work of Rottenburg (1956) and El-Hodiri and Quirk (1971, 1974). There are many more recent theoretical discussions within the literature on competitive balance including measuring the concept, its relationship to **demand** and its relationship to different league structures (North American versus European primarily). Fort and Maxcy (2003) suggested that the empirical literature on CB was made up of two parts: an analysis of competitive balance (ACB) itself, focusing on change in competitive balance over time as a result of change in the business practices and models of professional sport; and the relationship of CB to fan behaviour.

We shall now focus on exploring some of these issues within competitive balance in sport as mentioned above and comment on some of the most recent work being conducted in this field. The reader will see that there is still significant scope for research on competitive balance in a variety of sports in international contexts. The practical implications of understanding competitive balance for sport managers are also apparent when looking at how CB can affect the **effectiveness** and profitability of leagues and individual athletes. However, this is where the methodological debate continues and indicates that depending on how competitive balance is measured the evidence will vary as to whether or not it actually affects profitability.

Competitive balance is thought to be higher in North American leagues (e.g., the National Football League) as compared to some European sport leagues (e.g., Premier League Football). This is mainly due to the 'closed' **structure** (including rules and policies) of North American leagues, there being a greater emphasis on profit maximization and therefore the implementation of tools to ensure some balance in the strength of teams. These tools include measures such as salary caps, revenue sharing, and the draft system to recruit players to teams each year. By contrast, European sport league structures will often adopt a promotion and relegation system which emphasizes performance rather than profitability. Cain and Haddock (2005) provided an insightful and interesting discussion of how these systems developed and various implications for the development and management of sport within them. Understanding the different structures is important for developing a further understanding of how competitive balance operates. Giocoli (2007) suggested that rather than league structures being responsible for differences in competitive balance, teams within a league can have a variety of organizational goals and it is these different goals that can account for the differences in competitive balance. This concept argues that organizational objectives within a league can vary and it is this 'mixed case' that is significant to understanding competitive balance. Therefore, some teams within a league may have profit maximization as their key organizational goal whereas others may be focused on win maximization. Giocoli (2007: 246) illustrated this example using a discussion of the Italian football league, the *Serie A*, where 'in the face of the dramatic financial imbalances caused to teams by the rising cost of players' talent, a few clubs seem to have shifted to a profit-oriented pattern of behavior'.

Meanwhile Groot (2008) discussed the different dimensions of CB (see the table below), pointing out that there was more than one type of CB to be considered by researchers and practitioners. These included match uncertainty, seasonal uncertainty, and championship uncertainty, and for the appropriate league structure he added relegation uncertainty and European football uncertainty.

Table 2 Dimensions of Competitive Balance

Dimension of CB	Definition
Match	The uncertainty associated with a particular game. The higher the uncertainty, the greater the competitive balance.
Seasonal	The degree of uncertainty within a league in a given season.
Championship	The degree of uncertainty in becoming champions.
Relegation	The uncertainty associated with whether or not a team will be relegated at the end of a season.
European football	The uncertainty associated with which teams will qualify for the different European Cup competitions (the UEFA Cup and Champions League).

Researchers have long argued, and continue to debate, about how to measure competitive balance accurately. The literature surrounding this is immense and different debates will take place depending on the type of competitive balance that is being considered. Mizak et al. (2005) provided a review and critique of using standard deviations, Gini coefficients and the index of dissimilarity to assess CB in sport leagues. They suggested that each of the techniques was influenced by the introduction of more teams, unbalanced scheduling, and inter-league play. Utt and Fort (2002) concentrated on the problems with measuring competitive balance using Gini coefficients for within season competitions. The authors examined competitive balance in Major League Baseball and suggested that traditional methods of winning-percentage standard deviations provided a more accurate analysis of within–season CB. Owen and colleagues (2007) discussed measuring CB in professional team sports using the Herfindahl-Hirschman Index.

More recent research on competitive balance has focused on the impact of foreign players (Flores et al., 2010); the relationship between competitive balance and fan interest (Pivovarnik et al., 2008); optimal competitive balance (Fort and Quirk, 2010); and policy implications for competitive balance such as the effects of pool revenue sharing (Chang and Sanders, 2009). Some research on competitive balance has assumed that it is desirable while other research has been more critical of this assumption and has questioned whether CB is a requirement for team success. This is an interesting question to consider when examining the context of competitive balance in North American versus European sport models. The European sport model does not rely on competitive balance whereas the North American model does seem to take the concept more seriously.

An example of low competitive balance and high team (financial and fan) success can be found in the English Premier League. The majority of the research on competitive balance however assumes the former and thus is focused on identifying those factors which will have a significant effect and will reduce or increase balance and as a result will impact upon the team performance or success. Researchers are also interested in how CB serves to affect aspects of a successful sport organization such as attendance (see for example Meehan et al., 2007).

The reader may also be interested to know that the issue of competitive balance has been investigated across a wide variety of sports including baseball (Buraimo and Simmons, 2008), basketball (Morse et al., 2008), European football (Vrooman, 2007), American football (Lee, 2010), tennis (Del Corral, 2009), and rugby league and rugby union (Howarth and Robinson, 2008). As has already been mentioned, much of this work focuses on examining the evidence for factors affecting competitive balance in sport. This has resulted in a large and complex literature that is constantly evolving with the addition of new evidence that challenges the existing assumptions about how competitive balance affects the management of sport.

As various sports will have different league structures, financial structures, rules and historical developments, examining these sports has proven useful in developing our understanding of competitive balance. These studies have highlighted how a number of factors have had an impact on competitive balance in a particular sport, thereby demonstrating how managing sport can be unique to understanding the historical and structural complexities inherent in the game. Lee (2010: 77) has presented evidence to suggest that, contrary to previous work that indicated structural changes do not affect competitive balance, the effects of the 1993 collective bargaining agreement in the National Football League (NFL) 'included several innovations that might be expected to affect competitive balance'. Buraimo and Simmons (2008) challenged a conventional hypothesis concerning uncertainty of outcome (that uncertainty of outcome is not related to gate attendance) by examining attendances at Major League Baseball games. Perhaps unique to this sport, they suggested that fans at these games preferred to see their home team play an inferior team and win, rather than see a game that is predicted to be closer in competitive level and final score. Del Corral (2009) also examined the effects of seeded players in tennis, their gender and the court surface on competitive balance. The findings suggested that competitive balance was affected by a change in the seeding system for men but not for women.

Taking Major League Baseball as an example, researchers have studied the impact of various factors on competitive balance. Lewis (2008) looked at individual team incentives and their impact on managing competitive balance in sports leagues. This research focused on the financial management of teams and how populations and attendance rates impacted upon the financial management. Lee (2009) studied the effect of post-season restructuring on competitive balance and fan demand in Major League Baseball and demonstrated that restructuring had a positive effect on this fan demand. O'Reilly and colleagues (2008) used a new construct of 'hope' to attempt to link competitive balance with fan welfare and presented empirical support for their ideas through a market survey.

Overall, the reader should be aware that the literature on competitive balance is considerable and its content makes use of mathematics and statistical methods to investigate, measure and discuss the concept across a range of sports. There is also a considerable amount that focuses on the 'Big Four' American sports of baseball, ice hockey, football and basketball and a sizeable literature focusing on European sports (primarily football but also rugby). Interestingly, competitive balance has a long history of research yet there is still scant consensus on how to measure it or if it is required in professional sports leagues for leagues and teams to be successful. The North American professional sport system highly values competitive balance and actively manages it through mechanisms such as salary caps and revenue sharing. European leagues meanwhile tend to value winning and team performance over financial performance and so competitive balance has not traditionally been rigorously addressed.

To understand competitive balance more fully the reader may refer to the concepts of **demand** and **structure** that can be found elsewhere in the book.

FURTHER READING

For some further reading on this concept we would recommend the following:

Buraimo, B. and Simmons, R. (2008) Competitive balance and attendance in Major League Baseball: an empirical test of the uncertainty of outcome hypothesis. *International Journal of Sport Finance*, 3(3): 146–155.

Cain, L.P. and Haddock, D.D. (2005) Similar economic histories, different industrial structures: transatlantic contrasts in the evolution of professional sports leagues. *Journal of Economic History*, 65: 1116–1147.

Groot, L. (2008) *Economics, Uncertainty and European Football: Trends in Competitive Balance*. Cheltenham: Edward Elgar.

BIBLIOGRAPHY

Buraimo, B. and Simmons, R. (2008) Competitive balance and attendance in Major League Baseball: an empirical test of the uncertainty of outcome hypothesis. *International Journal of Sport Finance*, 3(3): 146–155.

Cain, L.P. and Haddock, D.D. (2005) Similar economic histories, different industrial structures: transatlantic contrasts in the evolution of professional sports leagues. *Journal of Economic History*, 65: 1116–1147.

Chang, Y.M. and Sanders, S. (2009) Pool revenue sharing, team investments and competitive balance in professional team sports: a theoretical analysis. *Journal of Sports Economics*, 10(4): 409–428.

Del Corral, J. (2009) Competitive balance and match uncertainty in Grand Slam tennis: effects of seeding system, gender and court surface. *Journal of Sports Economics*, 10(6): 563–581.

El-Hodiri, M. and Quirk, J. (1971) An economic model of a professional sports league. *Journal of Political Economy*, 79(6): 1302–1319.

El-Hodiri, M. and Quirk, J. (1974) The economic theory of a professional sports league. In R.G. Noll (ed.), *Government and the Sports Business*, 79: 33–80.

Flores, R., Forrest, D. and Tena, J.D. (2010) Impact on competitive balance from allowing foreign players in a sports league: evidence from European soccer. *Kylos: International Review for Social Sciences*, 63(4): 546–557.

Fort, R. and Maxcy, J. (2003) Competitive balance in sports leagues: an introduction. *Journal of Sports Economics*, 4(2): 154–160.

Fort, R. and Quirk, J. (1995) Cross-subsidization, incentives and outcomes in professional team sports. *Journal of Economic Literature*, XXXIII: 1265–1299.

Fort, R. and Quirk, J. (2010) Optimal competitive balance in single-game ticket sports leagues. *Journal of Sports Economics*, 11: 587–601.

Giocoli, N. (2007) Competitive balance in football leagues when teams have different goals. *International Review of Economics*, 54: 345–370.

Groot, L. (2008) *Economics, Uncertainty and European Football: Trends in Competitive Balance*. Cheltenham: Edward Elgar.

Howarth, A. and Robinson, T.A. (2008) The impact of salary cap in the European Rugby Super League. *International Journal of Business and Management*, 3(6): 3–7.

Lee, T. (2010) Competitive balance in the National Football League after the 1993 collective bargaining agreement. *Journal of Sports Economics*, 11(1): 77–88.

Lee, Y.H. (2009) The impact of postseason restructuring on the competitive balance and fan demand in Major League Baseball. *Journal of Sports Economics*, 10(3): 219–235.

Lewis, M. (2008) Individual team incentives and managing competitive balance in sports leagues: An empirical analysis of Major League Baseball. *Journal of Marketing Research*, 45(5): 535–549.

Meehan, J.W. (Jr.), Nelson, R.A. and Richardson, T.V. (2007) Competitive balance and game attendance in Major League Baseball. *Journal of Sports Economics*, 8(6): 563–580.

Mizak, D., Stair, A. and Rossi, A. (2005) Assessing alternative competitive balance measures for sports leagues: a theoretical examination of standard deviations, Gini coefficients, the index of dissimilarity. *Economic Bulletin*, 12(5): 1–11.

Morse, A., Shapiro, S., McEvoy, C. and Rascher, D. (2008) The effects of roster turnover on demand in the National Basketball Association. *International Journal of Sports Finance*, 3: 8–18.

O'Reilly, N., Kaplan, A., Rahinel, R. and Nadeau, J. (2008) 'If you can't win, why should I buy a ticket?': Hope, fan welfare and competitive balance. *International Journal of Sports Finance*, 3(2): 106–118.

Owen, P.D., Ryan, M. and Weatherston, C.R. (2007) Measuring competitive balance in professional team sports using the Herfindahl-Hirschman Index. *Review of Industrial Organization*, 31(4): 289–302.

Pivovarnik, T.P., Lamb, R.P., Zuber, R.A. and Gandar, J.M. (2008) Competitive balance and fan interest in the National Football League. *Journal of Economics and Economics Education Research*, 9(2): 75–98.

Rottenburg, S. (1956) The baseball players' labour market. *Journal of Political Economy*, 64(3): 242–258.

Utt, J. and Fort, R. (2002) Pitfalls of measuring competitive balance with Gini coefficients. *Journal of Sports Economics*, 3(4): 367–373.

Vrooman, J. (2007) Theory of the beautiful game: the unification of European football. *Scottish Journal of Political Economy*, 54(3): 314–354.

Conflict

> *Conflict is the potential or actual existence of differences of opinion accompanied by some emotional response in individual(s) and should be 'managed' but not necessarily discouraged.*

Conflict is inherent in all organizations and has been studied by scholars for many years (e.g., Fenn, 1971; Mouly and Sankaran, 1997; Temkin and Cummings, 1986; Whiteman, 2009). The generic management literature on conflict suggests that there are many definitions of the term, various ways of categorizing conflict (e.g., vertical and horizontal), assorted levels of conflict within organizations, and numerous sources of conflict (as well as management strategies to deal with these). Slack (1997) indicated some key points about the many different definitions of conflict when he suggested that it was important for the individuals and/or groups involved in a conflict situation to perceive that the conflict existed (although all perceived conflict is not necessarily real). He also highlighted that two or more parties had to be involved in presenting opposing views. There would also usually be some prevention of goal achievement which will result in some sort of emotional response such as anger, fear, or frustration. With these conditions evident, it can be confirmed that conflict exists and will need to be managed.

Researchers have studied the effects of different levels of conflict in organizations, resulting in the widely accepted theory of the relationship between conflict and effectiveness which states that there is an optimum level of conflict needed within organizations to maximize **effectiveness** and **efficiency**. Too little conflict results in stagnation and a lack of innovation, whereas too much conflict prevents progression towards **organizational goals** owing to disruptive behaviours. As for sources of conflict, researchers have identified some structural elements which can lead to conflict situations such as:

- differentiation (Lawrence and Lorsch, 1967);
- interdependence (Thompson, 1967);
- low formalization (Dawes and Massey, 2005);
- competition over resources (Deacon, 1993);
- differences in reward systems (Cliff, 1987);
- communication problems (Slack et al., 1994);
- role conflict (Prouty, 1988);
- and participative **decision making** (Cotton et al., 1988).

However, as Kolb and Putnam (1992) pointed out, these sources of conflict (and the conflict that results) may be seen as 'public', formal, and rationally observed. In other words, these sources of conflict can be managed (either proactively or reactively). Conflict management strategies include:

- the use of authority (usually a short-term solution);
- avoidance;
- separating or merging conflicting parties;
- increasing resources;
- integrating devices;
- confrontation/negotiation;
- job rotation;
- and third-party intervention.

For those managers seeking to increase conflict in their organizations to more optimum levels, researchers suggest creating competition, introducing 'new blood', and/or manipulating communications (Robbins, 1978). Bodtker and Jameson (2001) explored the role and use of emotion in conflict management strategies and demonstrated the importance of addressing emotion directly when managing organizational conflict. Knowing when to use the above-mentioned strategies can be difficult and researchers have attempted to provide suggestions on how to assess and manage conflict within organizations (see for example Jameson, 1999, and Ohbuchi and Suzuki, 2003).

Conflict has been studied in different types of organizations such as private, public and voluntary organizations, as well as through work that focuses on small groups (see Sell et al., 2004), yet there has not been any comprehensive review and comparison of the similarities and differences of conflict in these various organization **contexts**. Howell (1981) studied the behavioural styles used by agents in voluntary organizations and found that (in large, private, non-profit, human services organizations) 37 per cent of them identified avoidance as their primary conflict management style. This is in contrast to studies performed on profit-oriented business which indicated that avoidance was the least-utilized conflict management style, with agents preferring 'competition' tactics instead

(Phillips and Cheston, 1979). However, these studies did not differentiate between different kinds of conflict or take into account the conflict management styles used by volunteers versus those adopted by professional service workers.

Temkin and Cummings (1986) sought to investigate how conflict was managed using the Organizational Communication Conflict Instrument (OCCI) and statistical analysis of their data. Their study found that both volunteers and paid staff preferred non-confrontational conflict resolution methods in situations concerning organizational issues (consistent with Fenn, 1971; Howell, 1981; Rawls et al., 1975). Furthermore, they suggested that agents may respond emotionally to interpersonal conflict (e.g., when someone misinterprets their ideas, intentions, or actions) and more 'rationally' to conflicts involving organizational issues. Yet one criticism of the usefulness of these studies would focus on their lack of consideration for the influence of size, structure, and temporal context of the organizations they studied upon the type of conflict observed and the resultant conflict management strategy adopted.

The discussion above highlights the importance of understanding the nature of conflict and how to manage it. While conflict has been studied extensively in the organization theory literature it has not had the same attention within the management of sport. It is easy to think of sport as being conflict free, however this is not the case and sport organizations experience the same conflicts as organizations in other areas. For example, Macintosh and Whitson (1990) demonstrated how the differentiation (a component of **structure**) of Canadian national sport organizations resulted in conflict: this differentiation occurred as a result of new, professional staff bringing different goals to the organization that then led to clashes with volunteers who had traditionally managed the organization. Likewise Slack and colleagues (1994) revealed how the introduction of rational planning systems served to heighten conflict in Canadian national sport organizations to the detriment of the purpose for which the planning system was designed, while Amis et al. (1995: 1) argued that voluntary sport organizations were 'significantly more susceptible to conflict' due mainly to the interdependence of their structural characteristics.

There have been some authors who presented rich descriptions of conflict in sport organizations in Japan (Saeki, 1994), Islamic countries (Sfeir, 1985), and Namibia (Chappell, 2005), for example, which have mainly focused on the conflicts between culture, values, and the modernization of sport organizations. While these descriptions are welcome and useful to inform the reader of different international contexts in which sport is managed, they could perhaps do more to utilize theoretical models of conflict in order to better understand the imperatives of the situations and make suggestions for appropriate management strategies. Moriarty and Holman-Prpich (1987) proposed a model for analysing conflict and **change** through their examination of Canadian inter-university athletics but there have been few attempts to provide any subsequent work from sport management scholars. Slack and colleagues (1994) demonstrated how the **structural** (see **structure**) characteristics of **sport organizations** can lead to conflict in their work on rational planning systems as a source of organizational conflict.

As previously mentioned, the mainstream literature on conflict in organizations has proven extensive and continues to develop. Use of these theories to further our understanding of conflict in sport organizations is needed. The increasing size and complexity of the sport industry suggests a growing likelihood of conflict between **stakeholders**, requiring management to understand and effectively manage diverse conflict situations. Some exploratory work in sport focusing on the types and levels of conflict found in different sport organizations would be useful before undertaking further research investigating the implications of conflict for organization **effectiveness** and **efficiency**. There is also scant research into how those responsible for the management of sport currently perceive the role of conflict and which management strategies (if any) are employed by these managers and for what reasons. Managing conflict is also relevant to understanding how control in organizations is achieved given that highly conflictual organizations will require different **control** interventions from those organizations that suffer from stagnation due to a lack of conflict.

To understand conflict more fully, the reader may refer to the concepts of **change**, **stakeholders**, **effectiveness**, **efficiency**, **control**, **structure**, **decision making** and **sport organization**, and **organizational goals** that can be found elsewhere in this book.

FURTHER READING

For some further reading on this concept, we would recommend the following:

Amis, J., Slack, T. and Berrett, T. (1995) The structural antecedents of conflict in national sport organizations. *Leisure Studies*, 14: 1–16.

Rahim, M.A. (2010) *Managing Conflict in Organizations*. New Brunswick, NJ: Transaction.

Slack, T. and Parent, M. (2006) *Understanding Sport Organizations: The Application of Organization Theory*. Champaign, IL: Human Kinetics.

Tekleab, A.G., Quigley, N.R. and Tesluk, P.E. (2009) A longitudinal study of team conflict, conflict management, cohesion, and team effectiveness. *Group Organization Management*, 34(2): 170–205.

BIBLIOGRAPHY

Amis, J., Slack, T. and Berrett, T. (1995) The structural antecedents of conflict in national sport organizations. *Leisure Studies*, 14: 1–16.

Bodtker, A.M. and Jameson, J.K. (2001) Emotion in conflict formation and its transformation: applications to organizational conflict management. *International Journal of Conflict Management*, 12(3): 259–275.

Chappell, R. (2005) Sport in Namibia: conflicts, negotiations and struggles since independence. *International Review for the Sociology of Sport*, 40(2): 241–254.

Cliff, G. (1987) Managing organizational conflict. *Management Review*, 76(5)51–53.

Cosier, R.A. and Ruble, T.L. (1981) Research on conflict-handling: an experimental approach. *Academy of Management Journal*, 24: 816–831.

Cotton, J.L., Vollrath, D.A., Froggat, K.L., Lengnick-Hall, M.L. and Jennings, K.R. (1988) Employee participation: diverse forms and different outcomes. *Academy of Management Review*, 13(1): 8–22.

Dawes, P.L. and Massey, G.R. (2005) Antecedents of conflict in marketing's cross-functional relationship with sales. *European Journal of Marketing*, 39(11/12): 1327–1344.

Deacon, J. (1993) Blowing the whistle. *Maclean's*, December 6: 55.

Fenn, D.H. (1971) Executives as community volunteers. *Harvard Business Review*, 49: 10–16.

Howell, J.L. (1981) The identification, description and analysis of competencies focused on conflict management in a human services organization: an exploratory study. Doctoral dissertation, University of Massachusetts. *Dissertation Abstracts International*, 42(3-A): 933.

Jameson, J.K. (1999) Toward a comprehensive model for the assessment and management of intraorganizational conflict: developing the framework. *International Journal of Conflict Management*, 10(3): 268–294.

Kolb, D.M. and Putnam, L.L. (1992) The multiple faces of conflict in organizations. *Journal of Organizational Behaviour*, 13(3): 311–324.

Lawrence, P.R. and Lorsch, J.W. (1967) *Organization and Environment: Managing Differentiation and Integration*. Homewood, IL: R.D. Irwin.

Macintosh, D. and Whitson, D. (1990) *The Game Planners: Transforming Canada's Sport System*. Montreal: McGill-Queen's University Press.

Moriarty, D. and Holman-Prpich, M. (1987) Canadian interuniversity athletics: a model and method for analyzing conflict and change. *Journal of Sport Management*, 1: 57–73.

Mouly, V.S. and Sankaran, J.K. (1997) On the study of settings marked by severe superior–subordinate conflict. *Organization Studies*, 18(2): 175–192.

Ohbuchi, K. and Suzuki, M. (2003) Three dimensions of conflict issues and their effects on resolution strategies in organizational settings. *International Journal of Conflict Management*, 14(1): 61–73.

Phillips, E. and Cheston, R. (1979) Conflict resolution: what works? *California Management Review*, 11(4): 76–83.

Prouty, D.F. (1988) *In Spite of Us: My Education in the Big and Little Amateur and Olympic Sport in the U.S.* Brattleboro, VT: Vitesse.

Rawls, J.R., Ullrich, R.A. and Nelson, O.T. (1975) A comparison of managers entering or re-entering the profit and non-profit sectors. *Academy of Management Journal*, 18(4): 616–622.

Robbins, S.P. (1978) Conflict management and 'conflict resolution' are not synonymous terms. *California Management Review*, 21: 67–75.

Robbins, S.P. (1990) *Organization Theory: Structure, Design and Applications* (3rd edition). Englewood Cliffs, NJ: Prentice-Hall.

Saeki, T. (1994) The conflict between tradition and modernization in a sport organization. *International Review of Sport Sociology*, 29 (3): 301–313.

Sell, J., Lovaglia, M.J., Mannix, E.A., Samuelson, C.D. and Wilson, R.K. (2004) Investigating conflict, power and status within and among groups. *Small Group Research*, 35(1): 44–72.

Sfeir, L. (1985) The status of Muslim women in sport: conflict between cultural tradition and modernization. *International Review for the Sociology of Sport*, 20(4): 283–306.

Slack, T. (1997) *Understanding Sport Organizations: The Application of Organization Theory*. Champaign, IL: Human Kinetics.

Slack, T., Berrett, T. and Mistry, K. (1994) Rational planning systems as a source of organizational conflict. *International Review for the Sociology of Sport*, 29: 317–328.

Temkin, T. and Cummings, H.W. (1986) The use of conflict management behaviors in voluntary organizations: an exploratory study. *Nonprofit and Voluntary Sector Quarterly*, 15(1): 5–18.

Thompson, J.D. (1967) *Organizations in Action*. New York: McGraw-Hill.

Tjosvold, D. and Sun, H.F. (2002) Understanding conflict avoidance: relationship, motivations, actions and consequences. *International Journal of Conflict Management*, 13(2): 142–164.

Whiteman, G. (2009) All my relations: understanding perceptions of justice and conflict between companies and indigenous peoples. *Organization Studies*, 30(1): 101–120.

> *Context is a term that is used to describe a variety of elements or features which together provide an explanation for the existence of a phenomenon or the variation between phenomena.*

Context is arguably one of the most important concepts (if not *the* most important) in management and in doing management research. However, researchers do not usually focus on context as a concept in organizations. It is, rather, implicitly or explicitly considered when examining other concepts and has been recognized as an important variable in understanding organizations and how they operate. In relation to the concept of **control**, for instance, Johnson and Gill (1993) suggested that structure, culture and social, political/economic environments were important contextual features which influenced the control mechanisms adopted in organizations. Paying attention to context in this instance is vital as it indicates to managers which control mechanisms may be used effectively in different types of organizations or in different situations.

Daft (1989:17) defined context as 'the organizational setting which influences the structural dimensions' and recognized the importance of considering context in management and organization research (see for example Daft, 1989, 1996, 2008). The term 'context' has also been referred to in the literature as determinants, imperatives, or contingencies and different researchers have advocated different dimensions that together constitute an organization's context, which will vary, as mentioned above, depending on the concept(s) focused upon in the research. For example, four contextual features thought to influence organization **structure** are **strategy**, environment, size and **technology**.

At the most basic level different contexts may include, for example, public, private and voluntary sectors. Each sector has its own unique contextual features which influence the structure and operation of these organizations. The private sector is said to operate 'for profit': employees in an organization are paid and there is a legal framework, set by government, which controls for competition, fair trading and the social responsibilities of organizations in the private sector. The public sector (as well as the voluntary sector) also has a 'regulatory framework', which consists of government legislation to guide the operation of these organizations. However, public sector organizations do not operate for the profit of any individual or group of people such as shareholders. Public sector organizations are mainly reliant upon a government subsidy (from taxation) in order to provide services. They are under growing pressure from government because of restricted budgets. Increasingly they are subject to pressures similar to the commercial sector and therefore have arguably aligned with a private sector mentality of **efficiency, effectiveness**, and customer service.

The contextual factors of each sector mentioned above will include degrees of external environmental dynamism and complexity as well as technological complexity which will influence their operation. Students, researchers and practitioners should understand the contextual features and constraints of the sector they wish to study or work within and we would encourage the reader to consider a variety of sources when compiling an overview of important contextual features, relevant to their interests. Sources should also be contemporary as the contextual features and pressures on a sector can change over time. Of course, if it is the change in context over time that is of interest, it may well be worth examining studies from a historical and contemporary time period. Rashman, Withers and Hartley (2009) provided one such review of the literature focusing on understanding organizational learning and knowledge in public sector organizations, highlighting the complex contextual challenges for this sector.

A broader categorization of context dimensions can be found in the **strategy** literature which focuses on the political, economic, social, environmental, techno-logical, ecological and legal (PESTEL) factors influencing an organization's strategic development. These contextual features can provide explanations for differences in thinking about how organizations operate. For example, Gibson and colleagues (2003) examined team **effectiveness** in multi-national firms and argued that an explicit consideration of the team context, and specifically the cultural context, was needed in order to make any new meaningful contribution to the current base of knowledge. In the sport-management-related literature, there has also been a signifi-cant increase in the amount of attention being paid to context and identifying contextual features that are crucial for understanding the field. To some extent, all of the literature focused on the management of sport considers context as this concept has a considerable impact on research findings and conclusions (and issues such as the generalizability of research) although some authors discuss context more explicitly than others. For research attempting to explain 'why' something is happening or has occurred, an explicit discussion of contextual influences would be useful (before and after the data collection and analysis).

Explicit analysis of context and researchers' interest in doing this are increasing. Bamberger (2008) discusses how context has been studied in management research and the challenges associated with measuring context. He suggests that advances in computer software allow the examination of context as an important variable in developing management theories. An example of research which has explicitly examined the concept of context is that by Joshi and Roh (2009) who used meta-analysis to analyse the role of context in work team diversity research. They were able to use data from 8,757 teams in 39 studies conducted in various organizational settings to examine whether contextual factors (such as the industry, occupation, team) influenced the performance outcomes of relations-oriented and task-oriented diversity. Following Whetten's (2009) views, Child (2009) investigated the extent to which Chinese management features were context specific or context bound. As a result, he developed a method for measuring the context of Chinese management which considered material, ideational and institutional contextual features. Interestingly, this work recognizes different types of context and applies a theory of context measurement in making international comparisons of management practice.

Theodoraki and Henry (1994) examined the structure and context of national sport governing bodies in Britain and found that the global social context and the British social/economic context were influential in shaping how **sport organizations** in Britain have changed and currently operate with regard to structure. Another study by Amis and Slack (1996) examined the relationship between size and structure in the context of voluntary sport organizations, demonstrating how the nature of size and its influence on structure must consider the unique contextual features of voluntary sport organizations.

While many studies of organizations and of sport organizations consider contextual features as relevant, there has been no explicit focus on the concept and its role in research on the management of sport. Likewise, there has been no research that provides a synthesis of contextual factors as they are relevant to other concepts such as **change**, **control** or managing **conflict**. Researchers therefore often define context very differently and no common thoughts seem to exist on which contextual features should be taken into consideration when designing research investigations. This is indicative in research on sport organizations as well as the broader field of management. However, Weed (2005) provides a useful discussion of 'research synthesis methods' which can be used when attempting to understand diverse areas of research such as the management of sport or complex concepts which would benefit from a systematic method to analyse the existing knowledge base. While he acknowledges that research often begins with a search, review and synthesis of existing literature in order to identify the context in which the research project takes place, Weed goes on to suggest that some more systematic techniques of synthesis may be useful to sport management researchers. Systematic review, meta-analysis and meta-interpretation are three techniques he discusses as well as their potential to ensure a thorough use of existing literature. These techniques may also be used to examine contextual features more specifically across a body or bodies of literature in order to provide a rigorous comparison of contextual attributes that are key to a research investigation.

Overall, the explicit study of context has occurred in the mainstream management literature but not in the literature on the management of sport. This is unfortunate but also represents a considerable opportunity for further research and developing a new level of understanding in sport management research. Although a difficult concept to define, as it has so many meanings in different settings, context is increasingly being recognized as important enough to be considered explicitly rather than just implicitly in management and organization research.

To understand context more fully, the reader may refer to the concepts **sport organizations**, **structure**, **control**, **conflict**, **change** and **effectiveness** that may be found elsewhere in this book.

FURTHER READING

For some further reading on this concept, we would recommend the following:

Bamberger, P. (2008) Beyond contextualization: using context theories to narrow the micro-macro gap in management research. *Academy of Management Journal*, 51(5): 839–846.

Caza, A. (2000) Context receptivity: innovation in an amatuer sport organization. *Journal of Sport Management*, 14: 227–242.

Child, J. (2009) Context, comparison and methodology in Chinese management research. *Management and Organization Review*, 6(1): 57–73.

BIBLIOGRAPHY

Amis, J. and Slack, T. (1996) The size structure relationship in voluntary sport organizations. *Journal of Sport Management*, 10: 76–86.

context

Bamberger, P. (2008) Beyond contextualization: using context theories to narrow the micro-macro gap in management research. *Academy of Management Journal*, 51(5): 839–846.

Child, J. (2009) Context, comparison and methodology in Chinese management research. *Management and Organization Review*, 6(1): 57–73.

Daft, R.L. (1989) *Organization Theory and Design*. St. Paul, MN: West.

Daft, R. (1996) *Organizational Performance*. New York: Wiley.

Daft, R. (2004) Theory Z: opening the corporate door for participative management. *Academy of Management Executive*, 18(4): 117–121.

Daft, R.L. (2008) *Management*. Cincinnati, OH: South-Western College Publishing.

Gibson, C.B., Zellner-Bruhn, M.E. and Schwab, D.P. (2003) Team effectiveness in multinational organizations. *Group and Organization Management*, 28(4): 444–474.

Johnson, P. and Gill, J. (1993) *Management Control and Organizational Behaviour*. London: Paul Chapman.

Joshi, A. and Roh, H. (2009) The role of context in work team diversity research: a meta-analytic review. *Academy of Management Journal*, 52(3): 599–627.

Rashman, L., Withers, E. and Hartley, J. (2009) Organizational learning and knowledge in public service organizations: a systematic review of the literature. *International Journal of Management Reviews*, 11(4): 463–494.

Theodoraki, E. and Henry, I.P. (1994) Organizational structures and contexts in British national governing bodies of sport. *International Review for the Sociology of Sport*, 29: 243–265.

Weed. M. (2005) Research synthesis in sport management: Dealing with chaos in the brickyard. *European Sport Management Quarterly*, 5: 77–90.

Whetten, D.A. (2009) An examination of the interface between context and theory applied to the study of Chinese organizations. *Management and Organization Review*, 5(1): 29–55.

Control

> *Control is a complex and multi-dimensional phenomenon in organizations that can be studied at individual, group, organizational or field levels of analysis, and is highly context dependent.*

Delbridge and Ezzamel (2005: 603) suggested that 'control lies at the heart of organization theory'. The concept has certainly be given extensive attention in the mainstream management and organizational literature but has rarely been explicitly addressed by scholars who study the management of sport. Generally, the attention paid to control in organizations has focused firstly on control of the individual and has then moved on to focus on the control of organizations themselves (Birnberg, 1998). As with most areas of academic study, early researchers have focused on defining the concept of control and identifying different types or categories of control mechanisms in organizations. Tannenbaum (1962: 3) referred to control as a process whereby a person or group intentionally affects what another person, group or organization will do, and considered control as 'an inevitable correlate of organization'.

Essentially, early definitions were concerned with control in order to produce efficiency and effectiveness among employees and facilitate the attainment of organizational goals. Control was viewed as a management-led activity and did little to consider the role of other organizational actors in the process of control as important in influencing management or the organization. Researchers in the 1970s began to theorize about different types of control in addition to having a singular focus on observable individual/group action. For example, Reeves and Woodward (1970) suggested a **typology** of control systems with two dimensions. The personal-mechanical dimension referred to whether control was exercised directly by one individual over another or whether an organizational mechanism (such as a cost control system) was used to control behaviour. The unitary-fragmented dimension referred to whether integrated control systems were employed organization wide or whether different organization sub-units employed different control systems. It was therefore recognized that different controls may operate within organizations and the origins of that control may spring from an individual or from a system/procedure (e.g., an operating manual). This early conceptualization focused on how control may operate rather than specifying mechanisms through which it was actually enacted.

Researchers have also differentiated between different types of control systems (as opposed to specific control mechanisms) within organizations and how these systems may influence behaviour. For example, Ouchi and Johnson (1978) proposed two ideal types of organization control: type A and type Z control. The type A organization was thought to maintain control through highly scrutinized systems and procedures such as the American companies in Ouchi and Johnson's study. The type Z organization (e.g., Japanese companies) exerted control through the socialization of employees and was thought to be effective where the turnover of staff was low, allowing the organization to focus on the coordination between organizational units rather than the high specialization and formal monitoring which would be found in the type A organization.

Since the 1980s, research on control in organizations has gathered momentum and the complexity of this concept has become increasingly apparent. New categorizations and contexts have emerged in the literature which can help to expand our thinking on the variety of controls that operate in organizations and how these differ between organizations with different **structures** and industry sectors. The importance of context therefore was relatively undisputed during this time, fuelling further interest in informal control mechanisms and a variety of organizational contexts.

Some researchers embraced a more critical perspective of control and began to question the unobtrusive and even ideological forms (such as gender, race, and class) of control in organizations. Again, while extremely useful in providing a new perspective of organizations and control, these studies assumed negative connotations of the control process in organizations, seeking instances and evidence of domination and a **power** imbalance. Yet, the role of power and domination are important factors in control, and perhaps more so in some organizational contexts than others, yet they are only one aspect of control and as mentioned previously a single-factor focus fails to conceptualize control in sufficiently broad enough terms to move towards an explanation of how it occurs and why this happens in a particular way in an organization.

Some research has begun to investigate the relationship between mechanisms of control, providing more dynamic theories of control and recognizing the importance of the contextual features of organizations to advancing our understanding of such a complex concept. Most recently, studies of control have acknowledged the salience of considering the temporal context of control and encouraged more longitudinal studies to take into consideration the historical development of control, rather than attempting to isolate minimum periods of time to explain a concept (control) which itself is constantly changing and evolving within organizations.

Outside of the mainstream organization theory literature there exists a plethora of research (as evidenced below) which has implications for the study and understanding of control but which to date has rarely been considered in relation to the mainstream literature or as a separate but related body of literature itself. Single-factor studies have had a very specific focus on, for example, the controlling nature of language in organizations (Boden, 1994; Tompkins and Cheney, 1985), culture (e.g., Inzerilli and Rosen, 1983), trust (e.g., Lane and Bachmann, 1988), emotion (Fineman, 2000), ideology (Oliga, 1989) and identification (Alvesson and Willmott, 2002), but have not thoroughly addressed the broader concept of organization control. Furthermore, as Kimberly (1979) and Aldrich (1999) noted, scholars who have studied control have tended to focus on large commercial organizations, examining the characteristics and effects of control without giving attention to the development and **change** over time of control mechanisms. However, more problematic here is that the 'explicit discussion and debate of organization control has become increasingly less

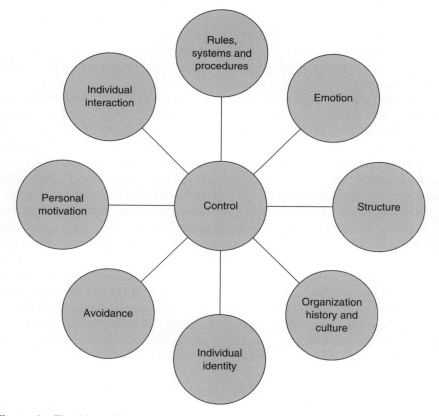

Figure 3   The Many Different Components of Control Within Organizations

common' (Delbridge and Ezzamel, 2005: 603), as these are being replaced by studies dissecting the control concept and examining its components in isolation rather than in context. After these many decades of research on control there is still little consensus on what control actually *is* within organizations. This is because control is not one thing or another; it is many different things, as can be seen in the figure below.

There has been little research which focuses on control in sport organizations explicitly and is grounded in the organization theory literature. Pitter (1990) constructed a case study to explore the concepts of power and control in a small amateur sport club. However, the study presented a narrow view of control and power as related to the ability to influence or secure some desired outcome. Nonetheless, his work is exemplary of the application of organization theory and appropriate theoretical frameworks to understanding the operation of sport organizations, demonstrating the interdependent relationships between power, control and organization structure. Byers, Henry and Slack (2007) presented some broader views on the concept of control in voluntary sport clubs and suggested this concept as one which required further exploration in the sport management literature. They developed a holistic conception of control and investigated the occurrence of administrative, social and self control mechanisms operating in small local sport clubs. Although these clubs, consistent with studies of sport clubs elsewhere, were relatively informal, use of all three types of control mechanisms was found. In addition to this, the authors noted how the mechanisms were employed, tactically, strategically, or systemically, while also pointing to the importance of the development of these mechanisms and their uses over time as key to understanding how control was exerted in these sport clubs. Byers (2013) went on to provide a more extensive account of control in sport clubs and demonstrated that this is still an under-researched field.

One could argue that much of the literature on the management of sport is about the concept of control. For example, feminist sport management literature addresses gender issues about the control of men's and women's sexuality (see for example Hall, 1988; Hoeber, 2007; Shaw and Hoeber, 2003; Shaw and Slack, 2002). Another example is Mason, Thibault and Misener (2006) who examined the control of decision making by focusing on corruption on the International Olympic Committee (IOC) using agency theory. Agency theory proved useful by highlighting the importance of stakeholders and their interests in sport organizations and the authors were able to make some useful suggestions for reform in the IOC to improve the accountability and function of the organization. It may contribute to our understanding of control, however, if more studies identified the concept explicitly and therefore took into consideration some of the wider knowledge on the concept which exists, and a further understanding of control in sport organizations may emerge. This may in effect help researchers who study the management of sport to demonstrate a contribution to the wider field of management knowledge as well as provide new insights into our field specifically. When focusing research on control it is necessary to distinguish between an examination of control mechanisms and considering how and why control mechanisms occur.

To understand control more fully, the reader may refer to the concepts of **change, structure, decision making, power, organizational culture** and **context** that can be found elsewhere in this book.

control

FURTHER READING

For some further reading on this concept, we would recommend the following:

Byers, T., Slack, T. and Henry, I.P. (2007) Understanding control in voluntary sport organizations. In M.M. Parent and T. Slack (eds), *International Perspectives on the Management of Sport*. London: Elsevier.

Byers, T. (2013, forthcoming) Using critical realism: a new perspective on control of volunteers in sport clubs. *European Sport Management Quarterly*, February.

Delbridge, R. and Ezzamel, M. (2005) The strength of difference: contemporary conceptions of control. *Organization*, 12(5): 603–618.

Johnson, P. and Gill, J. (1993) *Management Control and Organizational Behaviour*. London: Paul Chapman.

BIBLIOGRAPHY

Aldrich, H.E. (1999) *Organizations Evolving*. Thousand Oaks, CA: Sage.

Alvesson, M. and Willmott, H. (2002) Identity regulation as organisation control: producing the appropriate individual. *Journal of Management Studies*, 39 (5): 619–644.

Birnberg, J.G. (1998) Some reflections on the evolution of organizational control. *Behavioural Research in Accounting*, 10: 27–47.

Boden, C. (1994) *The Business of Talk*. Oxford: Polity/Blackwell.

Byers, T., Henry, I.P. and Slack, T. (2007) Understanding control in voluntary sport organizations. In T. Slack and M. Parent (eds), *International Perspectives on the Management of Sport*. London: Elsevier.

Delbridge, R. and Ezzamel, M. (2005) The strength of difference: contemporary conceptions of control. *Organization*, 12(5): 603–618.

Fineman, S. (ed.) (2000) *Emotion in Organizations*. London: Sage.

Hall, M.A. (1988) The discourse of gender and sport: from femininity to feminism. *Sociology of Sport Journal*, 5(4): 330–340.

Hoeber, L. (2007) Exploring the gaps between meanings and practices in gender equity in a sport organization. *Gender Work and Organization*, 14(3): 259–280.

Inzerilli, G. and Rosen, M. (1983) Culture and organizational control. *Journal of Business Research*, 11: 281–292.

Kimberly, J.R. (1979) Issues in the creation of organizations: initiation, innovation and institutionalization. *Academy of Management Journal*, 22: 437–457.

Lane, C. and Bachmann, R. (1988) *Trust Within and Between Organizations*. Oxford: Oxford University Press.

Mason, D.S., Thibault, L. and Misener, L. (2006) Research and reviews – an agency theory perspective on corruption in sport: the case of the International Olympic Committee. *Journal of Sport Management*, 20: 52.

Oliga, J.C. (1989) *Power, Ideology and Control*. London: Plenum.

Ouchi, W.G. and Johnson, J.B. (1978) Types of organizational control and their relationship to emotional well being. *Administrative Science Quarterly*, 23(2): 293–317.

Pitter, R. (1990) Power and control in an amateur sport organization. *International Review for the Sociology of Sport*, 25(4): 309–321.

Reeves, R.K. and Woodward, J. (1970) The study of managerial control. In J. Woodward (ed.), *Industrial Organization: Behaviour and Control*. Oxford: Oxford University Press. pp. 37–56.

Shaw, S. and Hoeber, L. (2003) 'A strong man is direct and a direct woman is a bitch': gender discourses and their influence on employment roles in sports organizations. *Journal of Sport Management*, 17(4): 347–375.

Shaw, S. and Slack, T. (2002) 'It's been like that for donkey's years': the historical construction of gender relations in sport organisations. *Culture, Sport, Society*, 5: 86–106.

Tannenbaum, A.S. (1962) Control in organizations: individual adjustment and organizational performance. *Administrative Science Quarterly*, 7: 236–257.

Tompkins, P.K. and Cheney, G. (1985) Communication and unobtrusive control. In R. McPhee and P.K. Tompkins (eds), *Organizational Communication: Traditional Themes and New Directions*. Beverly Hills, CA: Sage.

Corporate Social Responsibility (CSR)

> *Corporate Social Responsibility (CSR) can be defined as the economic, legal, ethical and/or discretionary/philanthropic activities undertaken by an organization, activities which form the basis of that organization's relationship with its societal or community stakeholders.*

Focusing on corporate social responsibility (CSR) is a growing trend by both academics and practitioners. Yet, as Carroll (1999: 291) noted, 'The concept of CSR has had a long and diverse history in the literature.' CSR, as we understand it today, dates back to the 1950s, where we saw a proliferation of definitions that lasted for twenty years thereafter. The 1980s saw some attempts at measuring CSR and researchers tried to integrate various perspectives and examine alternative approaches (e.g., **stakeholder** theory, business **ethics**, and corporate citizenship) throughout the 1990s (see Carroll, 1999, for more information). Waddock (2004: 10) defined CSR as 'the subset of corporate responsibilities that deals with a company's voluntary/discretionary relationships with its societal and community stakeholders'. For both Carroll (1991) and Wood (1991), there were four possible CSR domains, which Carroll presented in a pyramid format:

- *Economic*: the base of the pyramid where we find the maximization of earnings, a strong competitive position, and operating efficiency.
- *Legal*: the second level where we find operations in line with government expectations, regulations and the law.
- *Ethical*: the third level where we find organizations operating 'in a manner consistent with expectations of societal mores and ethical norms' (p. 41);
- *Discretionary/philanthropic*: the top of the pyramid – where we find organizational performance being in line with society's philanthropic and voluntary/charitable expectations.

Gallagher and Goodstein (2002) argued that organizational ethics/corporate social responsibility should include the following elements: integrity in the focal organization's mission and core values; a responsibility towards stakeholders; and institutional reflection on the crucial choices that have the potential for broad implications. In addition, McWilliams and Siegel (2001: 117) concluded that 'there is an "ideal" level of CSR, which managers can determine via cost–benefit analysis … [but] that there is a neutral relationship between CSR and financial performance'.

Nevertheless, CSR is today seen as an umbrella concept. More precisely, the literature describes three CSR-related sub-concepts or logics (see notably Frederick, 1994): CSR_1, CSR_2, and CSR_3 or CC. CSR_1 is the traditional corporate social responsibility view of corporate philanthropy/stewardship responsibility to the community and other stakeholders. CSR_2 refers to corporate social responsiveness which emphasizes 'corporate action, proaction, and implementation of a social role' (Carroll, 1991: 40). As such, CSR_2 covers the methods and mechanisms pertaining to corporate social responsibility. Finally, CSR_3 was coined as corporate social rectitude but has since then been supplanted by the term 'corporate citizenship' (CC) to better reflect the rights, duties, and social implications of the organizations towards the community for this third sub-concept (see also Matten and Crane, 2005; Walker and Parent, 2010). Lockett et al. (2006) suggested that the most popular issues addressed in CSR research within management journals have been concerned with ethics and the environment. These authors reviewed literature published between 1992 and 2002, acknowledging that research on CSR was largely driven by agendas in the business environment and by continuing scientific interest. They suggested that the single largest source of references on CSR was from the management literature.

It is also important to note that there is a difference between CSR and CSP (corporate social performance). Wood (1991) provided a model of CSP that included the following: principles of CSR (legitimacy, public responsibility and managerial discretion), processes of corporate social responsiveness (environmental assessment, stakeholder management and issues management), and outcomes of corporate behaviour (social impacts, social programs, and social policies). This illustrated the links between CSR and CSP. Nevertheless, CSP can be seen as the more instrumental point of view, one which Carroll (1991: 40) described as 'an inclusive and global concept to embrace corporate social responsibility, responsiveness, and the entire spectrum of socially beneficial activities of businesses'. However, the literature seems split as to the actual benefits of using a CSP approach, part of the problem seemingly being CSP's multidimensional nature which results in, notably, measurement problems – making comparisons between studies difficult. Waddock and Graves (1997) addressed this challenge empirically and their results indicated that good stakeholder relationships were positively related to CSP. Russo and Fouts (1997) found a positive relationship between an organization's proactive stance on environmental performance and its financial performance; and Turban and Greening (1997) found that organizations with higher CSP rates had more positive reputations and thus were more attractive potential employers. Yet Clarkson (1995), in his review of a ten-year research programme, stated that 'in the normal course of conducting their business, corporate managers do not think or act in terms of the concepts of corporate social responsibilities and responsiveness, nor of social issues and performance' (p. 98). Also, Gerde (2000) did not find any support indicating that organizations designed around the concept of justice had higher CSP ratings. She suggested that this lack of support could be due to measurement problems, or to the fact that most (just) organization designs could already be in place because of external expectations or because of institutional mimetic isomorphism. Another suggested reason here was that the external environment had put pressure on the organization so that the concept of justice was already present in the organization (before the study) thanks to the environment's expectations or through institutional mimetic isomorphism. This of course should be further explored through empirical research. For a wider reading of corporate responsibility and the literature surrounding this concept, Lee (2008) presented a review of the theories of CSR and made some suggestions for future research in the field.

CSR as an area of study in sport management is, in contrast, relatively recent. Breitbarth and Harris (2008: 179) examined CSR in professional football, arguing 'that an increased awareness and integration of CSR into the football business fosters the competitiveness of the game and creates additional value for its stakeholders'. Meanwhile Walker and colleagues (Kent and Walker, 2009; Sartore-Baldwin and Walker, 2011; Walker and Kent, 2009a, 2009b; Walker and Parent, 2010; Walker, Kent and Rudd, 2007; Walker, Heere, Parent and Drane, 2010) have also examined corporate social responsibility in the sport industry. They looked at CSR in golf, NASCAR, the National Football League (NFL) and the National Hockey League (NHL). Some of the key findings included the fact that CSR seemed to be an important predictor of consumer outcome – this included a willingness to make financial sacrifices, patronage intentions, and reputation. Awareness of a sport organization's socially responsive initiative can influence consumers' intentions – for which **image** is a strong mediator of this relationship. Finally, CSR was found to be a key aspect of a sport organization's overall business **strategy**, and it was viewed positively by most fans of the organization.

Babiak and Wolfe (2009) examined CSR in professional sport. Their research used qualitative methods to explore the determinants (internal and external factors) of CSR initiatives. Results showed that external drivers such as key constituents, the interconnectedness of the field, and pressures from the league were more important determinants of CSR initiatives than were internal resources that were available to deliver the initiatives. Based on their preliminary findings, the authors proposed a framework of CSR adoption that predicted the type of initiative a professional sports organization was likely to adopt and they suggested a research agenda based on that framework.

A related concept to CSR is (business) sustainability. Sustainability is often defined as 'managing the triple bottom line of corporate environmental, social and financial performance' (Network for Business Sustainability, 2009: 1). However, the Network for Business Sustainability – a network which brings together those interested in sustainability from academia, government, and industry (see www.nbs.net) – defines 'business sustainability as resilient businesses that create value, healthy ecosystems and strong communities' (Network for Business Sustainability, 2009: 2). Sustainability has only recently emerged in sport management research. For example, Lindsey (2008) offered frameworks which could be used to examine sustainability in sports development. Nevertheless, sustainability is being used by sport managers notably in relation to green facilities (e.g., the Leadership in Energy and Environmental Design or LEED certification) and green games (see for example, the Vancouver Organizing Committee for the 2010 Olympic and Paralympic Winter Games' sustainability reports). We therefore hope to see sport management research related to sustainability in facilities and events in the future.

To understand corporate social responsibility more fully, the reader may refer to the concepts of **strategy**, **stakeholders**, **image** and **ethics** that can be found elsewhere in this book.

FURTHER READING

For some further reading on this concept, we would recommend the following:

International Journal of Management Reviews (IJMR) (2010) Special Issue: Corporate Social Responsibility, March, 12(1): 1–105.

Lim, S.J. and Phillips, J. (2008) Embedding CSR values: the global footwear industry's evolving governance structure. *Journal of Business Ethics*, 81: 143–156.

Smith, A.C.T. and Westerbeek, H.M. (2007) Sport as a vehicle for developing corporate social responsibility. *Journal of Corporate Citizenship*, 25: 43–54.

BIBLIOGRAPHY

Babiak, K. and Wolfe, R. (2009) Determinants of corporate social responsibility in professional sport: internal and external factors. *Journal of Sport Management*, 23: 717–742.

Breitbarth, T. and Harris, P. (2008) The role of corporate social responsibility in the football business: towards the development of a conceptual model. *European Sport Management Quarterly*, 8(2): 179–206.

Carroll, A.B. (1991) The pyramid of corporate social responsibility: toward the moral management of organizational stakeholders. *Business Horizons*, 34: 30–48.

Carroll, A.B. (1999) Corporate social responsibility: evolution of a definitional construct. *Business and Society*, 38(3): 268–295.

Clarkson, M.B.E. (1995) A stakeholder framework for analyzing and evaluating corporate social performance. *Academy of Management Review*, 20: 92–117.

Frederick, W.C. (1994) From CSR1 to CSR2. *Business and Society*, 33(2): 150–164.

Gallagher, J.A. and Goodstein, J. (2002) Fulfilling institutional responsibilities in health care: organizational ethics and the role of mission discernment. *Business Ethics Quarterly*, 12(4): 433–450.

Gerde, V.W. (2000) Stakeholders and organization design: an empirical test of corporate social performance. In J.M. Logsdon, D.J. Wood and L.E. Benson (eds), *Research in Stakeholder Theory, 1997–1998: The Sloan Foundation Minigrant Project*. Toronto, ON: The Clarkson Centre for Business Ethics.

Kent, A. and Walker, M.B. (2009) Testing a schema for strategic corporate philanthropy in the sport industry. *International Journal of Sport Management*, 11(3): 1–26.

Lee, M.-D.P. (2008) A review of the theories of corporate social responsibility: its evolutionary path and the road ahead. *International Journal of Management Reviews*, 10: 53–73.

Lindsey, I. (2008) Conceptualising sustainability in sports development. *Leisure Studies*, 27(3): 279–294.

Lockett, A., Moon, J. and Visser, W. (2006) Corporate social responsibility in management research: focus, nature, salience and sources of interest. *Journal of Management Studies*, 43(1): 115–136.

Matten, D. and Crane, A. (2005) Corporate citizenship: toward an extended theoretical conceptualization. *Academy of Management Review*, 30(1): 166–179.

McWilliams, A. and Siegel, D.S. (2001) Corporate social responsibility: a theory of the firm perspective. *Academy of Management Review*, 26(1): 117–127.

Network for Business Sustainability (2009) Business sustainability. Retrieved 27 September 2009, from http://www.nbs.net/Knowledge.aspx?TopicId=5e890507-621c-4548-b3bf7e55b03d5451

Russo, M.V. and Fouts, P.A. (1997) A resource-based perspective on corporate environmental performance and profitability. *Academy of Management Journal*, 40(3): 534–559.

Sartore-Baldwin, M. and Walker, M. (2011) The process of organizational identity: What are the roles of socially responsive behaviors, organizational image, and identification? *Journal of Sport Management*, 25(5): 489–505.

Turban, D.B. and Greening, D.W. (1997) Corporate social performance and organizational attractiveness to prospective employees. *Academy of Management Journal*, 40(3): 658–72.

Waddock, S. (2004) Parallel universes: companies, academics, and the progress of corporate citizenship. *Business and Society Review*, 109: 5–42.

Waddock, S. and Graves, S. (1997) The corporate social performance–financial performance link. *Strategic Management Journal*, 18(4): 303–319.

Walker, M.B. and Kent, A. (2009a) CSR on tour: attitudes towards corporate social responsibility among golf fans. *International Journal of Sport Management*.

Walker, M.B. and Parent, M.M. (2010) Toward an integrated framework of corporate social responsibility, responsiveness, and citizenship in sport. *Sport Management Review*, 13: 198–213.

Walker, M.B. and Kent, A. (2009b) Do fans care? Assessing the influence of corporate social responsibility on consumer attitudes in the sport industry. *Journal of Sport Management* 23(6): 746–769.

Walker, M.B., Kent, A. and Rudd, A. (2007) Consumer reactions to strategic philanthropy in the sport industry. *Business Research Yearbook: Global Business Perspectives*, 14(2): 926–32.

Walker, M.B., Heere, B., Parent, M.M. and Drane, D. (2010) Social responsibility and the Olympic Games: the mediating role of consumer attributions. *Journal of Business Ethics*, 95(4): 659–680.

Wood, D.J. (1991) Corporate social performance revisited. *Academy of Management Review*, 16(4): 691–718.

Corruption

> *Corruption is described as a state, process, and outcome pertaining to the intentional undertaking of illegal, immoral or unethical activity by one or more actors for their personal gain.*

The year 2005 was a good year for so-called bad companies. Mokhiber and Weissman (2005) suggested that the ten worst companies for that year were BP, Delphi, DuPont, ExxonMobil, Ford, Halliburton, KPMG, Roche, Suez and W.R. Grace. Corruption is certainly an increasingly visible phenomenon, with various scandals being seen almost daily in the media, depicting major corporations such as Enron, Tyco, WorldCom and Parmalat, as well as institutions like the Catholic Church, as undertaking corrupt acts.

A quick search of an academic database will allow the retrieval of thousands of articles on corruption. A large portion of these will relate to governments, politics, and elections. However, there is definitely a growing concern within the management literature pertaining to corruption, which is typically associated with business **ethics**, corporate **governance**, and/or institutionalized processes and activities. This proliferation in research may be due to what has been happening in the business world, even if academics have been somewhat slow to join in the conversation (Ashforth et al., 2008).

In the management literature, corruption has been defined as a violation of one's entrusted organizational and/or societal norms for personal, sub-unit/group or organizational gain (cf. Ashforth and Anand, 2003; den Nieuwenboer and Kaptein, 2008; Sherman, 1980). Lange (2008: 710) defines corruption as 'the pursuit of individual interests by one or more organizational actors through the intentional misdirection of organizational resources or perversion of organizational routines', while O'Higgins (2006) argues that corruption is a self-reinforcing cycle. Ashforth et al. (2008) add that corruption is both a state and a process, and that, as a strong and provocative term, it is a useful addition to the arsenal of associated concepts currently being examined by scholars, such as unethical behaviour, counterproductive work behaviour, organizational misbehaviour and dysfunctional deviance. This would allow for a more complete picture of the phenomenon to be understood, as these associated terms are, they argue, typically dissected in a static and atomistic manner. They add that corruption needs to be studied using a wider lens, a societal and global perspective. A range of theories is being used to examine corruption, including:

- **corporate social responsibility**
- **ethics**
- trust violation theory
- social identity theory
- institutional theory
- **leadership**
- deontic justice
- disengagement
- **control**
- Foucault
- and policy literature.

(See, for example, Beugré, 2010; den Nieuwenboer and Kaptein, 2008; Everett et al., 2006; Lange, 2008; Manz et al., 2008; Martin et al., 2009; Misangyi et al., 2008; Moore, 2008; Sherman, 1980.)

The causes of corruption have also been of interest to researchers. Some have argued that it is due to the nature of the organization being 'schizophrenic' or as having a multiple personality disorder. Bakan (2004) goes deeper into this phenomenon in his book *The Corporation: The Pathological Pursuit of Profit and Power*, as well as the 2003 documentary *The Corporation* by Mark Achbar, Jennifer Abbott and Joel Bakan (see also Mokhiber and Weissman, 2003). In addition, researchers have argued that corruption can be due to individual and/or organizational characteristics, as well as environmental factors (see for example Baucus and Near, 1991; den Nieuwenboer and Kaptein, 2008; Pinto et al., 2008; Rabl and Kühlmann, 2008; Sung, 2003; Trevino and Youngblood, 1990). Anand and colleagues (2004) suggested that corrupt individuals are often, in fact, upstanding members of the community, caring parents, and givers to charity. The authors propose that individuals continue in their corrupt behaviours by rationalizing their actions and using socialization tactics for integrating organizational new-comers. Anand and colleagues elaborate further on rationalizations and sociali-zation tactics in their article. Zyglidopoulos et al. (2009) support the concept of rationalization for increasing corrupt behaviour. At an organizational level, den Nieuwenboer and Kaptein (2008) suggest three downward spirals as an explanation for the proliferation of corruption, which highlight the dynamic process perspective of corruption: a spiral of divergent norms, a spiral of pres-sures, and a spiral of opportunity.

How to counter corruption is an important part of current research being under-taken. In a review of the current debate, Calderón and colleagues (2009) suggest that there should be a better investment climate worldwide, but also firm self-regulation. Halter et al. (2009) also suggest transparency, as well as communication and compliance with a code of conduct by the organization as well as its buyers/suppliers, as strategies to decrease corruption. Lange (2008) presents eight types of controls for corruption – bureaucratic controls, punishment, incentive alignments, legal/regulatory sanctioning, social sanctioning, vigilance controls, self controls, and concertive controls – whereas Lindgreen (2004) presents five actions for dealing with corruption: no action, withdrawals from markets, a decentralized **decision-making** process, the establishment of an anti-corruption code, and mutual commitment through an integrity pact. De Graaf (2007) warns, however, that the theoretical lens used to examine a case of corruption will determine to a certain extent the solutions proposed: 'Different causal chains lead to different discourses on corruption prevention and corruption control' (2007: 39). This is a crucial point considering the suggestion earlier that corruption may be best viewed and under-stood from a wide perspective rather than any narrow theoretical lenses. This sug-gests that a multi-disciplinary view of corruption would be more fruitful than solely relying on any one theory or academic body of literature (e.g., sociology, ethics) to define and analyse issues related to corruption.

An increasing number of studies are also focusing on various countries/states and cross-cultural analyses (e.g., Davis and Ruhe, 2003; Hooker, 2009; Hustead, 2002; Treisman, 2000; Venard, 2009; Venard and Hanafi, 2008), as there are cul-tural differences related to perceptions of (un)ethical behaviour (Bierstaker, 2009). In a comparison between Australia, Indonesia, India and Singapore, Cameron and colleagues (2009) examined cultural differences in individual decision making in an experimental corruption game. They found that there was greater variation in the propensity to punish corrupt behaviour than there was to engage in corrup-tion. Their study is an interesting one as it tries to examine the reasons for differ-ences in perceptions of culture, including institutional and environmental changes taking place in these countries.

Sport management researchers have argued that corruption goes against some of the fundamental characteristics of sport that make it such a popular and lucra-tive industry, namely its uncertainty of outcome (**competitive balance**). More precisely, Gorse and Chadwick (2010) argued that corruption, on or off the field, takes that uncertainty away. In sport, corruption has been found to go back to antiquity with corrupt practices being uncovered during the ancient Olympics.

More contemporary examples include the 1919 Baseball World Series (i.e., the Chicago White Sox team taking bribes), the 1988 Seoul Olympic Games (Ben Johnson's doping scandal), performance-enhancing drugs within the cycling world, and the 2010 Delhi Commonwealth Games' corruption allegations. Two of the more popular topics of study within sport covering corruption have been related to the International Olympic Committee (IOC) and the *Fédération Internationale de Football Association* (FIFA). Given the range of corrupt behaviours found in sport, Gorse and Chadwick suggest that corruption in sport should be defined as 'any illegal, immoral or unethical activity that attempts to deliberately distort the result of a sporting contest for the personal material gain of one or more parties involved in that activity'.

In relation to the IOC and the Olympic Games, corruption abounds. Andrew Jennings (Jennings, 2000; Simson and Jennings, 1992), in his role as whistleblower, has been blacklisted and his books have been banned for outing the corruption that he alleges exists within the organization. A few notable examples of corruption and whistleblowers include:

- *The candidate city bribing of IOC members*: the whistleblower on the 2002 Olympic Games bidding process, that was ultimately won by Salt Lake City, was Swiss IOC member Marc Holder (The Associated Press, 2006).
- *United States Olympic Committee (USOC) CEO corruption*: besides the 2002 Salt Lake City bidding scandal, USOC CEO Lloyd Ward was plagued with alleged ethical and management transgressions, such as awarding contracts to his brother's company. The pressure from a key Olympic sponsor, John Hancock (financial services company), forced **changes** within the USOC (Slack and Parent, 2006).
- *Block voting by figure skating judges*: at the 2002 Salt Lake City Olympic Games, the International Skating Union's Technical Committee chair, Sally Stapleford, confronted French judge Marie-Reine Le Gougne who then involved the president of the French skating organization and the Russians. Block voting by figure skating judges, especially in the ice dancing, has also been denounced by a Canadian judge, Jean Senft.

Such corruption in the IOC has also been investigated by Mason et al. (2006) who used agency theory to explore the issue. They proposed changes which could decrease corruption, such as the formation of a board overseeing the IOC by its stakeholders, a board which would have the sanctioning power to counter IOC members' transgressions. Maenning (2002) also examined corruption in the Olympic family, as well as doping. He argued that reducing the surpluses of host cities, increasing transparency in the bidding process, and improving the incentives for corruption-free behaviour would decrease corruption in the Olympic family. In addition, financial penalties for athletes caught doping should be considered for this type of transgression.

Professional sports are another ripe area of study for corruption researchers. For example, Declan Hill (2008) presented evidence of match fixing in football/soccer at the highest levels of the sport: the Olympic Games, European Champions League, and World Cup tournaments. He then went on to study why certain leagues seemed to have more match fixing than others (Hill, 2010). Dietl and colleagues (2010) studied professional sumo wrestling and noted the varying levels of corruption that had been discovered over the years and the impact that the 'promotion through the ranks' structure had on sumo wrestlers' incentives to rig matches.

Lisa Kihl and colleagues have been investigating corruption in college sports. She uses grounded theory to explore the impact of academic corruption on newly hired coaching staff (Kihl and Richardson, 2009) and student-athletes (Kihl et al., 2008) in men's basketball. Wells and Carozza (2000) also explored corruption at the college level.

The impact of corruption on other stakeholders is also of interest to sport management researchers. Mazanov and Connor (2010) examined the impact of scandal and corruption on sports teams, particularly in relation to marketing and **sponsorship**. Gorse and Chadwick (2010) also examined the impact of corruption on sponsors. They suggested that the impact of this on sponsors depended on the level of media interest, the nature/frequency/severity of the transgression, and the degree of association or closeness between the transgression and the sponsor's business/target market. The answer to this dependence will determine how severely a sponsor deals with the situation.

Finally, McLaren (2008: 15) examined the various attempts to curb corruption and what needed to be done in order to 'stop sport from becoming an entertainment'. This may in part be due to the role the media play in diffusing, maintaining, and undermining corruption in sport (Numerato, 2009).

To understand corruption more fully, the reader may refer to the concepts of **competitive balance, ethics, governance, corporate social responsibility, changes, leadership, control, decision making, sport marketing** and **sponsorship** that can be found elsewhere in this book.

FURTHER READING

For some further reading on this concept, we would recommend the following:

Fleming, P. and Zyglidopoulos, S. (2009) *Charting Corporate Corruption: Agency, Structure and Escalation.* Cheltenham, UK: Edward Elgar.

Gorse, S. and Chadwick, S. (2010) Conceptualising corruption in sport: implications for sponsorship programmes. *European Business Review*, July/August: 40–45.

Senior, I. (2006) *Corruption – The World's Big C: Cases, Causes, Consequences, Cures.* London: Institute of Economic Affairs.

Maenning, W. (2005) Corruption in international sports and sport management: forms, tendencies, extent, and countermeasures. *European Sport Management Quarterly*, 5(2): 187–225.

BIBLIOGRAPHY

Anand, V., Ashforth, B.E. and Joshi, M. (2004) Business as usual: the acceptance and perception of corruption in organizations. *Academy of Management Executive*, 18(2): 39.

Ashforth, B.E. and Anand, V. (2003) The normalization of corruption in organizations. *Research in Organizational Behavior*, 25: 1–52.

Ashforth, B.E., Gioia, D.A., Robinson, S.L. and Trevino, L.K. (2008) Re-viewing organizational corruption. *Academy of Management Review*, 33(3): 670.

Bakan, J. (2004) *The Corporation: The Pathological Pursuit of Profit and Power*. Toronto: Penguin Books.

Baucus, M.S. and Near, J.P. (1991) Can illegal corporate behavior be predicted? An event history analysis. *Academy of Management Journal*, 34: 9–36.

Beugré, C. (2010) Resistance to socialization into organizational corruption: a model of deontic justice. *Journal of Business and Psychology*, 25(3): 533.

Bierstaker, J.L. (2009) Differences in attitudes about fraud and corruption across cultures. *Cross Cultural Management*, 16(3): 241.

Calderón, R., Álvarez-Arce, J. and Mayoral, S. (2009) Corporation as a crucial ally against corruption. *Journal of Business Ethics*, 87: 319.

Cameron, L., Chaudhuri, A., Irkal, N. and Gangadharan, L. (2009) Propensities to engage in and punish corrupt behaviour: experimental evidence from Australia, India, Indonesia and Singapore. *Journal of Public Economics*, 93(7–8): 843–851.

Davis, J.H. and Ruhe, J.A. (2003) Perceptions of country corruption: antecedents and outcomes. *Journal of Business Ethics*, 43(4): 275.

de Graaf, G. (2007) Causes of corruption: towards a contextual theory of corruption. *Public Administration Quarterly*, 31(1): 39–86.

den Nieuwenboer, N.A. and Kaptein, M. (2008) Spiralling down into corruption: a dynamic analysis of the social identity processes that cause corruption in organizations to grow. *Journal of Business Ethics*, 83(2): 133–146.

Dietl, H.M., Lang, M. and Werner, S. (2010) Corruption in professional sumo: an update on the study of Duggan and Levitt. *Journal of Sports Economics*, 11(4): 383–396.

Everett, J., Neu, D. and Rahaman, A.S. (2006) The global fight against corruption: a Foucaultian, virtues-ethics framing. *Journal of Business Ethics*, 65(1): 1.

Gorse, S. and Chadwick, S. (2010) Conceptualising corruption in sport: implications for sponsorship programmes. *The European Business Review*, July/August: 40–45.

Halter, M., de Arruda, M. and Halter, R. (2009) Transparency to reduce corruption? *Journal of Business Ethics*, 84: 373.

Hill, D. (2008) *The Fix: Soccer and Organized Crime*. Toronto: McClelland and Stewart.

Hill, D. (2010) A critical mass of corruption: why some football leagues have more match-fixing than others. *International Journal of Sports Marketing and Sponsorship*, 11(3): 221–235.

Hooker, J. (2009) Corruption from a cross-cultural perspective. *Cross Cultural Management*, 16(3): 251.

Hustead, B.W. (2002) Culture and international anti-corruption agreements in Latin America. *Journal of Business Ethics*, 37(4): 413.

Jennings, A. (2000) *The Great Olympic Swindle: When the World Wanted its Games Back*. London: Simon and Schuster.

Kihl, L.A. and Richardson, T. (2009) 'Fixing the mess': a grounded theory of a men's basketball coaching staff's suffering as a result of academic corruption. *Journal of Sport Management*, 23(3): 278–304.

Kihl, L.A., Richardson, T. and Campisi, C. (2008) Toward a grounded theory of student-athlete suffering and dealing with academic corruption. *Journal of Sport Management*, 22(3): 273–302.

Lange, D. (2008) A multidimensional conceptualization of organizational corruption. *Academy of Management Review*, 33(3): 710.

Lindgreen, A. (2004) Corruption and unethical behavior: report on a set of Danish guidelines. *Journal of Business Ethics*, 51(1): 31.

Maenning, W. (2002) On the economics of doping and corruption in international sports. *Journal of Sports Economics*, 3(1): 61–89.

key concepts in
sport management

Manz, C., Anand, V., Joshi, M. and Manz, K. (2008) Emerging paradoxes in executive leadership: a theoretical interpretation of the tensions between corruption and virtuous values. *Leadership Quarterly*, 19(3): 385.

Martin, K., Johnson, J. and Cullen, J. (2009) Organizational change, normative control deinstitutionalization, and corruption. *Business Ethics Quarterly*, 19(1): 105.

Mason, D.S., Thibault, L. and Mizener, L. (2006) An agency theory perspective on corruption in sport: the case of the International Olympic Committee. *Journal of Sport Management*, 20(1): 52–73.

Mazanov, J. and Connor, J. (2010) The role of scandal and corruption in sports marketing and sponsorship. *International Journal of Sports Marketing and Sponsorship*, 11(3): 183–198.

McLaren, R.H. (2008) Corruption: its impact on fair play. *Marquette Sports Law Review*, 19(1): 15–38.

Misangyi, V.F., Weaver, G.R. and Elms, H. (2008) Ending corruption: the interplay among institutional logics, resources, and institutional entrepreneurs. *Academy of Management Review*, 33(3): 750.

Mokhiber, R. and Weissman, R. (2003) Multiple corporate personality disorder: the 10 worst corporations of 2003. *Multinational Monitor*, 24(12): 9.

Mokhiber, R. and Weissman, R. (2005) The 10 worst corporations of 2005. *Multinational Monitor*, 26(11/12): 10.

Moore, C. (2008) Moral disengagement in processes of organizational corruption. *Journal of Business Ethics*, 80(1): 129.

Numerato, D. (2009) The media and sports corruption: an outline of sociological understanding. *International Journal of Sport Communication*, 2(3): 261–273.

O'Higgins, E.R.E. (2006) Corruption, underdevelopment, and extractive resource industries: addressing the vicious cycle. *Business Ethics Quarterly*, 16(2): 235.

Pinto, J., Leana, C.R. and Pil, F.K. (2008) Corrupt organizations or organizations of corrupt individuals? Two types of organizational-level corruption. *Academy of Management Review*, 33(3): 685.

Rabl, T. and Kühlmann, T. (2008) Understanding corruption in organizations: development and empirical assessment of an action model. *Journal of Business Ethics*, 82(2): 477.

Sherman, L.W. (1980) Three models of organizational corruption in agencies of social control. *Social Problems*, 27: 478–491.

Simson, V. and Jennings, A. (1992) *Dishonoured Games: Corruption, Money and Greed at the Olympics*. London: Simon and Schuster.

Slack, T. and Parent, M.M. (2006) *Understanding Sport Organizations: The Application of Organization Theory* (2nd edn). Champaign, IL: Human Kinetics.

Sung, H.-E. (2003) Fairer sex or fairer system? Gender and corruption revisited. *Social Forces*, 82(2): 703–723.

The Associated Press (2006, October 18) Olympic corruption whistleblower Marc Hodler dies. Retrieved 17 January 2009, from http://www.cbc.ca/news/story/2006/10/18/olympics-hodler.html

Treisman, D. (2000) The causes of corruption: a cross-national study. *Journal of Public Economics*, 76: 399–457.

Trevino, L.K. and Youngblood, A. (1990) Bad apples in bad barrels: a causal analysis of ethical decision-making behavior. *Journal of Applied Psychology*, 75: 378–385.

Venard, B. (2009) Organizational isomorphism and corruption: an empirical research in Russia. *Journal of Business Ethics*, 89(1): 59.

Venard, B. and Hanafi, M. (2008) Organizational isomorphism and corruption in financial institutions: empirical research in emerging countries. *Journal of Business Ethics*, 81(2): 481.

Wells, J.T. and Carozza, R.B. (2000) Corruption in collegiate athletics. *Internal Auditor: Journal of the Institute of Internal Auditors*, 57(2): 38–45.

Zyglidopoulos, S., Fleming, P. and Rothenberg, S. (2009) Rationalization, overcompensation and the escalation of corruption in organizations. *Journal of Business Ethics*, 84: 65.

Critical Theory and Critical Management Studies

> Critical theory is a research perspective that encourages paying attention to inequalities and power relations when studying management and organizations.
>
> Critical management studies is a broad field of study which advocates perspectives such as critical theory in the study of management.

In trying to understand 'critical' theory (CT) and its significance within the management of sport, it is necessary to explain how this differs from critical management studies (CMS). Alvesson and Willmott (1992) provided an edited volume of papers which discussed both these concepts and demonstrated how critical theory could be used in the analysis and development of management. They examined CT using a research perspective developed by the Frankfurt school and its followers (e.g., Habermas) that sought to recognize inequalities and power relations in the analysis of a phenomenon. It therefore provided a '*critical-constructive* intellectual counterpoint to mainstream management studies' (1992: 9 emphasis in original). CMS is a broader concept which encourages perspectives such as critical theory in order to provide advances in our knowledge of management practice beyond the rationalistic and function perspectives which have been more commonly employed in the analysis of management issues. Other schools of thought which are encompassed in CMS include labour process theory, feminist organization studies, radical humanist approaches, and 'critical' versions of postmodernism (Spicer et al., 2009). The origins, variations, benefits and purpose of CMS are discussed by Spicer and colleagues who contribute to the CMS literature by challenging the cynicism often associated with much of CMS by suggesting that:

> ... CMS cannot only seek to undermine, question and perhaps destroy given theoretical edifices. Instead, we suggest that the task of CMS should involve asserting quite clearly what it wants. This would transform CMS from a negative enterprise into one which seeks to rearticulate and re-present new ways of managing and organizing. This would hopefully empower CMS researchers to not only engage in systematic dismantling of existing managerial approaches, but also try to construct new and hopefully more liberating ways of organizing. (2009: 555)

Critical theory has been used in the mainstream literature to look at issues concerning management (cf. Burrell, 2009; Clegg and Dunkerly, 1980), marketing (cf. Firat et al., 1987), and accounting (cf. Laughlin, 1987). These issues are often related to sources of inequality or power relations where these are seen as helpful to understanding how organizations operate. Sources of inequality may include

key concepts in
sport management

gender relations, class structure, sexual orientation or dominant ideologies (such as those favoured by 'management'). An example of the use of CT in the analysis of a management/organizational issue is studies on organizational **control**. Within the organization theory literature, a focus on ideology as control (Czarniawska-Joerges, 1988) grew in popularity, as well as the examination of ideology, **power** and the control function (Oliga, 1989). The underpinnings of this work can be partially attributed to the culture literature, yet there was also a growing interest among academics in critical theory generally and the ability of more critical perspectives to advance our understanding of organization control by recognizing the intangible mechanisms which serve to control organizations and actors. A critical perspective of control acknowledges the value of formal control processes, functions and, for example, hierarchical structures, but also conceives that contemporary mechanisms of control are quite often far less obtrusive than formal, administrative mechanisms (see Jermier, 1998). The critical perspective also encouraged a view of control as domination (see for example Storey, 1983) rather than a function of the organization. The critical perspective of control has led researchers to focus on communication, meaning, identity and the dialectic of control in the workplace (see for example Mumby, 2001).

Critical theorists examining control in organizations sought to challenge and to be sceptical of overly rational or observable explanations and viewpoints of the control phenomenon. While there is considerable diversity within the critical theorist tradition (see for example Best and Kellner, 1991; Calhoun, 1995; Layden, 1994; Tong, 1989), critical theorists generally discuss the misuse of power in society and organizations and the resultant domination and mistreatment of individuals and groups. Focusing on control from a critical perspective, Jermier (1998) argued that forms of organization control were often insidious and unobtrusive rather than traditional practices of blatant hierarchical control, given individuals' increasing resistance to such infringements on freedom of choice. He also believed that modern forms of organizational control were often disguised as emancipatory but in fact constituted new management practices, innovative technologies and organizational experiments which provided for more thorough control for societal/organizational elites.

Sport and sport organizations are often seen as clean and unbiased, yet as Slack (2009) notes, sport and sport organizations like other phenomena that we find in social life are 'subject to the inequalities of race, gender, economics and politics'. It may be *inter alia* the relationship between players and owners, fans and owners, players and fans, or different factions of the organization. Critical theorists study these relationships. Critical theory is commonly used in feminist research (cf. Acker, 1990) and has been used in work on sport management (cf. Shaw and Cameron, 2008). With the exception of feminist-inspired studies of the relationship between women and men in sport, organization researchers have not used the critical approach extensively in their work. Frisby (2005) recognized the value of critical theory to the development of research on the management of sport when she suggested that critical social science was under-utilized. This, she suggested, may be because a critical approach often highlights the bad, the ugly, or the negative side of sports.

However, Frisby notes that this can be beneficial in the quest to understand all aspects of the management of sport, including the negative, and to work towards improving practices within organizations. Amis and Silk (2005) presented a special issue of the *Journal of Sport Management* that sought to promote critical and innovative approaches to the study of sport management. This highlighted an important aspect of adopting a 'critical' approach in that adopting such an approach will involve theoretical and methodological issues. The methodological challenges associated with using critical social science were discussed throughout the special issue and provided a contribution to the debate of using critical perspectives to understand the management of sport.

Nauright and Pope's (2009) *The New Sport Management Reader* contained articles which used a critical approach to the management of sport. Their book is a more recent example of work in sport management which uses a critical approach. It covers a wide range of topics including governance and policy, sport marketing and sponsorship, human rights, media culture and sports tourism, as well as sport events. A major strength of the book is its very useful case studies which explore the critical aspects of the management of sport.

In summary, critical theory and critical management studies have a long history in the general management literature but have been only marginally attended to by sport management scholars. The use of critical approaches, drawing from critical theory and the vast literature that continues to develop on CMS, represents a key area for further research and development in the sport management literature. Students and academics may contribute to understanding not only the management of sport but also CT and CMS if their work is also grounded in mainstream literature developments. This suggests that there is a need to move beyond the use of critical theory for analysing gender issues or focusing on methodological issues of epistemology and ontology in sport, and to opt for a more thorough engagement with key issues in the development and criticisms of critical theory and how sport management research may assist in advancing CT generally.

To understand critical management more fully, the reader may refer to the concepts of **power**, **ethics** and **control** that can be found elsewhere in this book.

FURTHER READING

For some further reading on this concept, we would recommend the following:

Frisby, W. (2005) The good, the bad and the ugly: critical sport management research. *Journal of Sport Management*, 19(1): 1–12.

Jermier, J.M. (1998) Introduction: critical perspectives on organizational control. *Administrative Science Quarterly*, 43: 235–256.

Nauright, J. and Pope, S. (2009) *The New Sport Management Reader*. West Virginia: Fitness Information Technology.

BIBLIOGRAPHY

Acker, J. (1990) Hierarchies, jobs, bodies: a theory of gendered organizations. *Gender and Society*, 4(2): 139–158.

Alvesson, M. and Willmott, H. (eds) (1992) *Critical Management Studies*. London: Sage.

Amis, J. and Silk, M. (2005) Rupture: promoting critical and innovative approaches to the study of sport management. *Journal of Sport Management*, 19(4): 355–366.

Best, S. and Kellner, D. (1991) *Postmodern Theory: Critical Interrogations*. London and New York: Macmillan and Guilford Press.

Burrell, G. (2009) Critical Management Studies: progress and prospects. In M. Alvesson, H. Willmott and D. Burton (eds), 'Critical marketing theory: the blueprint?', *European Journal of Marketing*, 35 (5/6): 722–743.

Calhoun, C. (1995) *Critical Social Theory*. Cambridge, MA: Blackwell.

Clegg, S. and Dunkerly, D. (1980) *Organization, Class and Control*. London: Routledge and Kegan Paul.

Czarniawska-Joerges, B. (1988) *Ideological Control in Non-ideological Organizations*. New York: Praeger.

Firat, A.F., Dholakia, N. and Bagozzi R.P. (eds) (1987) *Philosophical and Radical Thought in Marketing*. Lexington, MA: D.C. Heath. pp. xvii–xviii.

Frisby, W. (2005) The good, the bad and the ugly: critical sport management research. *Journal of Sport Management*, 19(1): 1–12.

Jermier, J.M. (1998) Introduction: critical perspectives on organizational control. *Administrative Science Quarterly*, 43: 235–256.

Laughlin, R.C. (1987) Accounting systems in organisational contexts: a case for critical theory. *Accounting, Organizations and Society*, 12(5): 479–502.

Layden, D. (1994) *Understanding Social Theory*. London: Sage.

Mumby, D.K. (2001) Power and politics. In F. Jablin and L.L. Putnam (eds), *The Handbook of Organizational Communication*. Thousand Oaks, CA: Sage. pp. 585–623.

Nauright, J. and Pope, S. (2009) *The New Sport Management Reader*. Morgantown, WV: Fitness Information Technology.

Obel, C., Bruce, T. and Thompson, S. (eds) (2008) *Outstanding: Research about Women and Sport in New Zealand*. Waikato, NZ: Wilf Malcolm Institute. pp. 7–30.

Oliga, J.C. (1989) *Power, Ideology and Control*. London: Plenum Press.

Shaw, S. and Cameron, J. (2008) 'The best person for the job': gender suppression and homologous reproduction in senior sport management. In C. Obel, T. Bruce and S. Thompson (eds) *Outstanding Research About Women and Sport in New Zealand*. Hamilton: The University of Waikato. pp. 211–226.

Slack, T. (2009) Foreword. In J. Nauright and S. Pope (eds), *The New Sport Management Reader*. Morgantown, WV: Fitness Information Technology.

Spicer, A., Alvesson, M. and Karreman, D. (2009) Critical performativity: the unfinished business of critical management studies. *Human Relations*, 62(4): 537–560.

Storey, J. (1983) *Managerial Prerogative and the Question of Control*. London: Routledge and Kegan Paul.

Tong, R. (1989) *Feminist Thought: A Comprehensive Introduction*. London: Routledge.

Decision Making

Decision making is a process that is undertaken at various levels or conditions of uncertainty by individuals and groups. Many different theories of how the decision-making process occurs have been proposed by scholars and some of these are discussed below.

Decision making is a concept – central to organization theory – which has been addressed by researchers in a wide variety of business and sporting situations. It can be studied by underpinning theories from psychology, sociology, mathematics, anthropology and management studies. Whichever underpinning theoretical base is used, decision making is most often viewed as a 'process' which takes place within individuals, groups and organizations (noted as different 'levels' of analysis). It is commonly accepted that decisions are made under varying conditions of uncertainty and from this a number of approaches have been developed to help understand how various decisions are and should be made in different situations.

A widely contested model of individual decision making is the 'rational model' which suggests that decisions in organizations are taken in a logical, systematic manner after a consideration of the problem, all its alternative solutions, and the implementation of a final solution (see the figure below).

 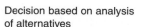

Identification of alternatives   Evaluate all alternatives   Decision based on analysis of alternatives

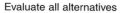

Figure 4   Rational Decision-Making Process

By contrast, another individual model of decision making is the 'administrative model' or what is known as 'bounded rationality', introduced by Nobel Laureate Herbert Simon (1945). This theory recognizes that individuals are not rational, and that all decisions are bounded by each person's past experiences, time limitations, personal preferences, and emotional and cognitive capacities. Managers therefore will most often strive for an optimum solution/decision but will not, and indeed cannot, consider all the options, and nor will they often give their comprehensive consideration to each perceived alternative. Individual decision making is therefore a process limited by a multitude of factors, as indicated by the figure on bounded rationality below. All the alternatives are neither identified nor assessed fully.

Time   Emotions

Past Experience   Cognitive Capacity

Decision Making

Figure 5   Bounded Rationality in Decision Making

Also popular and well documented in organization theory is the 'naturalistic decision making' (NDM) approach which is commonly regarded as a combination of 'non-standard' individual decision making models (Connolly and Koput, 1997). Gore et al. (2006) reviewed the similarities and differences between studies in NDM, making suggestions for future research to advance the knowledge base for decision making in organizations. Decisions in organizations are often made within groups and are rarely the domain of a single individual, and as a result, studies of organizational-level decisions have also emerged. Various models of decision making have been identified, including 'management science' (Leavitt et al., 1973; Markland, 1983); the Carnegie model (Cyert and March, 1963); the structuring of unstructured processes (Mintzberg et al., 1976); the Garbage Can model (Cohen et al., 1972); and the Bradford studies (e.g., Butler et al., 1979/80; Wilson et al., 1986) (for a further explanation of the five models see Slack and Parent, 2006).

Research on the process of decision making has developed through the expanding range of **contexts** that are of interest to scholars. Specifically, researchers have noted differences in decision making and the factors which influence how it occurs according to different cultural values (Tsang, 2004), different organization environments (Oliver and Roos, 2005) and prior behaviour/behavioural knowledge (Betsch et al., 2002). There have been many models which describe organization decision making (for a detailed exploration of various perspectives see Shapira, 1997) and individual decision making (some recent work focuses on 'sensemaking', such as Czarniawska, 2006; Waterman, 1990; Weick, 1995). For an in-depth discussion of the concept of sensemaking see Weick et al. (2005). The authors consider sensemaking as essential and 'central because it is the primary site where meanings materialise that inform and constrain identity and action' (p. 409). By identifying the central features of sensemaking, they also discuss future research which could enhance the sensemaking perspective. For instance, research focusing on sensemaking needs to consider the role of **power**, politics and inequality in accessing resources in order to address questions about how decisions are made and tasks are accomplished within organizations.

Some more recent studies in decision making include Dane and Pratt's (2007) exploration of 'intuition' and its role in managerial decision making, where intuition is seen as the ability to collate information quickly and effectively. After a critical review to more fully define intuition, the authors suggest that intuition is 'affectively charged judgments that arise through rapid, nonconscious, and holistic associations' (p. 40). Intuition and the factors influencing intuition are discussed as a potential means of helping managers make fast and accurate decisions. However the authors also suggest that there is very little known about the nonconscious aspect of human thought processes and this is where future research may focus in order to more fully develop an understanding of the role of intuition in decision-making practices.

The literature on decision making in sport is considerably less developed yet a number of different perspectives have been adopted in an attempt to understand the variety of decision-making situations. The management science approach has been widely used to examine individual athlete and team decisions and performance issues (see Farina et al., 1989; Farmer et al., 2007; Iyer and Sharda, 2009; Rulence-Paques et al., 2005; Sindik and Vidak, 2008). These studies focus not on management- or organization-level decisions but on athletes and teams. There is of course some relevance here for those sport managers who are concerned with the direct management and coaching of athletes, because this research looks specifically at the psychological and interpersonal relations among teams that affect physical performance.

There are also some studies in the management of sport which 'mention' the concept of decision making but fail to draw on any related theories from organization studies research to analyse the process, context or factors that influence decision making in sport. This is mainly because decision making has been treated as though it has a secondary importance to the other concepts investigated and/or measured. For example, Stewart and Smith (2008) developed a model to explain the factors which influence decisions by athletes to take performance-enhancing drugs. Granted, the focus of this article was on taking a more contextualized approach to understanding 'drugs in sport' and to this end it was a useful one. However, to extend the ideas presented, future research may take this rich contextual information through one of the numerous decision-making models in an attempt to understand why and how decisions are made in this situation.

Pawlak and Przybysz (1983) and Winkler (1984) also provide rich detailed descriptions of factors affecting the management (and decision making) of sport in Poland and Germany respectively, but do so without making any reference to management decision-making models. On the other hand, a growing interest in economic development and decisions related to building sport stadia is currently emerging (e.g., Fedderson et al. (2006) and Friedman and Mason (2004)) with the former underpinned by finance theory and the latter by stakeholder theory and a view of decision making as constitutive of power relations.

Another aspect of decision making in sport organizations which has also received attention is the gender equity of decision-making structures and practices. Hoeber (2007) analysed the explanations of organization members to explore gaps between the meanings and practices of gender equity in a Canadian university athletic department, finding gender inequalities embedded in formal decision-making structures. There is considerable scope for further research on decision making in sport organizations. Most recently, Soares and colleagues (2010) focused specifically on the decision-making process in attempting to understand the political factors when managing voluntary sport associations in Madeira, Portugal. To date, the majority of research has focused on sport performance and not the management of sport, with a few notable exceptions as mentioned above. The reader may also be interested in decision making in sporting events and if so could examine the work by Parent (2010) for a discussion of the parameters, drivers and strategies that are used in decision making at major events over time.

Those who are interested in pursuing research on decision making in the management of sport should first look to the general management literature for suitable frameworks and theories to apply to **sport organizations**. Research that demonstrates the value of this approach includes Sack and Johnson's (1996) examination of how decisions were made in the context of the Volvo International Tennis Tournament being awarded to Connecticut in 1989, and Kikulus and colleagues' (1995) examination of decision making in Canadian national sport organizations.

To understand decision making more fully, the reader may refer to the concepts of **power**, **context**, and **sport organizations** that can be found elsewhere in this book.

FURTHER READING

For some further reading on this concept, we would recommend the following:

Nutt, P.C. and Wilson, D.C. (eds) (2009) *Handbook of Decision Making*. Chichester: Wiley.

Slack, T. and Parent, M. (2006) *Understanding Sport Organizations: The Application of Organization Theory*. Champaign, IL: Human Kinetics.

Soares, J., Correia, A. and Rosado, A. (2010) Political factors in the decision-making process in voluntary sport associations. *European Sport Management Quarterly*, 10(1): 5–29.

BIBLIOGRAPHY

Betsch, T., Haberstroh, S. and Hohle, C. (2002) Explaining routinized decision making: a review of theories and models. *Theory and Psychology*, 12(4): 453–488.

Butler, R.J., Astley, W.G., Hickson, D.J., Mallory, G.R. and Wilson, D.C. (1979/80) Strategic decision making: concepts of content and process. *International Studies of Management and Organization*, 9: 5–36.

Cohen, M.D., March, J.G. and Olsen, J.P. (1972) A garbage can model of organizational choice. *Administrative Science Quarterly*, 17: 1–25.

Connolly, T. and Koput, K. (1997) Multiple approaches to naturalistic decision making. In Z. Shapira (ed.), *Organizational Decision Making*. New York: Cambridge University Press.

Cyert, R.M. and March, J.G. (1963) *A Behavioural Theory of the Firm*. Englewood Cliffs, NJ: Prentice-Hall.

Czarniawska, B. (2006) A golden braid: Allport, Goffman and Weick. *Organization Studies*, 27: 1661–1674.

Dane, E. and Pratt, M.G. (2007) Exploring intuition and its role in managerial decision making. *Academy of Management Review*, 32(1): 33–54.

Farina, R., Kochenberger, G.A. and Obremski, T. (1989) The computer runs the bolder boulder: a simulation of a major running race. *Interfaces*, 19: 48–55.

Farmer, A., Smith, J.S. and Miller, L.T. (2007) Scheduling umpire crews for professional tennis tournaments. *Interfaces*, 37(2): 187–196.

Fedderson, U., Maennig, W. and Borcherding, M. (2006) The novelty effect of new soccer stadia: the case of Germany. *International Journal of Sport Finance*, 1(3): 174–188.

Friedman, M.T. and Mason, D.S. (2004) A stakeholder approach to understanding economic development decision making: public subsidies for professional sport facilities. *Economic Development Quarterly*, 18(3): 236–254.

Gore, J., Banks, A., Millward, L. and Kyriakidou, O. (2006) Naturalistic decision making and organizations: reviewing pragmatic science. *Organization Studies*, 27(7): 925–942.

Hoeber, L. (2007) Exploring the gaps between meanings and practices of gender equity in a sport organization. *Gender, Work and Organization*, 14(3): 259–280.

Iyer, S.R. and Sharda, R. (2009) Predictions of athletes' performance using neural networks: an application in cricket team selection. *Expert Systems with Applications*, 36: 5510–5522.

Kikulus, L., Slack, T. and Hinings, B. (1995) Does decision making make a difference? Patterns of change within Canadian national sport organizations. *Journal of Sport Management*, 9: 273–299.

Leavitt, H.J., Dill, W.R. and Eyring, H.B. (1973) *The Organizational World*. New York: Harcourt Brace Jovanovich.

Markland, R.E. (1983) *Topics in Management Science*. New York: Wiley.

Mintzberg, H., Raisinghani, D. and Theoret, A. (1976) The structure of 'unstructured' decision processes. *Administrative Science Quarterly*, 21: 246–275.

Oliver, D. and Roos, J. (2005) Decision-making in high-velocity environments: the importance of guiding principles. *Organization Studies*, 26(6): 889–913.

Parent, M.M. (2010) Decision making in major sporting events over time: parameters, drivers, and strategies. *Journal of Sport Management*, 24(3): 291–318.

Pawlak, G. and Przybysz, T. (1983) Research on the problems of the functioning of the Polish Fencing Association as a sport organization. *International Review for the Sociology of Sport*, 18: 71–93.

Rulence-Paques, P., Fruchart, E., Dru, V. and Mullet, E. (2005) Cognitive algebra in sport decision-making. *Theory and Decision*, 58(4): 387–406.

Sack, A. and Johnson, A.T. (1996) Politics, economic development and the Volvo International Tennis Tournament. *Journal of Sport Management*, 10: 1–14.

Shapira, Z. (1997) *Risk Taking: A Managerial Perspective*. New York: Russell Sage.

Slack, T. and Parent, M. (2006) Understanding sport organizations (2nd edition). Champaign, IL: Human Kinetics.

Simon, H. (1945) *Administrative Behavior: A Study of Decision-making Processes in Administrative Organization*. New York: Macmillan.

Sindik, J. and Vidak, N. (2008) Application of game theory in describing efficacy of decision making of sportsmen's tactical performance in team sports. *Interdisciplinary Descriptions of Complex Systems*, 6(1): 53–66.

Soares, J., Correia, A. and Rosado, A. (2010) Political factors in the decision-making process in voluntary sport associations. *European Sport Management Quarterly*, 10(1): 5–29.

Stewart, B. and Smith, A. (2008) Drug use in sport: implications for public policy. *Journal of Sport and Social Issues*, 32(3): 278–298.

Tsang, E.W.K. (2004) Towards a scientific enquiry into superstitious business decision-making. *Organization Studies*, 25(6): 923–946.

Waterman, R. (Jr) (1990) *Adhocracy: The Power to Change*. Memphis: Whittle Direct Books.

Weick, K. (1995) *Sensemaking in Organizations*. London: Sage.

Weick, K.E., Sutcliffe, K.M. and Obstfeld, D. (2005) Organizing and the process of sensemaking. *Organization Science*, 16(4): 409–421.

Wilson, D.C., Butler, R.J., Cray, D., Hickson, D.J. and Mallory, G.R. (1986) Breaking bounds of organization in strategic decision making. *Human Relations*, 39: 309–332.

Winkler, J. (1984) On the structural change in voluntary organizations: the case of the 'German Sports Association' ('DSB'). *International Review for the Sociology of Sport*, 19: 31–46.

Demand

> Demand for sport products and services refers to the strength and quantity of desire by individuals and groups to consume those products and services provided by sports teams, facilities and businesses.

Demand is a concept which has been studied primarily by economists interested in measuring consumer interest in a given product or service. Practitioners may be interested in demand to aid them in making investment decisions for new products and services or to improve their understanding of current business performance. Demand, in the context of the management of sport, is a concept which has been of great interest to economists, sport business entrepreneurs, and those working in or studying sport operations management (facility and event operations). As a central concept in the study of sport economics/finance, demand is closely related to other key issues in the management of sport such as **competitive balance** (Andreff and Syzmanski, 2006; Goosens and Kesenne, 2007), uncertainty of outcome (Benz et al., 2009), and market size (Buraimo and Simmons, 2009). The literature on demand has broadly focused on different forms of demand (e.g., demand for sports facilities, activities, professional leagues, players/labour, different styles of competition), the effects of demand on related markets for products and services, and the effects of various market conditions or other environmental influences on the demand for sport. In managing the business of sport, practitioners would need to understand how demand affects the supply of goods and services and what factors will affect the demand for those goods and services. Yet research has demonstrated a significant difficulty in studying demand, namely accurately measuring the demand for a product, a sport, or a related service. The application of generic consumer theory is not easily achieved, particularly in relation to spectator sports (Simmons, 2006).

Considering the demand for spectator sports, Simmons (2006) has suggested that there are several unique features to these that require attention in order to analyse demand. First, the event as a product is uncertain to some extent. This uncertainty can be present in the form of who will win and who will lose, or in the performance of individual players. Second, spectator sports are subject to *partisanship* or *habit persistence*. For example, fans will identify with a team but their strength of identification may vary over time. This variation in fan identification can create unpredictability in their behaviour, something which those who are managing sport will need to be aware of when calculating demand. Third, sport events are the core product but they are also sold along with many complementary products for consumption. As these are not available for the consumption of broadcast sport, they are unique to the live sport event product and should be considered when estimating demand for the event as a product.

For further details of the principles of sports economics and the concept of demand, the reader can access Andreff and Syzmanski's (2006) *Handbook on the Economics of Sport*. The authors cover the demand for sport itself, as well as for spectator sports, sports broadcasting, and sport media coverage. Specifically focused on professional sport, Borland and Macdonald (2003) also provide a review of the literature on demand from an international perspective. In doing so they also present a conceptual framework for examining the sources and determinants of the demand for professional sports events/contests and review the empirical evidence for several sources of demand, such as attendance at sporting events, broadcasting, sponsorship, and merchandising. Their framework suggests five categories of determinants of demand for sporting contests: economic (e.g., the costs associated with attendance, fan income); consumer preferences (e.g., habits, conspicuous consumption, the 'bandwagon effect'); quality of viewing (e.g., viewing facilities, weather conditions, timing of the contest); the sporting contest (e.g., significance of the contest, uncertainty of outcome); and supply capacity (determined by the stadium size).

While much of the research on demand for sport focuses on the demand for 'professional sport', there is also an interest in the demand for and consumption of sport in the form of active participation in sporting activities (Lera-Lopez and Rapun-Garate, 2007). Humphreys and Ruseski (2009) examined the market for sports participation, viewing and sports spectating in the United States, while Downward and Riordan (2007) explored the decision to participate and frequency of participation in sporting activities in the United Kingdom. Other authors have looked at the demand for team sports (see Byon et al., 2009) and the demand for 'aggressive play' in English Premier League football (Jewel, 2009).

Some have also looked at the effects of demand on labour markets (Rosen and Sanderson, 2001). Frick (2007) suggested that the majority of research in this area has been on American professional sport, but that due to changes in the market and increasing popularity European football is also attracting the attention of researchers. Kesenne (2007) examined the effects of changes in the European football labour market on competitive balance in European football. Many authors have noted and provided some analysis of the movement of football players from African nations into Europe and the effects this has had on the sport (Darby, 2009; Darby et al., 2007). Goddard and Wilson (2007) also examined racial discrimination in English professional football based on an analysis of players' career progressions.

Sport business owners need to know what the demand for their service or products is if they are to maintain profitability. However, such demand is not always straightforward to measure and this area of research is constantly developing. Economists have focused on this aspect in their research on demand, and the debate still continues as to how to effectively and efficiently measure the demand (and related concepts such as competitive balance) for sports products and services. This is therefore an interesting research area for students and has clear practical applications to sport business practice.

To understand demand more fully, the reader may refer to the concept of **competitive balance** and **corruption** that can be found elsewhere in this book.

FURTHER READING

For some further reading on this concept, we would recommend the following:

Buraimo, B. and Simmons, R. (2009) Market size and attendance in English Premier League football. *International Journal of Management and Marketing*, 6(2): 200–214.

Downward, P. and Rasciute, S. (2010) The relative demands for sport and leisure in England. *European Sport Management Quarterly*, 10(2): 198–214.

Frick, B. (2007) The football players' labor market: empirical evidence from the major European leagues. *Scottish Journal of Political Economy*, 54(3): 422–446.

BIBLIOGRAPHY

Andreff, W. and Syzmanski, S. (2006) *Handbook on the Economics of Sport*. Cheltenham: Edward Elgar.

Benz, M., Brandes, L. and Franck, E. (2009) Do soccer associations really spend on a good thing? Empirical evidence on heterogeneity in the consumer response to match uncertainty of outcome. *Contemporary Economic Policy*, 27(2): 216–235.

Borland, J. and Macdonald, R. (2003). Demand for sport. *Oxford Review of Economic Policy*, 19(4): 478–502.

Buraimo, B. and Simmons, R. (2009) Market size and attendance in English Premier League football. *International Journal of Management and Marketing*, 6(2): 200–214.

Byon, K.K., Zhang, J.J. and Connaughton, D.P. (2009) Dimensions of general market demand associated with professional team sports: development of a scale. *Sport Management Review*, 13(2): 142–157.

Darby, P. (2009) Ghanaian football labour migration to Europe: preliminary observations. In *Labour Market Migration in European Football: Key Issues and Challenges*. Birkbeck Sport Business Centre Research Papers. pp. 149–163.

Darby, P., Akindes, G. and Kirwin, M. (2007) Football academies and the migration of African football labor to Europe. *Journal of Sport and Social Issues*, 31(2): 143–161.

Downward P. and Riordan, J. (2007) Social interactions and the demand for sport: an economic analysis. *Contemporary Economic Policy*, 25: 518–537.

Frick, B. (2007) The football players' labor market: empirical evidence from the major European leagues. *Scottish Journal of Political Economy*, 54(3): 422–446.

Goddard, J. and Wilson, J.O.S. (2007) Racial discrimination in English professional football: evidence from an empirical analysis of players' career progression. *Cambridge Journal of Economics*, 33(2): 295–316.

Goosens, K. and Kesenne, S. (2007) National dominance in European football leagues. In M.M. Parent and T. Slack (eds), *International Perspectives on the Management of Sport*. London: Butterworth-Heinemann.

Humphreys, B.R. and Ruseski, J.E. (2009) Estimates of the dimensions of the sports market in the US. *International Journal of Sports Finance* 4(2): 94–113.

Jewel, T. (2009) Estimating demand for aggressive play: the case of English Premier League Football. *International Journal of Sport Finance*, 4(3): 192–210.

Kesenne, S. (2007) The peculiar international economics of professional football in Europe. *Scottish Journal of Political Economy*, 54(3): 388–399.

Lera-Lopez, F., Rapun-Garate, M. (2007) The demand for sport: sport consumption and participation models. *Journal of Sport Management*, 21(1): 103–122.

Rosen, S. and Sanderson, A. (2001) Labour markets in professional sports. *The Economic Journal*, 111(469): 47–68.

Simmons, R. (2006) The demand for spectator sports. In W. Andreff and S. Szymanski (eds), *Handbook on the Economics of Sport*. Cheltenham: Edward Elgar.

Effectiveness or Efficiency

Effectiveness refers to the extent to which goals are achieved.

Efficiency considers whether resources have been optimized in achieving goals.

Within the tradition that emphasizes the importance of **organizational goals**, a distinction needs to be made between the concepts of organizational effectiveness and organizational efficiency. *Effectiveness* means the extent to which an organization achieves its goals. *Efficiency*, on the other hand, takes into account the amount of resources used to produce the desired output. It is often measured in economic terms, usually as the ratio of inputs to outputs. However, as Mintzberg (1982: 104) notes, 'Because economic costs can usually be more easily measured than social costs, efficiency often produces an escalation in social costs.' While efficiency is a goal for all organizations, an efficient organization is not necessarily effective. Likewise, an organization may be effective in that it achieves its goal(s) but it may not be efficient in its use of resources to achieve those goals.

Research on effectiveness in organizations has been conducted from several perspectives, including rational goal, open systems, internal process, participant satisfaction, competing values, and multiple constituencies (Atkinson and Maxwell, 2007; Cameron, 1986; Herman and Renz, 1998; Ostroff and Schmitt, 1993; Quinn and Rohrbaugh, 1983). Some more recent research focuses on effectiveness in relation to a variety of concepts such as culture (Gregory et al., 2009), leadership (Yukl, 2008), strategy implementation (Neilson et al., 2008) and identity (Paulsen et al., 2009). The generic literature is considerably more diverse and those interested in studying effectiveness should search for literature related to the context in which they are interested (e.g., small firms, groups, the industry sector) in order to learn about the effectiveness studies that have been conducted and which approaches to the subject are most common.

Stewart (2010) discussed Data Envelopment Analysis (DEA) as a widely recognized tool for measuring organizational efficiency, and offered an extension to the model to include top management goals. Broadly, the efficiency literature is concerned with studies focused on determinants of organizational efficiency such as information technology (Seol et al., 2008).

There have been several studies in sport management which have specifically looked at effectiveness or efficiency (see below), but these are also concepts that are examined more implicitly in many studies. Efficiency and effectiveness are attracting increasing interest owing to the rising level of competition and decreasing resources within the sport industry. Cunningham (2002) measured the effectiveness of strategic types (as defined by Miles and Snow, 1978) and organization achievement (athletic achievement, student athlete graduation rates, and compliance with Title IX regulations). This research considered the **context** of intercollegiate athletes in the USA and provided a review of previous attempts to define and measure the concept of effectiveness in the management of sport literature and in the wider field of management (e.g., Connolly et al., 1980; Koski, 1995; Papadimitriou and Taylor, 2000).

Some more recent studies include Shilbury and Moore (2006) who examined organizational effectiveness in Australian national Olympic sport organizations, but who also provided a thorough review of literature pertaining to measuring effectiveness in organizations, including four different conceptual definitions for effectiveness which as a result altered how effectiveness could be measured. In addition

Papadimitriou (2007) attempts to empirically verify effectiveness measures for Greek national sport organizations, suggesting five dimensions which are argued to clearly reflect the five constituent groups considered in the study. Babiak (2009) compares the effectiveness criteria used by a Canadian non-profit sport organization and its multiple cross-sectoral partners using a qualitative case study method. The central focus of her work was measuring the effectiveness of interorganizational relationships (IOR). These **networks** were seen by sport organizations as an essential **strategy** for reducing external environmental uncertainty and gaining access to valuable resources. It was therefore deemed important to examine how various sector organizations (public, private and voluntary) measured the effectiveness of partnerships and which criteria they used to evaluate those partnerships. The results indicated that there were some similarities but also some inconsistencies in how the organizations viewed and evaluated the effectiveness of a network.

Lewis et al. (2009) measures the contributions of capability and efficiency to effectiveness in major league baseball teams from 1901 to 2002. Team capability is measured with offensive and defensive statistics using Network Data Envelopment Analysis to produce efficiency scores that were representative of managerial performance. Effectiveness was defined as the teams' winning percentage. Both capability and efficiency were found to be significant contributors to performance/effectiveness, with capability being of greater importance. However, when the authors examined post-season performance, this was held to be unrelated to capability and managerial performance.

The effectiveness concept has also been studied in relation to other concepts such as 'leadership' and 'management'. Kotter (1990) differentiated between managers and leaders by specifying the difference between effective managers and effective leaders. Effective managers, according to Kotter, could plan, budget, organize and control staff as well as solve problems, whereas effective leaders would be able to inspire, direct, and motivate people. Here, research was directed at the effectiveness of individuals rather than the organization as a whole.

The most significant earlier work on the effectiveness of sport organizations is that of Chelladurai and his associates. Chelladurai et al.'s (1987) article in the *Journal of Sport Management* presents an interesting perspective on integrating approaches to effectiveness into a comprehensive framework. His work with Szyszlo and Haggerty in the same year also produced a psychometric scale for determining effectiveness in national sport organizations, while his research with Haggerty (1991) focused primarily on the differences between professionals and volunteers in their perceptions of process effectiveness.

Barros (2003) also looked at efficiency in Portuguese sport organizations implementing government-subsidized training programmes. The results of his study indicated that **sport policy** changes were needed, from an incentive regulation policy to one based on a governance environment framework. The concept of efficiency has been examined in the context of Premier League Football clubs (Barros and Leach, 2007), with the results indicating variable efficiencies across clubs. There is another related body of literature which examines 'performance' rather than effectiveness and at times uses the terms interchangeably. Although this is ill-defined, we discuss

performance management here as a separate concept in order to highlight the growing body of research which is emerging.

The concepts of efficiency and effectiveness are thoroughly considered in the generic organization literature and there are some good examples of studies conducted on sport organizations. However, as organizations are always changing so too might the factors which contribute to their efficiency or effectiveness. It is therefore vital to consider **context** when conducting studies of efficiency and effectiveness, and there is scope for further work on defining the concepts in different contexts and developing appropriate indicators to measure the concepts in order to further discuss their implications for managers.

To understand efficiency and effectiveness more fully, the reader may refer to the concepts of **organizational goals**, **performance management**, **networks**, **strategy**, **sport policy** and **context** that can be found elsewhere in this book.

FURTHER READING

For some further reading on this concept, we would recommend the following:

Babiak, K.M. (2009) Criteria of effectiveness in multiple cross-sectoral interorganizational relationships. *Evaluation and Programme Planning*, 32(1): 1–12.

Barros, C.P. (2003) Incentive regulation and efficiency in sport organizational training activities. *Sport Management Review*, 6(1): 33–52.

Barros, C.P. and Leach, S. (2007) Technical efficiency in the English Football Association Premier League with a stochastic cost frontier. *Applied Economics Letters*, 14(10): 731–741.

Lewis, H.F., Lock, K.A. and Sexton, T.R. (2008) Organizational capability, efficiency and effectiveness in Major League Baseball: 1901–2002. *European Journal of Operational Research*, 197(2): 731–740.

BIBLIOGRAPHY

Atkinson, M. and Maxwell, V. (2007) Driving performance in a multi-agency partnership using outcome measures: a case study. *Measuring Business Excellence*, 11(2): 12–22.

Babiak, K.M. (2009) Criteria of effectiveness in multiple cross-sectoral interorganizational relationships. *Evaluation and Programme Planning*, 32(1): 1–12.

Barros, C.P. (2003) Incentive regulation and efficiency in sport organizational training activities. *Sport Management Review*, 6(1): 33–52.

Barros, C.P. and Leach, S. (2007) Technical efficiency in the English Football Association Premier League with a stochastic cost frontier. *Applied Economics Letters*, 14(10): 731–741.

Bayle, E. and Madella, A. (2002) Development of a taxonomy of performance for national sport organizations. *European Journal of Sport Science*, 2(2): 1–21.

Bayle, E. and Robinson, L. (2007) A framework for understanding the performance of national governing bodies of sport. *European Sport Management Quarterly*, 7(3): 249–268.

Cameron, K. (1986) Effectiveness as a paradox: consensus and conflict in conceptions of organizational effectiveness. *Management Science*, 32(5): 539–553.

Chelladurai, P. (1987) Multidimensionality and multiple perspectives of organizational effectiveness. *Journal of Sport Management*, 1: 37–47.

Chelladurai, P. and Haggerty, T.R. (1991) Measures of organizational effectiveness in Canadian national sport organizations. *Canadian Journal of Sport Science*, 16: 126–133.

Chelladurai, P., Szyszlo, M. and Haggerty, T.R. (1987) Systems-based dimensions of effectiveness: the case of national sport organizations. *Canadian Journal of Sport Science*, 12: 111–119.

Connolly, T., Conlon, E.J. and Deutsch, S.J. (1980) Organizational effectiveness: a multiple constituency approach. *Academy of Management Review*, 5: 211–217.

Cunningham, G.B. (2002) Examining the relationship among Miles and Snow's strategic types and measures of organizational effectiveness in NCAA Division I athletic departments. *International Review for the Sociology of Sport*, 37(2): 159–175.

Frisby, W. (1986) The organizational structure and effectiveness of voluntary organizations: the case of Canadian sport governing bodies. *Journal of Park and Recreation Administration*, 4(3): 61–74.

Gregory, B.T., Harris, S.G., Armenakis, A.A. and Shook, C.L. (2009) Organizational culture and effectiveness: a study of values, attitudes and organizational outcomes. *Journal of Business Research*, 62(7): 673–679.

Herman, R.D. and Renz, D.O. (1998) Nonprofit organizational effectiveness: contrasts between especially effective and less-effective organizations. *Nonprofit Management and Leadership*, 9(1): 23–38.

Koski, P. (1995) Organization effectiveness of Finnish sport clubs. *Journal of Sport Management*, 9: 85–95.

Kotter, J.P. (1990) *Change: How Leadership Differs from Management*. New York: The Free Press.

Lewis, H., Lock, K. and Sexton, T. (2009) Organizational capability, efficiency, and effectiveness in Major League Baseball: 1901–2002. *European Journal of Operations Research*, 197: 731–741.

Madella, A. (1998) La performance di successo delle organizzazioni: Spunti di riflessione per gestire effecemente la societa di athletica leggers. *Athleticastudi*, 1: 2–3.

Miles, R.E. and Snow, C.C. (1978) *Organizational Strategy, Structure and Process*. New York: McGraw-Hill.

Mintzberg, H. (1982) A note on that dirty word 'efficiency'. *Interfaces*, 12: 101–105.

Neilson, G.L., Martin, K.L. and Power, E. (2008) The secrets to successful strategy execution. *Harvard Business Review*, 86(6): 60–70.

Ostroff, C. and Schmitt, N. (1993) Configurations of organizational effectiveness and efficiency. *Academy of Management Journal*, 36(6): 1345–1361.

Papadimitriou, D. (2007) Conceptualizing effectiveness in a non-profit organizational environment: an exploratory study. *International Journal of Public Sector Management*, 20(7): 571–587.

Papadimitriou, D. and Taylor, P. (2000) Organizational effectiveness of Hellenic national sports organisations: a multiple constituency approach. *Sport Management Review*, 3: 23–46.

Pattanayak, B., Gupta, V. and Niranjana, P. (eds) (2002) *Creating Performing Organizations: International Perspectives for Indian Managers*. New Delhi: Sage. pp. 151–177.

Paulsen, N., Maldonado, D., Callan, V.J. and Ayoko, O. (2009) Charismatic leadership, change and innovation in an R&D organization. *Journal of Organizational Change Management*, 22(5): 511–523.

Quinn, R.E. and Rohrbaugh, J. (1983) A spatial model of effectiveness criteria: towards a competing values approach to organizational analysis. *Management Science*, 29(3): 363–377.

Seol, H., Lee, H., Kim, S. and Park, Y. (2008) The impact of information technology on organizational efficiency in public services: a DEA-based DT approach. *Journal of the Operational Research Society*, 59: 231–238.

Shilbury, D. and Moore, K.A. (2006) A study of organizational effectiveness for national Olympic sporting organizations. *Nonprofit and Voluntary Sector Quarterly*, 35(1): 5–38.

Stewart, T.J. (2010) Goal-directed benchmarking for organizational efficiency. *Omega*, 38: 534–539.

Wolfe, R., Hoeber, L. and Babiak, K. (2002) Perceptions of the effectiveness of sport organizations: the case of intercollegiate athletics. *European Sport Management Quarterly*, 2: 135–156.

Yukl, G. (2008) How leaders influence organizational effectiveness. *The Leadership Quarterly*, 19(6): 708–722.

Employability

> Employability is the extent to which individuals possess the skills, competencies or attributes which will enable them to gain and maintain employment in a given industry.

Employability is a concept of concern to students, academic staff, employers, and governments. Students seek out education and training courses in order to increase their employability; academic staff/educators attempt to embed employability into their programmes, and employers are always looking for individuals with the right skills and attributes to be effective in their organizations. Research has tended to focus on defining employability (and examining employability in different contexts), the relationship between employability and other work-related constructs, and employability pedagogy.

Research focusing on defining employability in various **contexts** has revealed that the concept is highly context dependent. Nicholls (2005) discussed the employability of history students; Thornham and O'Sullivan (2004) likewise examined the employability of media studies students; and Major (2006) examined employability in the context of travel, tourism, and hospitality students. Nicholls (2005) proposed to investigate the employability skills that students claimed to possess upon entering an educational programme, thereby raising questions about whether higher education was focusing on the development of the correct set of skills for students. Thornham and O'Sullivan (2004) presented the findings of a three-year funded UK research project that had been designed to investigate the meanings and perceptions of employability held by teachers, students, graduates, and employers, as related to the media studies curriculum. Comparing these studies it is evident that employability can vary from one subject area to another, and various groups of people will hold different perspectives on the meaning of employability.

There has been considerable academic debate regarding how to define employability. The authors listed above and others such as Lees (2002) have noted that broadly speaking employability is concerned with the skills, knowledge and attitudes which underpin an individual's ability to possess the capability to gain employment, maintain that employment, and progress in their desired career path. It is not surprising then that research has identified different skills and attributes as necessary for employability in different subject areas and job contexts. It is these skills and knowledge which may vary across sectors when we investigate the employability requirements for students.

Fugate et al. (2004) presented a further view of employability as a 'psycho-social' construct with three dimensions: career identity, personal adaptability, and social and human capital. Defining employability as a proactive and multi-dimensional construct, the authors go on to compare and contrast employability with other concepts such as job loss and job search. Other authors have given a focus to defining employability without seeking to examine its relationship with other concepts.

Yorke (2006b) provided a comprehensive account of the concept by defining what it was and what it was not. He suggested that employability was not merely a set of transferable skills that enabled an individual to obtain employment. He defined employability as:

> a set of achievements – skills, understandings and personal attributes – that makes graduates more likely to gain employment and be successful in their chosen occupations, which benefits themselves, the workforce, the community and the economy.(2006b: 8)

This definition recognizes employability as concerned with gaining employment, maintaining employment, and gaining new employment if necessary. Yorke argues that transferable skills are a key contributor to employability, but so too are the personal qualities, beliefs and experience that individuals possess.

Pedagogical research on employability is concerned with identifying and testing methods of developing employability in undergraduate and postgraduate students. Pool and Sewell (2007) provided a practical framework for developing employability by examining existing research into employability issues and the experience of the authors involved. Their model is theoretical and requires empirical testing. Yorke (2006a), on behalf of the Higher Education Academy (www.heacademy. ac.uk), supplied a more comprehensive edited series of papers concerned with embedding employability in the curriculum. Within this, many contemporary issues were addressed and these included:

Series 1

- Employability and higher education: what it is – what it is not.
- Employability: judging and communicating achievements.
- Embedding employability into the curriculum.
- Entrepreneurship and higher education: an employability perspective.
- Employability and work-based learning.
- Pedagogy for employability.

Series 2

- Work-related learning in higher education.
- Employability for research postgraduates.
- Employability and part-time students.
- Ethics and employability.
- Career development learning and employability.
- Personal development planning and employability.
- Embedding employability in the context of widening participation.

In the context of sport management, there has actually been very little research in comparison to the application of employability as discussed in the variety of settings mentioned above. A few notable exceptions here include Becket and Kemp

(2006) in their edited volume of papers that examined various aspects of employ-ability in the hospitality, leisure, sport, and tourism sectors in England. Within this, Keech (2006) was the only author to focus explicitly on employability in sport management programmes, through examining the employability benefits to undergraduate sport management students of undertaking a work placement/ work-related learning programme. This research discussed the student perspective and offered suggestions for best practice when integrating a work-based programme within a sport management undergraduate curriculum. Jowdy et al. (2004) exam-ined work-based undergraduate experience and suggested an integral approach to sport management internships, underpinned by Wilber (1995, 2000a, 2000b). The paper also provides an important discussion of internships in the context of experiential learning.

Horch and Schutte (2003) examined the 'competencies' of sport managers in German sport clubs and federations. Competencies were referred to as the knowl-edge skills or attitudes required to conduct activities leading to the successful engage-ment of an individual's career. There have also been a number of articles published in the *Journal of Sport Management* focusing on internships, interns, and curricular content, with the intention being to provide guidelines for programmes preparing undergraduate and graduate students for careers in sport management (see Brown, 1990; Chouinard, 1993).

Griffiths and Reiner (2010) described how the University of Glamorgan, in consultation with key stakeholders, developed a sport development degree to meet industry and government expectations of graduate employability. Petry and col-leagues (2008) presented a broader view of issues in higher education in sport management in their edited volume looking at sport in Europe. Within this, Camy and Madella (2008) specifically addressed 'employability' in sport but not just the management of sport. They took a slightly different approach to the concept of employability, adopting the definition put forth by CEDEFOP (2000):

> ... the degree of adaptability an individual demonstrates in finding and keeping a job and updating occupational competencies/skills. Employability depends not only on adequacy of knowledge and competencies/skills of individuals but also on the incen-tives and opportunities offered to individuals to seek employment.

The authors therefore argue that employability can be demonstrated by having a good balance between job availability and employment demand. They then go on to give an overview of the employability of sport graduates in the EU by discussing the relationship between the job market in sport and sport-related sectors and the sport training and education system.

Although there has been considerable research on employability generally, there has been limited research which focuses specifically on sport/leisure. There is there-fore considerable scope for further research on this concept in the **context** of the management of sport. As we have recommended with other concepts, the generic literature provides a valid starting-point for understanding the concept as well as a foundation for forming research questions related to sport. However, given the considerable context dependence of employability, it is necessary to consider also the relevant characteristics of the sport industry when researching employability.

To understand employability more fully the reader may refer to the concept of **context** that can be found elsewhere in this book.

FURTHER READING

For some further reading on this concept, we would recommend the following:

Camy, J. and Madella, A. (2008) Higher education and employability in sport. In K. Petry, K. Froberg, A. Madella and W. Tokarski (eds), *Higher Education in Sport in Europe: From Labour Market Demand to Training Supply*. Maidenhead: Meyer and Meyer Sport.

Horch, H.D. and Schutte, N. (2003) Competencies of sport managers in German sport clubs. *Managing Leisure*, 8: 70–84.

Yorke, M. (ed.) (2006) *Learning and Employability Series 1 and 2*. The Higher Education Academy, Learning and Teaching Support Network (LTSN) and the Enhancing Student Employability Coordination Team (ESECT), Oxford.

BIBLIOGRAPHY

Becket, N. and Kemp, P. (eds) (2006) *Enhancing Graduate Employability in Business and Management, Hospitality, Leisure, Sport, Tourism*. Newbury: Threshold.

Brown, S. (1990) Selecting students for graduate academic success and employability: a new research direction for sport management. *Journal of Sport Management*, 4(2): 133–146.

Camy, J. and Madella, A. (2008) Higher education and employability in sport. In K. Petry, K. Froberg, A. Madella and W. Tokarski (eds), *Higher Education in Sport in Europe: From Labour Market Demand to Training Supply*. Maidenhead: Meyer and Meyer Sport.

CEDEFOP (2000) *An Age of Learning: Vocational training policy at European level: vocational training policy report 2000*, Thessaloniki, CEDEFOP.

Chouinard, N. (1993) Some insights on meaningful internships in sport management: a cooperative education approach. *Journal of Sport Management*, 7(2): 95–100.

Fugate, M., Kinicki, A.J. and Ashforth, B. (2004) Employability: a psycho-social construct, its dimensions and applications. *Journal of Vocational Behavior*, 65(1): 14–38.

Griffiths, R. and Reiner, P. (2010) Designing a degree programme 'fit' for the sport industry. *Journal of Applied Research in Higher Education*, 2(1): 47–57.

Horch, H.D. and Schutte, N. (2003) Competencies of sport managers in German sport clubs. *Managing Leisure*, 8: 70–84.

Jowdy, E., MacDonald, M. and Spence, K. (2004) An integral approach to sport management internships. *European Sport Management Quarterly*, 4(4): 215–233.

Keech, M. (2006) Placements and employability in sport and leisure management. In N. Becket and P. Kemp (eds), *Enhancing Graduate Employability in Business Management, Hospitality, Leisure, Sport and Tourism*. Newbury: Threshold.

Lees, D. (2002) Graduate Employability: Literature Review. Available at http://www.palatine.ac.uk/files/emp/1233.pdf (last accessed 12/01/2011).

Major, B. (2006) Enhancing travel, tourism and hospitality management graduates' employability. In N. Becket and P. Kemp (eds), *Enhancing Graduate Employability in Business and Management, Hospitality, Leisure, Sport, Tourism*. Newbury: Threshold. pp. 125–132.

Nicholls, D. (2005) *The Employability of History Students*. Glasgow: Higher Education Academy Subject Centre for History, Classics and Archaeology.

Petry, K., Froberg, K., Madella, A. and Tokarski, W. (2008) *Higher Education in Sport in Europe: From Labour Market Demand to Training Supply*. Maidenhead: Meyer and Meyer Sport.

Pool, L.D. and Sewell, P. (2007) The key to employability: developing a practical model of graduate employability. *Education + Training*, 49(4): 277–289.

Thornham, S. and O'Sullivan, T. (2004) Chasing the real: 'employability' and the media studies curriculum. *Media, Culture and Society*, 26(5): 717–736.

Wilber, K. (1995) An informal overview of transpersonal studies. *Journal of Transpersonal Psychology*, 27(2): 107–129.

Wilber, K. (2000a) *Sex, Ecology, Spirituality: The Spirit of Evolution*, 2nd edn. Boston: Shambhala.

Wilber, K. (2000b) *A Theory of Everything*. Boston: Shambhala.

Yorke, M. (ed.) (2006a) *Learning and Employability Series 1 and 2*. The Higher Education Academy, Learning and Teaching Support Network (LTSN), and the Enhancing Student Employability Coordination Team (ESECT), Oxford.

Yorke, M. (2006b) Employability in higher education: what it is and what it is not. Available: http://www.heacademy.ac.uk/assets/York/documents/ourwork/tla/employability/id116_employability_in_higher_education_336.pdf (last accessed 12/01/11).

Entrepreneurship

> *Entrepreneurship refers to the act of an entrepreneur who undertakes risk and innovation for the purpose of economic benefit in business transactions.*

Audretsch (2002) provided a comprehensive review of the literature pertaining to entrepreneurship, noting the interdisciplinary nature of the subject. That is, entrepreneurship does not easily correspond to one academic subject area such as economics, marketing, or finance. Rather, it is a 'multifaceted, complex social and economic phenomenon' (2002: 1). There is also a significant body of literature on small business management which addresses entrepreneurship and related concepts. Mullen et al. (2009) noted that there have been considerable advances both theoretically and methodologically in the small business–entrepreneurship literature, and they discussed trends in the research methods underpinning this before making recommendations on how to make further advances in the field. Their recommendations were based on their analysis of 665 research articles published between 2001 and 2008 in the *Journal of Small Business Management*, *Journal of Business Venturing* and *Entrepreneurship Theory and Practice*.

Research has proposed that there are different types of entrepreneurship such as social and strategic forms. Various definitions of social entrepreneurship have been developed in a number of different contexts including not-for-profit organizations, private and public sector organizations, and combinations of all three (Christie and Honig, 2006). Short et al. (2009), in their review of the social entrepreneurship literature, suggested that more rigorous research methods and empirical studies were

key concepts in sport management

necessary to provide advancements in the field. They also suggested that the concept was informed by areas of interest which were common to many management scholars and so more mainstream literature and theory should be used in framing research questions about social entrepreneurship.

Kyrgidou and Hughes (2009) discussed strategic entrepreneurship (SE) as a relatively new concept, providing a discussion of its origins, key components, and possible future research direction. They did this by reviewing the literature on entrepreneurship and **strategy** separately before moving on to a discussion of SE as the interdependence between the two bodies of knowledge. They concluded by defining SE as a process with four components:

1 An entrepreneurial mindset, culture and leadership that supported the search for entrepreneurial opportunity.
2 The strategic management of resources involving managing the bundling, structuring and leverage of financial, human, and social capital.
3 The application of creativity to develop innovations and novel combinations in order to achieve radical and incremental innovation.
4 The formation and execution of competitive advantages.

While entrepreneurship has commonly been referred to as an action, process, or activity, there is also a suggestion that it can be considered as a stock of capital, 'since it reflects a number of different factors and forces, legal, institutional and social, which create a capacity for this activity' (Hofstede et. al., 2002). Entrepreneurship is often considered to be a private sector business activity and as Kearney and colleagues (2009) noted, one that is primarily concerned with small to medium-sized enterprises. However, the authors also pointed out that the concept of entrepreneurship has also appeared in the public administration literature with increasing frequency over the last two decades and so they included a comparative analysis of public and private sector entrepreneurship, highlighting the key differences and similarities in order to provide practical advice for public sector entrepreneurs. Some notable differences between public and private sector entrepreneurship were identified along with several key dimensions, including:

- innovation
- risk taking
- proactivity
- political environment
- complexity
- munificence
- dynamism
- structure/formalization
- decision making
- control
- rewards/motivation
- performance measurement.

The research concludes that entrepreneurship is beneficial to the public sector and should be encouraged for increased organizational **performance management**. The challenge for managers in the public sector is recognizing how the unique context of the sector translates into similarities and differences between public and private entrepreneurship and addressing this **context** via their management policies and behaviour.

Harms et al. (2009) suggest that a key topic in entrepreneurship research was the analysis of new venture performance (NVP) and **change**. They also suggested that the configuration approach to studying change was useful given the diverse and complex nature of new venture performance: that is, configuration theory assists in identifying different types of organizations and the interrelationships between personal, structural, environmental, and strategic factors relevant to new venture success. They suggested caution on considering the specific **context** of new ventures when applying configuration theory to explain change or performance.

Slotte-Kock and Coviello (2009) examined how the entrepreneurship literature has addressed the issue of **networks** and in particular the use of 'process' in understanding networks. They drew on Hoang and Antoncic's (2003) critique of the network literature in entrepreneurship research before assessing other approaches to network analysis and proposing their own framework for the analysis of the various processes associated with network development.

There is very little research published on entrepreneurship in sport and considerable scope to develop a further understanding of the process and types of entrepreneurship in sport businesses, as only a few articles have addressed this issue and primarily through case studies. Gorse and colleagues (2010) provide a case study analysis of entrepreneurship in sport through their examination of Red Bull. Their work documented the development of the Red Bull brand and discussed the implications of the success of the brand development for other sport companies wishing to do the same for their products. Tergesen and Argue (2010) focus more specifically on the entrepreneurship concept through an examination of the five dimensions of entrepreneurship activity at Brooks Sports, a footwear and apparel company based in Washington, DC. Ratten (2010, 2011) has also written about sport-based entrepreneurship, developing a conceptual framework intended for future research and discussing different forms of entrepreneurship in sport.

As can be seen from the preceding discussion of entrepreneurship, research on the concept spans many different literatures, from a pure focus on entrepreneurship processes and practices to examining the concept in international business and in understanding change and networks. Research on entrepreneurship is developing rapidly, perhaps due to its increasingly important role in society. While we have tried to give a short overview of the complexity of this concept, the reader would benefit from Acs and Audretsch's (2010) edited volume which covers the topic comprehensively and provides a useful historical context to the development of entrepreneurial research. Blackburn and Kovalainen (2009) also supply a review of research in small firms and entrepreneurship that seeks to stimulate the debate around the agendas, methodologies, and methods used in such research. They suggest that although entrepreneurship offers a rich and lucrative setting for research, future studies need to take a more critical perspective in order to provide new insights on the concept in practice. Research on entrepreneurship in sport is quite far behind the mainstream literature and so there is considerable scope to develop further understanding. The sport entrepreneurship literature goes some way to considering developments in the mainstream literature but has not yet yielded the theoretical and methodological accomplishments that Blackburn and Kovalainen (2009) highlight.

To understand entrepreneurship more fully the reader may refer to the concepts of **change**, **context**, **networks**, and **strategy** that can be found elsewhere in this book.

FURTHER READING

For some further reading on this concept, we would recommend the following:

Acs, Z.J. and Audretsch, D.B. (eds) (2010) *Handbook of Entrepreneurship Research*. London: Springer.

Blackburn, R. and Kovalainen, A. (2009) Researching small firms and entrepreneurship: past, present and future. *International Journal of Management Reviews*, 11(2): 127–148.

Gorse, S., Chadwick, S. and Burton, N. (2010) Entrepreneurship through sports marketing: a case analysis of Red Bull in sport. *Journal of Sponsorship*, 3(4): 348–357.

Mullen, M.R., Budeva, D.G. and Doney, P.M. (2009) Research methods in the leading small business-entrepreneurship journals: a critical review with recommendations for future research. *Journal of Small Business Management*, 47(3): 287–307.

BIBLIOGRAPHY

Acs, Z.J. and Audretsch, D.B. (eds) (2010) *Handbook of Entrepreneurship Research*. London: Springer.

Audretsch, D.B. (2002) *Entrepreneurship: A Survey of the Literature*. Report prepared for European Commission, Enterprise Directorate General. London: Institute for Development Strategies, Indiana University & Centre for Economic Policy Research (CEPR).

Blackburn, R. and Kovalainen, A. (2009) Researching small firms and entrepreneurship: past, present and future. *International Journal of Management Reviews*, 11(2): 127–148.

Christie, M. and Honig, B. (2006) Social entrepreneurship: new research findings. *Journal of World Business*, 41(1): 1–5.

Gorse, S., Chadwick, S. and Burton, N. (2010) Entrepreneurship through sports marketing: a case analysis of Red Bull in sport. *Journal of Sponsorship*, 3(4): 348–357.

Harms, R., Kraus, S. and Schwarz, E. (2009) The suitability of the configuration approach in entrepreneurship research. *Entrepreneurship and Regional Development*, 21(1): 25–49.

Hoang, H. and Antoncic, B. (2003) Network-based research in entrepreneurship: a critical review. *Journal of Business Venturing*, 18(2): 165–187.

Hofstede, G., Noorderhaven, N.G., Thurik, A.R., Wennekers, A.R.M., Uhlaner, L. and Wildeman, R.E. (2002) Culture's Role in Entrepreneurship. In J. Ulijn & T. Brown (eds), *Innovation, Entrepreneurship and Culture: The Interaction Between Technology, Progress and Economic Growth*. Brookfield: Edward Elgar.

Kearney, C., Hisrich, R.D. and Roche, F. (2009) Public and private sector entrepreneurship: differences, similarities or a combination? *Journal of Small Business and Enterprise Development*, 16(1): 26–46.

Kyrgidou, L.P. and Hughes, M. (2009) Strategic entrepreneurship: origins, core elements and research directions. *European Business Review*, 22(1): 43–63.

Mullen, M.R., Budeva, D.G. and Doney, P.M. (2009) Research methods in the leading small business-entrepreneurship journals: a critical review with recommendations for future research. *Journal of Small Business Management*, 47(3): 287–307.

Ratten, V. (2010) Sport-based entrepreneurship: towards a new theory of entrepreneurship and sport management. *International Entrepreneurship and Management Journal*, 7(1): 57–69.

Ratten, V. (2011) A social perspective of sports-based entrepreneurship. *International Journal of Entrepreneurship and Small Business*, 12(3): 314–326.

Short, J.C., Moss, T.W. and Lumpkin, G.T. (2009) Research in social entrepreneurship: past contributions and future opportunities. *Strategic Entrepreneurship Journal*, 3: 161–194.

Slotte-Kock, S. and Coviello, N. (2009) Entrepreneurship research on network processes: a review and ways forward. *Entrepreneurship: Theory and Practice*, 34(1): 31–57.

Tergesen, S. and Argue, E. (2010) Run happy: entrepreneurship at Brooks Sports. *International Journal of Sport Management and Marketing*, 7(1–2): 132–143.

Ethics

> *Ethics is a branch of philosophy that considers moral issues related to right and wrong. These issues can be discussed in a wide variety of contexts, for example business, sport, or society, and ethical issues may be unique to these individual contexts.*

According to Argandona (2008) one of the first serious attempts to integrate ethics into management was the work of Juan Antonio Perez Lopez (1986 [1934]). Since these beginnings, research has emerged offering a range of practical 'how to' models and instructions for managers (e.g., Chryssides and Kaler, 1996; Steare, 2006) to philosophical and theoretical debates focusing on the very notion and role of ethics in management and organizations (e.g., Hancock, 2008; Long and Driscoll, 2008).

There is a distinct body of literature focused on business ethics which has existed for over thirty years as an area of applied philosophy which suggests that businesses should demonstrate a degree of social responsibility (Bowie, 2002). Business ethics therefore emerged as a challenge to economic theories of the firm which favoured shareholder needs and profit maximization. The predominant approach which continues to challenge the profit/shareholder wealth maximization model is stakeholder theory, first introduced by Freeman (1984). Laplume and colleagues (2008) provided a comprehensive review of this literature, but it was Kaler (2003, 2006) who examined the usefulness of the stakeholder approach to business ethics.

The stakeholder approach highlights that managers make decisions by considering the implications of their choice for various groups of stakeholders, with a concern for the interests of others as opposed to their own self-interest (Jones et al., 2007). While the literature on business ethics is concerned with a variety of related topics and literatures such as **corporate social responsibility**

(Bos et al., 2006; Lund-Thomsen, 2008) and **critical management studies** (CMS) (Brewis and Wray-Bliss, 2008), the aim of much of this work is to produce comprehensive guidance which effectively influences daily business behaviour and **decision making** (see Boatright, 1993; Frederick, 1995; Margolis and Phillips, 1999; Pucetaite and Lamsa, 2008; Soule, 2002).

Integrative social contracts theory has arguably been the most encouraging approach for achieving a set of norms capable of guiding business agents (Donaldson and Dunfee, 1995, 1999; Van Oosterhout et al., 2006). However, many other perspectives have underpinned business ethics research in an attempt to prescribe how ethics can be integral to business function, such as the Kantian perspective (Bowie, 1999), egoism (Beauchamp and Bowie, 2004), utilitarianism (Sartorios, 1975; Singer, 1976; Smart, 1973), virtue ethics (Solomon, 1992), Rawlsian fairness (Rawls, 1971), rights theories (Logsdon and Wood, 2002), and the ethics of care, derived from 'feminist ethics in general and Gilligan (1982) in particular' (Jones et al., 2007: 139).

The above theories and perspectives are applied across a wide range of issues in the study of business ethics. Broadly, these issues are concerned with decision making, and as noted in the previous discussion, attempt to guide decision-making agents in taking the 'right' decisions. Research has focused on a number of different 'levels' such as functional areas of business, including management education, marketing finance, human resources, operations and strategic management, but with some overlap with ethical issues between these functions (Bowie, 2002). Another important topic in business ethics is management responsibility to the environment: DesJardins (2002) presents an overview of this topic and of the environment as a silent stakeholder.

Another issue in business ethics is relativism (Dunfee and Donaldson, 2002) which examines the extent to which business conduct should retain corporate values in international **contexts**. Dunfee and Donaldson (2002) discuss universal norms of conduct, international agreements, and legitimate reasons for divergences from these guidance measures. This indicates another topic of business ethics which is **governance** and the relationship between ethics and legal imperatives (Cranor, 2002). Finally, one of the most controversial topics in business ethics research concerns pedagogy and the debate which is centred on how and if ethical decision making and ethical behaviour can be taught (Sims, 2002; Solberg et al., 1995).

Some of the topics of interest in the mainstream business ethics literature can also be found in the context of the management of sport such as pedagogy issues (Zakus and Malloy, 2007). The stakeholder approach has also been utilized (Maguire, 2008) as well as concerns over (corporate) social responsibility (Persson, 2008) and critical management studies (Frisby, 2005). There has not however been direct use of the integrated social contracts theory or attention paid to relativism in the management of sport.

One of the first to embrace a concern for ethics in the management of sport was Earle F. Zeigler (see Zeigler, 1989, 2007) who was actively involved in promoting the development of a code of ethics for the North American Society of Sport Management. There are also a variety of issues, which arguably are ethical in nature (and at times possibly legal), that are unique to the management of sport and not found in traditional business or organization research. Doping and genetic modification have received much attention from researchers for example (Hanstad et al., 2008; Konig, 1995; Miah, 2004), while **corruption** and specifically match fixing are a reality in commercialized sporting contests (Alvad, 2008). Bockrath and Franke (1995: 243) suggested that 'discussions on ethics are booming' and provide an edited volume of ten research papers from an international selection of authors, examining a variety of issues in sport ethics concerned with recreational-, amateur-, and elite-level sport.

In addition DeSensi and Rosenburg (1996) provided an example of how ethics can be applied to the management of sport through a critical examination of ethical concepts. Their work gives a good introduction to basic concepts, ethical theories, personal and professional rights and ethical models, and the application of ethics to the functions of decision making, marketing, personnel management and sports law, as well as offering suggestions for some future issues in sports ethics that sport managers/students should consider. A very contemporary use of ethics theory in the context of the management of sport is Wenner's (2006, 2008) examination of the media, the Super Bowl, and how moral issues can become commercial issues.

Morgan (2007) also presents an edited volume of some key issues related to ethics in sport. Although this is not specifically aimed at the management of sport, it is useful for identifying discussion points for students and managers which are important to the development and integrity of sport. From broad discussions of the moral foundations and values of sport to more specific issues of fair play, sportsmanship, cheating, drugs, sexual inequality, disability and violence in sport, the text and its many contributors offer a sound starting-point for anyone who is interested in learning more about these issues in relation to sport, and should prompt some thoughtful questions on the management of these.

In summary, ethics is a crucial concept in business generally and in the management of sport specifically. Business ethics implies a degree of social responsibility from managers and staff. This may be perceived as being in opposition to traditional theories of business which favoured economic responsibility in decision making and behaviour, or ethical business practices could be seen as being economically advantageous for business but in the long rather than the short term. Issues in business ethics can also be found in the management of sport but there are also some ethical issues which are unique to sport such as fair play, drugs, and disability. While the subject of ethics in sport is interesting and has received considerable attention from researchers, the management implications are not often explicitly addressed. There is much scope for those interested in ethics related to the management of sport and we would suggest that any studies in this area consider the themes, concepts and perspectives which are currently being addressed in the mainstream literature to inform any research on ethics within the context of sport management.

To understand ethics more fully the reader may refer to the concepts of **decision making, corruption, corporate social responsibility, critical management studies, governance** and **context** that can be found elsewhere in this book.

FURTHER READING

For some further reading on this concept, we would recommend the following:

Chryssides, G. and Kaler, J. (1996) *Essentials of Business Ethics*. Maidenhead: McGraw-Hill.
DeSensi, J. and Rosenberg, M. (1996) *Ethics in Sport Management*. Morgantown, WV: Fitness Information Technology.
Morgan, W.J. (2007) *Ethics in Sport*. Champaign, IL: Human Kinetics.

BIBLIOGRAPHY

Alvad, S. (2008) Corruption and match fixing in Bulgarian football. *Play the Game News*, available at http://www.playthegame.org/news/detailed/corruption-and-match-fixing-in-bulgarian-football.html (last accessed on 20/05/09).
Argandona, A. (2008) Integrating ethics into action theory and into organization theory. *Journal of Business Ethics*, 78: 435–446.
Beauchamp, T.L. and Bowie, N.E. (2004) *Ethical Theory and Business*. Upper Saddle River, NJ: Prentice-Hall.
Boatright, J.R. (1993) *Ethics and Conduct in Business*. Englewood Cliffs, NJ: Prentice-Hall.
Bockrath, F. and Franke, E. (1995) Is there any value in sports? About the ethical significance of sport activities. *International Review for the Sociology of Sport*, 30(3+4): 283–309.
Bos, N.D., Shami, N.S. and Naab, S. (2006) A globalization simulation to teach corporate responsibility: design features and analysis of student reasoning. *Simulation and Gaming*, 37(1): 56–72.
Bowie, N.E. (1999) *Business Ethics: A Kantian Perspective*. Malden, MA: Blackwell.
Bowie, N.E. (2002) *The Blackwell Guide to Business Ethics*. Oxford: Blackwell.
Brewis, J. and Wray-Bliss, E. (2008) Researching ethics: towards a more reflexive critical management studies. *Organization Studies*, 29(12): 1521–1540.
Chryssides, G. and Kaler, J. (1996) *Essentials of Business Ethics*. Maidenhead: McGraw-Hill.
Cranor, C.F. (2002) The regulatory context for environmental and workplace health protections: recent developments. In N.E. Bowie (ed.), *The Blackwell Guide to Business Ethics*. Oxford: Blackwell.
DesJardins, J.R. (2002) Environmental responsibility. In N.E. Bowie (ed.), *The Blackwell Guide to Business Ethics*. Oxford: Blackwell.
DeSensi, J. and Rosenberg, M. (1996) *Ethics in Sport Management*. Morgantown, WV: Fitness Information Technology.
Donaldson, T. and Dunfee, T.W. (1995) Integrative social contracts theory: a communitarian conception of economic ethics. *Economics and Philosophy*, 11: 85–112.
Donaldson, T. and Dunfee, T.W. (1999) *Ties that Bind: A Social Contracts Approach to Business Ethics*. Boston, MA: Harvard Business School Press.
Dunfee, T.W. and Donaldson, T.J. (2002) Untangling the knot of corruption: Global bribery viewed through the lens of integrative social contract theory. In N.E. Bowie (ed.) *The Blackwell Guide to Business Ethics*. Oxford: Blackwell Publishing.
Frederick, W.C. (1995) *Values, Nature, and Culture in the American Corporation*. New York: Oxford University Press.
Freeman, R.E. (1984) *Strategic Management: A Stakeholder Approach*. Boston, MA: Pitman.
Frisby, W. (2005) The good, the bad and the ugly: critical sport management research. *Journal of Sport Management*, 19(1): 1–12.
Gilligan, C. (1982) *In a Different Voice*. Cambridge, MA: Harvard University Press.
Hancock, P. (2008) Embodied generosity and an ethics of organization. *Organization Studies*, 29(10): 1357–1373.

Hanstad, D.V., Smith, A. and Waddington, I. (2008) The establishment of the World Anti-Doping Agency: a study of the management of organizational change and unplanned outcomes. *International Review for the Sociology of Sport*, 43(3): 227–249.

Jones, T.M., Felps, W. and Bigley, G.A. (2007) Ethical theory and stakeholder-related decisions: the role of stakeholder culture. *Academy of Management Review*, 31(1): 137–155.

Kaler, J. (2003) Differentiating stakeholder theories. *Journal of Business Ethics*, 46: 71–83.

Kaler, J. (2006) Evaluating stakeholder theory. *Journal of Business Ethics*, 69: 249–268.

Konig, E. (1995) Criticisms of doping: the nihilistic side of technological sport and the antiquated view of sport ethics. *International Review for the Sociology of Sport*, 30(3–4): 247–260.

Laplume, A.O., Sonpar, K. and Litz, R.A. (2008) Stakeholder theory: reviewing a theory that moves us. *Journal of Management*, 34(6): 1152–1189.

Logsdon, J.M. and Wood, D.J. (2002) Business citizenship: from domestic to global levels of analysis. *Business Ethics Quarterly*, 12(2): 155–187.

Long, B.S. and Driscoll, C. (2008) Codes of ethics and the pursuit of organizational legitimacy: theoretical and empirical contributions. *Journal of Business Ethics*, 77: 173–189.

Lund-Thomsen, P. (2008) The global sourcing and codes of conduct debate: five myths and five recommendations. *Development and Change*, 39(6): 1005–1018.

Maguire, J. (2004) Challenging the sports-industrial complex: human sciences, advocacy and service. *European Physical Education Review*, 10: 299–332.

Maguire, J. (2008) 'Real politic' or 'ethnically based': sport, globalisation, migration and nation-state policies. *Sport in Society*, 11(4): 443–458.

Margolis, J.D. and Phillips, R.A. (1999) Towards an ethics of organizations. *Business Ethics Quarterly*, 9: 619–638.

Miah, A. (2004) *Genetically Modified Athletes: Biomedical Ethics, Gene Doping and Sport*. London: Routledge.

Morgan, W.J. (2007) *Ethics in Sport*. Champaign, IL: Human Kinetics.

Perez Lopez, J.A. (1986 [1934]) Should businessmen behave ethically? Technical note. IESE. FHN-188-E, December. Reproduced under the title 'Deben los empresarios y directivos comportarse eticamente', in Perez Lopez (1998), Chapter 7.

Persson, H.T.R. (2008) Social capital and social responsibility in Denmark: more than gaining public trust. *International Review for the Sociology of Sport*, 43: 35–51.

Pucetaite, R. and Lamsa, A.M. (2008) Advancing organizational trust in a post-socialist context: role of ethics management tools. *Economics and Management*, 13: 381–388.

Rawls, J. (1971) *A Theory of Justice*. Cambridge, MA: Belknap.

Sartorios, R.E. (1975) *Individual Conduct and Social Norms: A Utilitarian Account of Social Union and Rule of Law*. Belmont, CA: Dickenson.

Sims, R.R. (2002) Business ethics teaching for effective learning. *Teaching Business Ethics*, 6(4): 393–410.

Singer, P. (1976) Freedom and utility in the distribution of health care. In R. Veatch and R. Bronson (eds), *Ethics and Health Policy*. Cambridge, MA: Boelinger.

Smart, J.J.C. (1973) Distribution, justice and utilitarianism. In J. Arthur and W.H. Shaw (eds), *Justice and Economic Distribution*, Englewood Cliffs, NJ: Prentice-Hall.

Solberg, J., Strong, K.C. and McGuire, C. Jr (1995) Living (not learning) ethics. *Journal of Business Ethics*, 14: 71–81.

Solomon, R.C. (1992) *Ethics and Excellence: Cooperation and Integrity in Business*. New York: Oxford University Press.

Soule, E. (2002) Managerial moral strategies: in search of a few good principles. *Academy of Management Review*, 27: 114–124.

Steare, R. (2006) *Ethicability: How to Decide What's Right and Find the Courage to Do It*. London: Roger Steare Consulting.

Van Oosterhout, J., Heugens, P. and Kaptein, M. (2006) The internal morality of contracting: advancing the contractualist endeavor in business ethics. *Academy of Management Review*, 31(3): 521–539.

Wenner, L.A. (2006) Recovering from Janet Jackson's breast: ethics and the nexus of media, sport and management. *Journal of Sport Management*, 18: 315–334.

Wenner, L.A. (2008) Super-cooled sports dirt: moral contagion and Super Bowl commercials in the shadows of Janet Jackson. *Television and New Media*, 9(2): 131–154.

Zakus, D.H. and Malloy, D.C. (2007) Critical and ethical thinking in sport management: philosophical rationales and examples of methods. *Sport Management Review*, 10: 133–158.

Zeigler, E.F. (1989) Proposed creed and code of professional ethics for the North American Society for Sport Management. *Journal of Sport Management*, 3(1): 2–4.

Zeigler, E.F. (2007) Sport management must show social concern as it develops tenable theory. *Journal of Sport Management*, 21: 297–318.

Globalization

> *Globalization is the economic, political, socio-cultural and temporal integration of people, values, goods and services enabled through advances in technology, travel and communication.*

Globalization surfaced as *the* buzzword of the 'Roaring Nineties' because it best captured the increasingly independent nature of social life on our planet. At the end of the opening decade of the twenty-first century there were millions of references to globalization in both virtual and printed space. (Steger, 2010: 1)

Essentially, through the process of globalization it is easier for people to communicate via the internet, mobile phones, and satellites and to be exposed to various cultures/values through these communication technologies as well as travel. This has enabled an expansion of people, businesses, and ideas across the globe and a deregulation of legal and political barriers to encourage this exchange. Western values and ideals from religion (e.g., Christianity) to cultural traditions (e.g., Christmas) can be found in Asian and European nations. Similarly cultural ideas from Asian business practices and European fashion and language are no longer confined to those countries but can be found in North America and Australasia as well.

Research on the concept of globalization has primarily been from a sociological or an economics perspective. Broadly, the purpose of this research has been to discuss the impacts of globalization on society, with many positive and negative effects identified. Rossi (2008) provides a useful edited text on globalization and the key theoretical and methodological issues related to the concept, and demonstrated that different theoretical approaches can yield different truths about the globalization movement and that adopting different methods of studying globalization is also imperative to understanding the concept's multiple aspects. More specifically, research has examined the impacts of globalization on elements of society such as, but not limited to:

- culture (United Nations Human Settlements Programme, 2004);
- the environment (Lofdahl, 2002);
- health (Lee, 2003);
- social policy (Baldock et al., 2007).

There is also interest in the effects of globalization on particular geographical areas including, but not limited to:

- Asia (Davies and Nyland, 2004);
- China (Wu, 2006);
- Europe (Weber, 2001).

Exploring the 'impacts' of globalization means looking at how the increased movement of people, capital, goods and ideas affects a culture (and the values and traditions associated with it), a national society, or a social/political system. Some benefits of globalization include increases in life expectancy for people in developing countries, a 60 per cent decline in child mortality in less than four decades, a doubling of grain yields in developing countries, and large increases in food supplies (Johnson, 2002).

Poli (2010) adopts a relationist view in attempting to understand globalization by examining the migration of football players throughout Europe. His work discussed three perspectives of globalization before examining the geography of the international flows of footballers and analysing the quantitative evolution of expatriate players in the five principal European leagues, in order to verify if the increase in international flows of players reflects a biased system of recruitment. The third part of his findings analyses the empirical functioning of transfer networks using three ideal-typical upward career paths of African players to the Premier League for illustration. The overall purpose of Poli's research is to 'show that the general tendency of increased international flow of athletes does not occur by itself, as a natural feature of the contemporary world, but concretely depends on the actions of a plurality of actors who, by the relations they build on a daily basis, are responsible for the interconnection between specific zones of departure and arrival' (2010: 492). He therefore suggests that globalization is not a force that is immune to changes in human behaviour, but is instead a structural process that is strongly linked to human action. While this is a useful discussion of the concept of globalization and sport, it does not extend to a discussion of the management implications of an increase in the migration of athletes or the dangers and benefits of this form of globalization for sport.

Miller et al. (2001: 131) describes globalization as:

a process through which space and time are compressed by technology, information flows, and trade and power relations, allowing distant actions to have increased significance at the local level.

Surrounding this definition is a thorough discussion of the social and political **context** of sport which emanates from the forces of globalization. More recently,

Rowe (2011) extends this discussion to critically evaluate the flow of media sport from the West to the East and back again. Considering new sport media, hybrid sport cultural forms, sport-related political controversies, and other contemporary issues in global sport media, Rowe provided an insightful analysis leading to projections for the future global sport media.

A debate which features throughout the sport globalization literature is the role and representation of women. Stevenson (2002), using **media** coverage of the Australian Tennis Open, investigated issues concerning the situation of women and their relationship to sport as consumers and participants. More broadly, the issue of gender and sport has also featured in considering the impacts of globalization.

Houlihan and Green (2008) discussed globalization as one of three pressures towards a convergence of **sport policy** and systems for elite **sport development** between countries. They recognized the significance of globalization in sport policy research, but also suggested that the concept had proven difficult to operationalize once the

> consideration moves from a simple cataloguing of effects to an analysis of forms ... causes ... and trajectories of globalization... . (2008: 10)

Houlihan and Green (2008) describe the globalization literature as 'eclectic' but also suggest that there is broad agreement on four issues:

1 Globalization should not be considered as a coherent, one-directional process.
2 The varying depth of social embeddedness is important in the analysis of cultural change and an overemphasis on the popularity of sports or events should be avoided.
3 The impact of globalization on policy in individual countries will vary due to differences in the 'reach' of global forces and differences in the responses to those forces.
4 The economic dimension of globalization in sport has garnered most interest in the last twenty-five years, with some of this being given to political and cultural aspects.

The other two pressures for a similarity in elite sport development systems discussed by Houlihan and Green were **commercialization** and governmentalization. They looked at how these concepts have impacted on sport and changed the way it is viewed and experienced by society in general, by athlete, and by those working in sport.

Overall, the literature on the globalization of sport has attempted to examine the process as it applies to sport and the impacts globalization has had on sport. Globalization has proven to be a considerable force, partly responsible for changes in the role of sport in society. It is often discussed alongside the concept of commercialization in attempting to analyse the change in sport from amateur to professional structures and systems, but perhaps more consideration of the cultural and political aspects of the concept would be useful for understanding its impact on sport and the management of sport, rather than, as the tendency has been, to concentrate on the economic element of globalization. The relationship between globalization, the media and sport has also received a great deal of attention and continues to do so. As sport responds to the forces of globalization the changes and challenges will also continue to evolve and so there is considerable scope for further research to understand how this can be managed.

To understand globalization more fully, the reader may refer to the concepts of **commercialization**, **context**, **sport development**, **media/broadcasting** and **sport policy** that can be found elsewhere in this book.

FURTHER READING

For some further reading on this concept, we would recommend the following:

Giulianotti, R. and Robertson, R. (2007) Special Issue: Sport and Globalization – Transnational Dimensions. *Global Networks*, 7(2): 107–247.
Poli, R. (2010) Understanding globalization through football: the new international division of labour, migratory channels and transnational trade circuits. *International Review for the Sociology of Sport*, 45(4): 491–506.
Rowe, D. (2011) *Global Media Sport: Flows, Forms and Futures*. London: Bloomsbury Academic.

BIBLIOGRAPHY

Andreff, W. (2008) Globalization of the sports economy. *Rivista Di Diritto Ed Economia Dello Sport*, 4(3): 13–32.
Baldock, J., Manning, N. and Vickerstaff, S. (eds) (2007) *Social Policy*. Oxford: Oxford University Press.
Davies, G. and Nyland, C. (eds) (2004) *Globalization in the Asia Region: Impacts and Consequences*. Cheltenham: Edward Elgar.
Houlihan, B. and Green, M. (2008) *Comparative Elite Sport Development: Systems, Structures and Public Policy*. London: Butterworth-Heinemann.
Johnson, D.G. (2002) Globalization: what it is and who benefits. *Journal of Asian Economics*, 13(4): 427–439.
Lee, K. (ed.) (2003) *Health Impacts of Globalization: Towards Global Governance*. Basingstoke: Palgrave Macmillan.
Lofdahl, C.L. (2002) *Environmental Impacts of Globalization and Trade: A Systems Study*. Cambridge, MA: MIT.
Miller, T., Lawrence, G., McKay, J. and Rowe, D. (2001) *Globalization and Sport: Playing the World*. London: Sage.
Poli, R. (2010) Understanding globalization through football: the new international division of labour, migratory channels and transnational trade circuits. *International Review for the Sociology of Sport*, 45(4): 491–506.
Rossi, I. (ed.) (2008) *Frontiers of Globalization*. New York: Springer.
Rowe, D. (2011) *Global Media Sport: Flows, Forms and Futures*. London: Bloomsbury Academic.
Steger, M.B. (2010) *Globalization: A Brief Insight*. New York: Sterling.
Stevenson, D. (2002) Women, sport and globalization: competing discourses of sexuality and nation. *Sport and Social Issues*, 26(2): 209–225.
Thibault, L. (2009) Globalization of sport: an inconvenient truth. *Journal of Sport Management*, 23(1): 1–20.
United Nations Human Settlements Programme (2004) *The State of the World's Cities 2004/2005: Globalization and Urban Culture*. Oxford: Earthscan.

key concepts in sport management

Weber, S. (2001) *Globalization and the European Political Economy.* New York: Columbia University Press.

Wu, Y. (2006) *Economic Growth, Transition and Globalization in China.* Cheltenham: Edward Elgar.

Governance

> *Governance is a concept that has been used to encompass the systems and organizations which regulate and control organizations.*

The concept of governance is not strictly found in the organization theory literature, but through an analysis of this term we can find that within organization theory, governance issues are often addressed using the concept of **control**. However, governance has been addressed rigorously in the management of sport and continues to be an important field of enquiry and so we will discuss some of the prominent literature and approaches to this concept below. The concept of governance has mostly been used to discuss control issues within voluntary organizations whereas 'control' is often used in reference to private and public sector organizations.

Hoye and Cuskelly (2007) suggest that the term 'sport governance' is the practice of governance in a sporting context. Kikulus (2000) describes governance in sport as the responsibility for the overall direction of the organization which is institutionalized within all clubs, national governing bodies, government agencies, sport service organizations and professional sport teams. Henry and Lee (2004) discussed three approaches to, and concepts of, 'governance' in sport; these were:

- systemic governance;
- organizational governance;
- political governance.

Systemic governance refers to the manner in which sport is controlled and organized, increasingly by global forces and international business/markets rather than local and national government. The concept of systemic governance highlights the trend of **globalization** in sport and the increasing complexity of sport organizations' external environment, given the multitude of political, economic and socio-cultural forces which act upon individual **sport organizations**. For example, in heavily commercialized sports such as European football, the North American 'Big Four' sport leagues, Formula 1 racing and English rugby stakeholders will play an essential role in influencing or governing the actions of organizations, players, coaches and other individuals. Within European football, broadcasters, the FA (Football Association), FIFA (Fédération Internationale de Football Association), and UEFA (Union des Associations Européennes de Football) will all have some influence over the development of the sport. Even entities such as the European Union are part of the systemic governance of football, as they will have influenced the regulation of player contracts for example.

Of course, systemic governance does not mean that sport is **powerless**. Some Formula 1 owners have used the threat of a breakaway league to influence the system within which they must operate. For those interested in this concept and the related concept of globalization, there is a considerable body of literature upon which to draw. Jozsa (2004) details much of the literature on the globalization of sport and provides an analysis of the foreign expansion of American professional sport leagues. He also presents a detailed analysis of the international strategies of five American professional sport leagues, why and how they have progressed as international sport businesses, and essentially addresses the concept of capitalism as well as globalization in relation to sport management. Silk and Andrews (2001) also provide a thorough examination of the globalization concept and issues related to the globalization of sport through multinational corporations. Added to this, for a contemporary view of the globalization concept in relation to sport, see Andrews and Ritzer (2007).

The second concept of governance discussed by Henry and Lee (2004) is organizational governance which refers to standards of management behaviour and ethical issues related to organizational operations. Also referred to as 'good governance' or 'corporate governance', this covers issues related to cultural perceptions of how to achieve **ethical** management and indeed what good governance means. Research on governance at an organizational level can be found in work on sport organizations and factors which affect their operation such as funding (e.g., Edwards et al., 2009) and policy (Skirstad, 2009). Other work in the literature has focused on gender issues in the governance of sport organizations (White and Kay, 2006) and there is also some explicit work which focuses on governance through examining the various legal aspects of how organizations are governed/controlled (e.g., Dietl et al., 2009). It is at the organizational level that researchers have examined boards within voluntary sport organizations and the various factors which serve to influence/control members and, as a result, influence the governance of organizations (e.g., Hoye and Cuskelly, 2003). Most recently, Ferkins and colleagues (2009) have examined the role of boards in the strategy formation of sport organizations.

The third concept is that of political governance, which is concerned with the influence of governments and governing bodies upon sport organizations. For a general review of international sport governance, Forster (2006) provides some interesting suggestions about the detrimental effect of **commercialization** on the sport governance system. He also argues that much of the sport governance literature is concerned with individual governing bodies, such as Jennings (2000) and Sugden and Tomlinson (1998), and as such focuses on internal governance. Other studies have noted the significance of international sport governing bodies (Boli and Thomas, 1999, 2001; Ronit and Schneider, 2000; Strange, 1996) but failed to provide any detailed analysis of their operation or influence.

Political governance is addressed primarily in the work of researchers focused on sports policy development by national and supra-national governments. Some of this research is concerned with the development of sport policy and with the comparison of sport policy intervention between various countries (Houlihan, 2005, 2007).

Other research has examined the relationship between central government sport policy and local, grassroots sports organizations (Skille, 2009).

A contemporary theme of the research on governance in sport focuses on the role of sport generally and sport governing bodies specifically (both national and local organizations) in developing social capital in communities. Groeneveld and colleagues (2010) present an edited volume which analysed seven European countries' sport governance structures and their relationship to social capital. They noted an increasing interest coming from the European Union and some individual European countries policy makers in sport's ability to generate social capital. Unfortunately there was little recognition by governments of sport's ability to encourage dysfunctional social behaviour and decreases in social capital. A focus on social capital highlighted the importance of **networks** and relationships in the analysis of governance.

In summary, sport governance is concerned with the organizing, power, and control of sport. The concept of governance can be examined on a variety of levels including organizational, national/international systems, and political influences. The governance of sport has changed drastically in recent years due to the increasing commercialization and globalization of sport. This means that a larger number of stakeholders, including government, private sector sponsors, governing bodies and the media, now play a role in controlling how sport is played and regulated. This affects not only professional sport but also small local clubs who are influenced by the government applying the pressure of commercialization to encourage them to be more professional in how they operate. Research into governance can be underpinned by related concepts from sociology such as social capital or concepts from organization studies such as control. Governance is also prevalent in the public administration and political studies literatures.

To understand governance more fully the reader may refer to the concepts of **control**, **globalization**, **sport organization**, **commercialization**, **power**, **networks** and **ethics** that can be found elsewhere in this book.

FURTHER READING

For some further reading on this concept, we would recommend the following:

Dietl, H.M., Franck, E., Hasan, T. and Lang, M. (2009) Governance of professional sports leagues: cooperatives versus contracts. *International Review of Law and Economics*, 29: 127–137.
Forster, J. (2006) Global sports organisations and their governance. *Corporate Governance*, 6(1): 72–83.
White, M. and Kay, J. (2006) Who rules sport now? White and Brackenridge revisited. *International Review for the Sociology of Sport*, 41: 465–473.

BIBLIOGRAPHY

Andrews, D.L. and Ritzer, G. (2007) The global in the sporting glocal. *Global Networks*, 7(2): 113–153.
Boli, J. and Thomas, G. (eds) (1999) *Constructing World Culture: International Nongovernmental Organisations Since 1875*. Stanford, CA: Stanford University Press.
Boli, J. and Thomas, G. (2001) INGOs and the organisation of world culture. In P. Diehl (ed.), *The Politics of Global Governance: International Organizations in an Interdependent World*, 2nd edn. Boulder, CO: Lynne Rienner. pp. 62–96.

Dietl, H.M., Franck, E., Hasan, T. and Lang, M. (2009) Governance of professional sports leagues: cooperatives versus contracts. *International Review of Law and Economics*, 29: 127–137.

Edwards, J.R., Mason, D.S. and Washington, M. (2009) Institutional pressures, government funding and provincial sport organizations. *International Journal of Sport Management and Marketing*, 6(2): 128–149.

Ferkins, L., Shilbury, D. and McDonald, G. (2009) Board involvement in strategy: advancing the governance of sport organizations. *Journal of Sport Management*, 23: 245–277.

Forster, J. (2006) Global sports organisations and their governance. *Corporate Governance*, 6(1): 72–83.

Groeneveld, M., Houlihan, B. and Ohl, F. (eds) (2010) *Social Capital and Sport Governance in Europe*. Abingdon: Routledge.

Henry, I. and Lee, P.C. (2004) Governance and ethics in sport. In J. Beech and S. Chadwick (eds), *The Business of Sport Management*. London: Prentice-Hall.

Houlihan, B. (2005) Public sector sport policy. *International Review for the Sociology of Sport*, 40(2): 163–185.

Houlihan, B. (2007) *Sport Policy: A Comparative Analysis of Stability and Change*. Oxford: Butterworth-Heinemann.

Hoye, R. and Cuskelly, G. (2003) Board-Executive relationships within voluntary sport organisations. *Sport Management Review*, 6: 53–74.

Hoye, R. and Cuskelly, G. (2007) *Sport Governance*. Oxford: Elsevier (Butterworth-Heinemann)

Jennings, A. (2000) *The Great Olympic Scandal: When the World Wanted its Games Back*. London: Simon and Schuster.

Jozsa, F.P., Jr (2004) *Sports Capitalism: The Foreign Business of American Professional Sports Leagues*. Gateshead: Athenaeum.

Kikulus, L. (2000) Continuity and change in governance and decision making in national sport organizations: institutional explanations. *Journal of Sport Management*, 14(4): 293–320.

Ronit, K. and Schneider, V. (eds) (2000) *Private Organisations in Global Politics*. London: Routledge.

Silk, M.S. and Andrews, D.L. (2001) Beyond a boundary? Sport, transnational advertising and the re-imaging of national culture. *Journal of Sport and Social Issues*, 25(2): 180–201.

Skille, E.A. (2009) State sport policy and voluntary sports clubs: the case of the Norwegian Sports City Programme as social policy. *European Sport Management Quarterly*, 9(1): 63–79.

Skirstad, B. (2009) Gender policy and organisational change: a contextual approach. *Sport Management Review*, 12(4): 202–216.

Strange, S. (1996) The retreat of the state: the diffusion of power in the world economy. *Cambridge Studies in International Relations*. Cambridge: Cambridge University Press.

Sugden, J. and Tomlinson, A. (1998) *FIFA and the Contest for World Football: Who Rules The People's Game?* Cambridge: Polity.

White, M. and Kay, J. (2006) Who rules sport now? White and Brackenridge revisited. *International Review for the Sociology of Sport*, 41: 465–473.

Image, Identity and Reputation

Whereas image is typically defined according to how organizational members think others see their organization (whether this is the image that has been projected or not) at a certain point in time, identity and reputation are defined over a longer term, with identity being how organizational members see themselves over the long term and reputation being how stakeholders see the organization over the long term (i.e., the accumulation of images providing an overall estimation).

Organizational image, identity and reputation are interrelated, and sometimes hard to differentiate: Dutton and Dukerich (1991) simply state that an organization's identity is defined as how organizational members see their organization, while Albert and Whetten (1985) define organizational identity as the characteristics of an organization which are central, distinctive, and enduring or constant. These characteristics allow an organization's members to define their organization and understand why it exists. However, the enduring aspect of identity has been questioned. Gioia et al. (2000) argue that identity should be seen as fluid and unstable and not enduring, because it is still a social construction (something created or 'constructed' by people in society) and social constructions do change. Soenen and Moingeon (2002) present five facets of an organization's identities:

- Professed identity or what organizational members say about their organization.
- Projected identity or what elements an organization uses to present itself to specific **stakeholders**.
- Experienced identity or what organizational members experience or believe, whether consciously or not, in relation to their organization.
- Manifested identity or the organization's historical identity, the elements which have characterized the organization over time (i.e., organizational reputation, see below).
- Attributed identity or what stakeholders ascribe to the organization.

Balmer and Greyser (2002) provide five types of identities (labelled the AC²ID test) thought to be present at the same time in a corporation:

- *Actual identity* or the current attributes of a corporation.
- *Communicated identity* or the controllable aspect seen as corporate communication.
- *Conceived identity* or the perceptual concepts or corporate image, reputation and branding.
- *Ideal identity* or the best positioning for an organization in a market for a certain timeframe.
- *Desired identity* or the aspects of a corporation which live in the hearts and minds of its leaders, i.e., their vision for the organization.

Balmer and Greyser (2003) later on differentiated organizational identity from corporate identity. They see organizational identity as what organizational members' affinities were, while they saw corporate identity as what the corporation's distinctive attributes were. For a more recent perspective, the reader is referred to Ashforth and colleagues (2008) who present a review of the literature on identity and identification by posing four fundamental questions around defining the term, its importance, and how and in what contexts it occured. Their analysis concluded with suggestions for future research into the dynamic aspects of identity and how identity can transform into 'over-identification' which can prove dysfunctional to organizations. They also call for more process-driven research, as well as research on identification in new **contexts**, identification in groups, teams, and other interrelationships.

Researchers have also provided many theoretical variations for the concept of organizational image. Dutton and Dukerich (1991) simply defined organizational image as how organizational members think others – who are external to the organization – see the organization. Gatewood et al. (1993) define an organization's image as what information was available as regards that organization, with various types of images being possible such as a corporate image or a recruitment image. Scott and Lane (2000) outlined two types of images in their stakeholder-based organizational identity construction framework: projected desired images and reflected **stakeholder** appraisals. Projected desired images are what organizational members want stakeholders to see about their organization whereas reflected stakeholder appraisals are what stakeholders perceive about, and send back to, the organization. Gioia et al. (2000) reviewed the literature and suggested that six forms of organizational images existed:

- Construed external image: how organizational members think others see their organization.
- A projected image: images created by the organization and communicated to stakeholders.
- A desired future image: how the organization wants organizational members and stakeholders to see the organization in the future.
- A corporate identity: internally and externally planned and consistent representations of how the organization wishes to be seen using logos and symbols.
- A transient impression: immediate or short-term impressions of observed or interpreted symbols by a targeted audience.
- A reputation; a longer-term, stable and collective judgment of an organization's actions and achievements by stakeholders.

Balmer and Greyser (2003) do not define organizational image, rather corporate image. They see corporate image as how a corporation's distinctive attributes are currently seen.

Fombrun (1996) saw reputation as a fragile, intangible asset originating from stakeholders' (customers', community's, investors', and employees') images of the corporation, which come from the corporation's identity (names, self-representation). For him, reputation is an overall estimation of the organization by its stakeholders, and their perceptions are based on the organization's ability to directly manage impressions or images; the organization's ability to build strong stakeholder relationships; and the organization's rumour management skills. Elsbach and Glynn (1996) offered different types of reputation that were possible for a given organization, including predatory, high quality, and distinctive. Balmer and Greyser (2003) defined corporate reputation not organizational reputation, and saw corporate reputation as how the corporation was seen over time.

Management researchers have looked at various aspects of organizational or corporate image, identity and reputation. Gioia (1998) suggested researchers use three perspectives in identity research: a functionalist perspective where identity is a social fact; an interpretive perspective where identity is not a given, it is socially constructed; and a post-modern perspective where the very idea of identity is questioned as simply being a linguistic manifestation that is enabled and produced through language.

Specific examples of research relating to image, identity and reputation include Fombrun's (1996) linear path argument for corporate identity which leads to images that in turn lead to reputation. Fombrun did add however that a corporation's image did not necessarily have to mirror the corporation's identity because image can be manipulated, for example through rumours. Meanwhile Podolny (1993) used investment banks to show how organizational status or reputation in a market could affect organizational actions, that reputation was a factor in strategic decision making. Gioia and Thomas (1996) found that top management team members' perceptions of identity and image, especially a desired future image, were key to members' sense-making processes. These perceptions were also the links between the organization's internal context and top management-team members' interpretations of issues faced by the organization. Golden-Biddle and Rao (1997) also warned that organizations can have more than one identity, which can cause commitment conflicts when issues arise which follow one identity but go against another.

In the literature on the management of sport, researchers have not so much tried to define or conceptualize organizational image, identity and/or reputation, as use them in relation to other aspects of interest. For example, Thannopoulos and Gargalianos (2002) explained how ticketing challenges for the 2000 Sydney Olympic Games caused damage to the organizing committee's image, in their *Facilities* article entitled 'Ticketing of large scale events: the case of Sydney 2000 Olympic Games'. In turn, Gwinner and Eaton (1999) showed how sponsoring an event can result in the event's image impacting on the sponsoring brand in their article from the *Journal of Advertising*, 'Building brand image through event sponsorship: the role of image transfer'. Whitson and Macintosh (1993) explained how cities will use hallmark events to gain a world-class image in their *Sociology of Sport Journal* article 'Becoming a world-class city: hallmark events and sport franchises in the growth strategies of Western Canadian cities'. Whitson and Macintosh (1996) went on to further explore this topic in their article 'The global circus: international sport, tourism, and the marketing of cities' in the *Journal of Sport and Social Issues*. Finally, Chalip et al. (2003) explored the 'Effects of sport event media on destination image and intention to visit' in their *Journal of Sport Management* article. However, Parent and Foreman (2007) did specifically explore image and identity in major sporting events, noting the presence of three identity referents.

As has been noted in the mainstream literature, the fluid, changing aspect of image, identity and reputation is interesting and under-researched. Sport scholars could use the sporting context to examine the dynamic aspect of these concepts as a new context for research. Within the management of sport there are also a variety of contexts which could be examined, such as differences in the public, private and voluntary sectors or those concerning image, identity or reputation in the development of amateur into professional sport. Sport is constantly changing and therefore makes a valid research site from which to learn about image, identity, and reputation.

To understand image, identity and reputation more fully, the reader may refer to the concepts of **context** and **stakeholders** that can be found elsewhere in this book.

FURTHER READING

For some further reading on this concept, we would recommend the following:

Ashforth, B.E., Harrison, S.H. and Corley, K.G. (2008) Identification in organizations: an examination of four fundamental questions. *Journal of Management*, 34: 325.

Fombrun, C.J. (1996) *Reputation: Realizing Value from the Corporate Image*. Boston, MA: Harvard Business School Press.

Gioia, D.A., Schultz, M. and Corley, K.G. (2000) Organizational identity, image, and adaptive instability. *Academy of Management Review*, 25(1): 63–81.

BIBLIOGRAPHY

Albert, S. and Whetten, D.A. (1985) Organizational identity. In L.L. Cummings and B.M. Staw (eds), *Research in Organizational Behavior* (Vol. 8). Greenwich, CT: JAI Press. pp. 263–295.

Ashforth, B.E., Harrison, S.H. and Corley, K.G. (2008) Identification in organizations: an examination of four fundamental questions. *Journal of Management*, 34: 325.

Balmer, J.M.T. and Greyser, S.A. (2002) Managing the multiple identities of the corporation. *California Management Review*, 44: 72–86.

Balmer, J.M.T. and Greyser, S.A. (2003) Prologue: new insights. In J.M.T. Balmer and S.A. Greyser (eds), *Revealing the Corporation: Perspectives on Identity, Image, Reputation, Corporate Branding, and Corporate-level Marketing*. New York: Routledge.

Chalip, L., Green, B.C. and Hill, B. (2003) Effects of sport event media on destination image and intention to visit. *Journal of Sport Management*, 17: 214–234.

Dutton, J.E. and Dukerich, J.M. (1991) Keeping an eye on the mirror: image and identity in organizational adaptation. *Academy of Management Journal*, 34: 517–554.

Elsbach, K.D. and Glynn, M.A. (1996) Believing your own 'PR': embedding identification in strategic reputation. In J.A.C. Baum and J.E. Dutton (eds), *Advances in Strategic Management* (Vol. 13). Greewich, CT: JAI Press. pp. 65–90.

Fombrun, C.J. (1996) *Reputation: Realizing Value from the Corporate Image*. Boston, MA: Harvard Business School Press.

Gatewood, R.D., Gowan, M.A. and Lautenschlager, G.J. (1993) Corporate image, recruitment image, and initial job choice decisions. *Academy of Management Journal*, 36(2): 414–427.

Gioia, D.A. (1998) From individual identity to organizational identity. In D. Godfrey (ed.), *Identity in Organizations: Building Theory through Conversation*. Thousand Oaks, CA: Sage. pp. 17–31.

Gioia, D.A. and Thomas, J.B. (1996) Identity, image and issue interpretation: sensemaking during strategic change in academia. *Administrative Science Quarterly*, 41: 370–403.

Gioia, D.A., Schultz, M. and Corley, K.G. (2000) Organizational identity, image, and adaptive instability. *Academy of Management Review*, 25(1): 63–81.

Golden-Biddle, K. and Rao, H. (1997) Breaches in the boardroom: organizational identity and conflicts of commitment in a nonprofit organization. *Organization Science*, 8(6): 593–611.

Gwinner, K.P. and Eaton, J. (1999) Building brand image through event sponsorship: the role of image transfer. *Journal of Advertising*, 28(4): 47.

Parent, M.M. and Foreman, P.O. (2007) Organizational image and identity management in large-scale sporting events. *Journal of Sport Management*, 21(1): 15–40.

Podolny, J.M. (1993) A status-based model of market competition. *American Journal of Sociology*, 98(4): 829–872.

Scott, S.G. and Lane, V.R. (2000) A stakeholder approach to organizational identity. *Academy of Management Review*, 25(1): 43–62.

Soenen, G. and Moingeon, B. (2002) The five facets of collective identities: integrating corporate and organizational identity. In G.S.B. Moingeon (ed.), *Corporate and Organizational*

Identities: Integrating Strategy, Marketing, Communication, and Organizational Perspectives. London: Routledge.

Thannopoulos, Y. and Gargalianos, D. (2002) Ticketing of large-scale events: the case of Sydney 2000 Olympic Games. *Facilities*, 20(1/2): 22.

Whitson, D. and Macintosh, D. (1993) Becoming a world-class city: hallmark events and sport franchises in the growth strategies of Western Canadian cities. *Sociology of Sport Journal*, 10(3): 221–240.

Whitson, D. and Macintosh, D. (1996) The global circus: international sport, tourism, and the marketing of cities. *Journal of Sport and Social Issues*, 20(3): 278–295.

Knowledge Transfer

> *Knowledge transfer is the process of sharing and exchanging knowledge between two or more actors.*

It is 'intrinsically difficult to define and value knowledge' (Sillince, 2006: 800), which is why there are many definitions of it. For example, the resource-based view of the firm sees knowledge as an asset or a 'thing', yet some researchers also treat it, perhaps more appropriately, as a process (Sillince, 2006). Knowledge within the knowledge management literature has been described as an input resource (i.e., knowledge from), as an output resource (i.e., knowledge to), and as a throughput or process (i.e., the link between knowledge from and knowledge to) (Assundani, 2005). Knowledge has also been defined rather simply as 'that which is known' (Grant, 1996: 110). In contrast, Cook and Brown (1999) suggest four forms of knowledge based on individual/group and explicit/tacit characteristics: concepts, stories, skills, and genres. In addition, depending on the reader's epistemological and ontological stance, they may challenge the concept of knowledge. For example, Foucault (see Burrell, 1988) describes the idea of power/knowledge and other postmodernists critique the concept of knowledge as a 'fundamental truth' (Assundani, 2005: 32): this is in contrast to, for example, Nonaka (1994), who defined knowledge as a justified truth or belief. Most subjectivists see knowledge creation or learning as being highly dependent on the social and physical conditions, as well as on practice (i.e., not only from a brain to another; it is not abstract) (Assundani, 2005).

Nevertheless, knowledge is quite often categorized as explicit or tacit, organizational or individual. Explicit knowledge is the more objective knowledge, such as product innovations. It is the know-what, the observable information that can be found in some tangible form (e.g., symbols, books, reports, manuals) (Assundani, 2005; Inkpen, 1996; Kogut and Zander, 1992). Tacit knowledge is of more interest to researchers and organizations seeking a competitive advantage as it is harder to transfer; it is non-codifiable, translucent, and usually developed unconsciously by an individual, depending on that person's experience in a given **context** or environment (Howells, 1996; Inkpen, 1996; Kogut and Zander, 1992; Lubit, 2001). Tacit knowledge is the know-how, and it is related to social relationships (Kogut and Zander, 1992). Thus, we can speak of social and human capital here (Assundani, 2005). Kogut and Zander (1992) also explain that knowledge is held not only by an individual (based on their experiences in a given context) but also by a community (group, organization, network, etc.) through interrelationships: knowledge is 'embedded in the organizing principles by which people cooperate within organizations' (Kogut and Zander, 1992: 383). As such, the context or environment is important when discussing tacit knowledge.

Moving away from knowledge as an asset or thing, researchers are examining knowledge as a process, practice, or system of knowing activity (Assundani, 2005; Sillince, 2006; Spender, 1996). We find knowledge transfer within this knowledge sharing and exchange process. Nonaka (1994) argued that there are four modes of knowledge conversion or knowledge transfer:

1 *Socialization*: from tacit knowledge to tacit knowledge.
2 *Externalization*: from tacit knowledge to explicit knowledge.
3 *Internalization*: from explicit knowledge to tacit knowledge.
4 *Combination*: from explicit knowledge to explicit knowledge.

Thus, we can see that knowledge can be transferred internally (intra-organizational) or externally (inter-organizational). The process of transferring knowledge can be done in three general ways: dyadic or person-to-person, published (i.e., written documentation), and group (i.e., a combination of knowledge seekers and sources being exchanged in an open environment) (Gray and Meister, 2004). Specific mechanisms can include the internet, databases, journals, training, conferences, and networks of contacts (Caloghirou et al., 2004). Regardless, the individual is key in the knowledge transfer process. There are various aspects to consider when wanting to transfer knowledge: knowledge characteristics (e.g., ambiguity), organizational characteristics (e.g., age, size, degree of decentralization), and network characteristics (e.g., structural, relational and cognitive capital) (van Wijk et al., 2008).

The Knowledge-Based View of the firm (KBV) is an approach which stems from the resource-based view of the firm, where the heterogeneous distribution of tangible and intangible resources that are rare, valuable, inimitable, and non-substitutable provide a competitive advantage to an organization (see Barney, 1991; Wernerfelt, 1984). It is thought that the intangible resources are key to gaining and maintaining that competitive advantage. One such intangible resource is knowledge, as described above. KBV is also a reaction to transaction cost economics (see Williamson, 1975, 1979) as knowledge has been argued to be the basis of an organization and KBV discusses knowledge transfer (Assundani, 2005). There is evidence that knowledge transfer, which is thought to 'foster capability development and exploitation of current competences', actually does have a positive impact on organizational innovation and performance (van Wijk et al., 2008: 845).

In sport management, we find very little research on knowledge and knowledge transfer. What we do find is notably related to national sport organizations and the Olympic Games. More precisely, Halbwirth and Toohey (2001) present, from a personal perspective, the growth and development of knowledge management within the Sydney Organizing Committee for the Olympic Games (SOCOG). They use an information management approach and consider the importance of technology in the analysis of explicit and tacit knowledge. They argue that 'accurate and accessible information can be managed effectively throughout a growing organization' like an Olympic Games organizing committee (2001: 91) and that an efficient information and knowledge flow is possible within such organizations through knowledge management processes, but it is also dependent on having an organizational culture that is receptive to these processes and a culture created and promoted by top executives within that organization.

In turn, O'Reilly and Knight (2007) discuss knowledge management best practices in the context of national sport organizations. In their exploratory study, they link intellectual demands (e.g., interdependence, routines), knowledge sourcing (e.g., one-to-one or dyadic, many-to-many or group), and best practices (e.g., use of intranet, publications, email) in arguing for a need to study knowledge management within non-profit sport organizations, notably national sport organizations in greater depth.

In addition, Frawley and Toohey (2009) examine how important prior knowledge of the Olympic Games and the Olympic context was for the Australian Olympic Committee in its negotiations with other Games partners (e.g., the host governments) once the bid was obtained. This prior knowledge allowed the Australian Olympic Committee to gain a strategic advantage. Given the emphasis that the International Olympic Committee places on its knowledge management programme, called the Olympic Games Knowledge Management (OGKM) programme, and the desire of other sport organizations for more efficient resource use, we would strongly urge sport management researchers to examine knowledge management processes. Besides KBV, another associated literature which may be of assistance in this matter is organizational learning (see for example Argote, 2005; Berends and Lammers, 2010; Garvin et al., 2008; Janowicz-Panjaitan and Noorderhaven, 2009; Karataş-Özkan and Murphy, 2010; McLaughlin et al.,2008; Rashman et al., 2009; Yang, 2007).

Research on knowledge transfer therefore relies on the researcher to clearly define the term 'knowledge' and also identify who or what is considered to hold that knowledge (i.e., a person, organization, group). Knowledge transfer implies that a process occurs whereby that knowledge passes from one person or thing to another. The process of knowledge transfer has been shown to be complex and can serve as a source of strategic competitive advantage for firms with knowledge at the centre of their corporate **strategy**. The impact of knowledge transfer on motivation is also thought to be positive and therefore contributes to effective organizations. Within the context of the management of sport, there is substantial scope for research on knowledge transfer. As with other concepts, we would encourage an examination of the mainstream literature in order to inform studies on the management of sport but also that the reader take into consideration the unique contextual elements of sport when forming research questions. Aside from the current research settings in sport, researchers could look at knowledge transfer in sport clubs, in partnerships (e.g., public–private), or in using social media.

To understand knowledge transfer more fully, the reader may refer to the concepts of **context** and **strategy** that can be found elsewhere in this book.

FURTHER READING

For some further reading on this concept, we would recommend the following:

Assundani, R.H. (2005) Catching the chameleon: understanding the elusive term 'knowledge'. *Journal of Knowledge Management*, 9(2): 31–44.

Frawley, S. and Toohey, K. (2009) The importance of prior knowledge: the Australian Olympic Committee and the Sydney 2000 Olympic Games. *Sport in Society*, 12(7): 947–966.

Kogut, B. and Zander, U. (1992) Knowledge of the firm, combinative capabilities, and the replication of technology. *Organization Science*, 3(3): 383–397.

Nonaka, I. (1994) A dynamic theory of organizational knowledge creation. *Organization Science*, 5(1): 14–37.

BIBLIOGRAPHY

Argote, L. (2005) Reflections on two views of managing learning and knowledge in organizations. *Journal of Management Inquiry*, 14(1): 43–48.

Assundani, R.H. (2005) Catching the chameleon: understanding the elusive term 'knowledge'. *Journal of Knowledge Management*, 9(2): 31–44.

Barney, J.B. (1991) Firm resources and sustained competitive advantage. *Journal of Management*, 17: 99–120.

Berends, H. and Lammers, I. (2010) Explaining discontinuity in organizational learning: a process analysis. *Organization Studies*, 31(8): 1045–1068.

Burrell, G. (1988) Modernism, postmodernism and organization analysis 2: the contribution of Michel Foucault. *Organization Studies*, 9: 221–235.

Caloghirou, Y., Kastelli, I. and Tsakanikas, A. (2004) Internal capabilities and external knowledge sources: complements or substitutes for innovative performance? *Technovation*, 24: 29–39.

Chappelet, J.-L. (2001) Risk management for large-scale events: the case of the Olympic Winter Games. *European Journal for Sport Management*, 8(Special Issue): 6–21.

Cook, S.D.N. and Brown, J.S. (1999) Bridging epistemologies: the generative dance between organizational knowledge and organizational knowing. *Organization Science*, 10(4): 381–400.

Frawley, S. and Toohey, K. (2009) The importance of prior knowledge: the Australian Olympic Committee and the Sydney 2000 Olympic Games. *Sport in Society*, 12(7): 947–966.

Garvin, D.A., Edmondson, A.C. and Gino, F. (2008) Is yours a learning organization? *Harvard Business Review*, 86(3): 109–124.

Grant, R.M. (1996) Toward a knowledge-based theory of the firm. *Strategic Management Journal*, 17(Winter Special Issue): 109–122.

Gray, P.H. and Meister, D.B. (2004) Knowledge sourcing effectiveness. *Management Science*, 50(6): 821–834.

Halbwirth, S. and Toohey, K. (2001) The Olympic Games and knowledge management: a case study of the Sydney Organising Committee of the Olympic Games. *European Sport Management Quarterly*, 1(2): 91–111.

Howells, J. (1996) Tacit knowledge, innovation and technology transfer. *Technology Analysis and Strategic Management*, 8(2): 91–106.

Inkpen, A.C. (1996) Creating knowledge through collaboration. *California Management Review*, 31(1): 123–140.

Janowicz-Panjaitan, M. and Noorderhaven, N.G. (2009) Trust, calculation, and interorganizational learning of tacit knowledge: an organizational roles perspective. *Organization Studies*, 30(10): 1021–1044.

Karataş-Özkan, M. and Murphy, W.D. (2010) Critical theorist, postmodernist and social constructionist paradigms in organizational analysis: a paradigmatic review of organizational learning literature. *International Journal of Management Reviews*, 12(4): 453–465.

Kogut, B. and Zander, U. (1992) Knowledge of the firm, combinative capabilities, and the replication of technology. *Organization Science*, 3(3): 383–397.

Lubit, R. (2001) Tacit knowledge and knowledge management: the keys to sustainable competitive advantage. *Organizational Dynamics*, 29(4): 164–178.

McLaughlin, S., Paton, R.A. and Macbeth, D.K. (2008) Barrier impact on organizational learning within complex organizations. *Journal of Knowledge Management*, 12(2): 107–123.

Nonaka, I. (1994) A dynamic theory of organizational knowledge creation. *Organization Science*, 5(1): 14–37.

O'Reilly, N.J. and Knight, P. (2007) Knowledge management best practices in national sports organisations. *International Journal of Sport Management and Marketing*, 2(3): 264–280.

Rashman, L., Withers, E. and Hartley, J. (2009) Organizational learning and knowledge in public service organizations: a systematic review of the literature. *International Journal of Management Reviews*, 11(4): 463–494.

Sillince, J.A.A. (2006) The effect of rhetoric on competitive advantage: knowledge, rhetoric and resource-based theory. In S.R. Clegg, C. Hardy, T.R. Lawrence and W.R. Nord (eds), *The SAGE Handbook of Organization Studies* (2nd edn). Thousand Oaks, CA: Sage. pp. 800–813.

Spender, J.C. (1996) Making knowledge the basis of a dynamic theory of the firm. *Strategic Management Journal*, 17(Winter Special Issue): 45–62.

van Wijk, R., Jansen, J.J.P. and Lyles, M.A. (2008) Inter- and intra-organizational knowledge transfer: a meta-analytic review and assessment of its antecedents and consequences. *Journal of Management Studies*, 45(4): 830–853.

Wernerfelt, B. (1984) A resource-based view of the firm. *Strategic Management Journal*, 5: 171–180.

Williamson, O.E. (1975) *Markets and Hierarchies: Analysis and Antitrust Implications*. New York: Free Press.

Williamson, O.E. (1979) Transaction-cost economics: the governance of contractual relations. *Journal of Law and Economics*, 22: 233–261.

Yang, J.T. (2007) The impact of knowledge sharing on organizational learning and effectiveness. *Journal of Knowledge Management*, 11(2): 83–90.

Leadership

> *Leadership is a complex notion that generally refers to an individual's ability to direct, motivate and 'lead' other individuals and groups in a desired direction or behavioural pattern.*

The concept of leadership is one with 'universal appeal' (Northouse, 2007: 12) and has been examined extensively in the mainstream management literature. We consider the large diversity of research and perspectives of leadership to give the reader an appreciation of the many ways this concept has been viewed. Early research depicted leadership as a trait, suggesting that good leaders are born with distinctive qualities that enable them to lead. This 'trait approach' was one of the first systematic attempts to study leadership and was used to study the 'innate' characteristics of leaders (see for example, Bass, 1990; Jago, 1982). Traits which have been associated with leadership include intelligence (e.g., Zaccaro et al., 2004), self-confidence (e.g., Kirkpatrick and Locke, 1991), determination (e.g., Stogdill, 1974), integrity (e.g., Mann, 1959) and sociability (e.g., Stogdill, 1948). However, this approach, whilst intuitive and conceptually appealing, has yet to yield a definitive list of leadership traits with findings from many of the studies ambiguous and uncertain (Northouse, 2007). Nonetheless, there is support for this approach and Judge et al. (2002) produced a meta-analysis of leadership studies, finding support for a relationship between the Big Five personality factors (see Goldberg, 1990; McCrae and Costa, 1987) of neuroticism, extraversion, openness, agreeableness, and conscientiousness and the concept of leadership, with extraversion being the most strongly suggestive personality trait of effective leaders.

An alternative perspective of leadership is as a process that can be learned (Jago, 1982), is contextually bound, and involves some degree of influence (Northouse, 2007). It is also thought that leaders can be formally appointed within an organization/group or they can emerge with the support and acceptance of others, with personality traits (such as confidence, dominance and intelligence) and gender-biased perceptions of the most important determinant factors in the process of emergence (Hoffman, 2004; Smith and Foti, 1998). Whether appointed or emergent, the concept of leadership is intimately related to **power** and therefore **control** within organizations. As a leader who is appointed, an individual has certain formal, administrative and legitimated influence mechanisms available to them (e.g., disciplinary procedures). An emergent leader arguably has stronger influence due to the support and acceptance of those who are being led, yet may face barriers from the formal systems and structure of leadership which are expected or have been designed by organizational hierarchical superiors. In both situations, various forms of power are enacted and will therefore play a role in organization control.

The conceptualization of leadership as a process has led to a considerable diversity of approaches which embrace this broad view. While it is beyond the scope of this book to provide an in-depth discussion of all approaches to leadership, it is useful to provide a brief account of this diversity in order to then progress to highlight studies which have examined leadership in the management of sport. The major approaches to leadership which have accepted that leadership is a process that can be learned and is contextually located include the skills approach, the style approach, the situational approach, the contingency approach, path–goal theory, leader–member exchange theory, and transformational leadership. The skills approach to leadership was first introduced by Katz (1955) as an alternative to the trait approach which dominated the literature. Rather than focusing on personality (trait approach), Katz (1955) and later Mumford et al. (2000) and Yammarino (1993) addressed leadership as developable skills that an effective leader must develop, such as technical skills (knowledge and proficiency in work-specific activities), humanistic skills (dealing with people), and conceptual skills (an ability to work with ideas rather than people or things). There are many criticisms of this approach including its lack of consideration for **context**, its similarities to trait models (and therefore being subject to the same criticisms as trait models), its weakness in offering predictive values and explaining how skills are causative of effective leadership, and how the breadth of the approach (including motivation, creative thinking, two types of intelligence ability, personality, conflict) is concerned with matters beyond the concept of leadership, thereby diluting the usefulness of this approach to explain leadership performance (Northouse, 2007).

Two research programmes constitute the basis of the style approach to leadership: the Ohio State studies and the Michigan studies. Yet the most widely known model of managerial behaviour and leadership style is Blake and Mouton's (1964, 1978, 1985) Managerial (Leadership) Grid, a model used to explain how leaders achieve organization goals through organizational tasks (and a concern for output/results) and through people within the organization.

Research on leadership styles has been criticized extensively (see for example Bryman, 1992; Yukl, 1994) as having no conclusive findings to indicate which style(s) is most appropriate/effective in which situation(s) (see Blake and McCanse, 1991; Musumi, 1985). The situational approach to leadership emerged in the 1970s to address this weakness and pointed out that there were no universally appropriate leadership styles (Bryman, 1992). There are two situational models which are most widely cited: path–goal theory and Hersey and Blanchard's (1984) situational theory. The path–goal theory model attempts to explain the effects various types of leadership will have under numerous work conditions, such as work that is stressful, tedious, complex, low in autonomy and/or frustrating. The path–goal model has been used in the sports coaching context by Chelladurai and Saleh (1978) to identify five types of leader behaviour: training behaviour, autocratic behaviour, democratic behaviour, social support, and rewarding behaviour. Athletes in, for example, team sports, preferred coaches who emphasized training behaviour (which is similar to the Ohio State studies' term 'initiating structure'). Unfortunately, this work only focused on athletes and not on managers or 'employees', volunteers, or other organizational actors.

Hersey and Blanchard's (1984) situational approach to leadership is based on task behaviour (again similar to the Ohio state concept of initiating structure) where the leader organizes how work is to be accomplished and relationship behaviour (similar to the concept 'consideration'), including open communication and supportive actions. This work was refined and a model by Blanchard (1985) and Blanchard, Zigarmi and Zigarmi (1985) resulted, called the Situational Leadership II model which consisted of four leadership styles. These four styles were dependent upon the development level of subordinates and a combination of either task behaviour or relationship behaviour by the leader. The four leadership styles differentiated the behavioural patterns of the person (leader) who attempted to influence others, including both supportive and directive behaviours.

Directive behaviours include, for example, setting goals, defining job roles, evaluation, and setting deadlines, often through one-way communication. Supportive behaviour includes two-way communication to enable workers to be comfortable with their role, situation, and other colleagues. Criticisms of the research lie in the ambiguous specification of the development levels. Also, a significant shortcoming of the situational leadership approaches is the lack of consideration for demographic and social/historical characteristics on the leader/manager. Vecchio and Boatwright (2002) demonstrated an inverse relationship between level of education, job experience, and directive leadership. In other words, employees with high levels of education and experience desired less structure and did not respond well to directive leadership. Their study also suggested that age and gender were related to employee acceptance of leadership styles, with males preferring directive leadership, females preferring supportive leadership, and older employees responding more favourably to directive leaders than the younger employees. However, there still lacks a consistent body of empirical evidence for the theoretical underpinnings of the situational approaches, and it would appear that while it is a practical approach and easy to apply, there is still much ambiguity and a lack of consideration for a broader context in the model.

Sometimes used interchangeably with 'situational' models is the contingency approach to leadership. However, where the situational models suggested that leadership effectiveness was dependent upon the relationship between leaders and followers, the contingency theory places greater emphasis on the context in which the leader is working. Fiedler (1964, 1967) and Fiedler and Garcia (1987) developed contingency theory by primarily studying military organizations, the results of which included empirical evidence of leadership style effectiveness for specified organizational contexts. This theory therefore provides a framework for matching an appropriate leadership style with a given organizational situation where styles are again depicted as 'task motivated' (goals setting, plans to achieve goals) and/or 'relationship motivated' (developing interpersonal relationships) and contingencies were characterized by leader–member relations, task structure, and position power.

The basic assumption of this theory can offer some insight as to why leaders may be ineffective in some situations and therefore account for sources of conflict in an organization by highlighting the importance of context to organization (and leadership) effectiveness. This is also the first leadership model to overtly recognize the importance of power in the process of leading, managing, and controlling within organizations and whether power is legitimate or lacking in a given situation. It does not, however, provide a sufficiently complex perspective of how power operates in organizational settings but goes some way to conceptualizing the complexity of organizational life and understanding how organizations are controlled.

Leader–Member Exchange Theory (LMX) emerged to offer a new conceptualization of leadership as a process focusing on the interactions between leaders and followers. Initial studies that formed this approach were concerned with the nature of differences between groups of subordinates who negotiated tasks and responsibilities with their leader (termed the 'in-group') and those who operated based on formal job descriptors (the 'out-group') (e.g., Dansereau et al., 1975; Graen, 1976; Graen and Cashman, 1975). Graen and Uhl-Bien (1995) then became concerned with how the theory related to organizational effectiveness, specifically looking at the quality of the leader–member relationship in comparison to positive outcomes for the leader, subordinates, groups, and the organization generally. The effects of high-quality leader–member exchanges included, for example, low employee turnover, positive performance evaluation, frequent promotions, increased organization commitment, faster career progression, positive attitudes to work and increased participation (Graen and Uhl-Bien, 1995; see also Liden et al., 1993). This work suggested that leaders were more effective if they could build positive relationships with employees.

LMX theory is based upon a fairly naïve view of communication and does not consider sufficiently the role of politics and power in the communication process. The model strongly suggests leaders should build trust, respect and interdependence in leader–subordinate relationships, but does little to explain how this occurs or the difficulties that may be encountered in developing these relationships. It also does little to recognize that interdependence can be a precursor to conflict situations. Finally, criticisms focused on measurement have been documented by Schriesheim et al. (2001), indicating that no empirical work has used dyadic measures to analyse the LMX process even though the basis of the theory encompasses a dyadic relationship between leaders and followers. This work also questions the content validity of the measurement scales, and Graen and Uhl-Bien (1995) questioned whether the standard scale should be uni-dimensional or multi-dimensional.

Despite criticisms and uncertainties in measurement and method, the LMX theory provided an important impetus to leadership research by suggesting that if leadership is viewed as a process that can be manipulated, then leadership can play an important role in change and transformation within organizations. Yukl (1999: 204) described how 'influencing major change in the attitudes and assumptions of organisation members and building commitment for the organisation's mission or objectives' constituted 'transformational leadership'. Other terms have been used to describe similar/related leadership approaches, including charismatic leadership (Conger and Kanungo, 1987, 1988), visionary leadership (Sashkin, 1988; Westley and Mintzberg, 1989), magic leadership (Nadler and Tushman, 1989), and transferential leadership (Pauchant, 1991). The term 'transformational leadership' was first suggested by Downton (1973) and emerged as a popular approach to leadership research following the work of political sociologist James MacGregor Burns (1978). He distinguished between transactional and transformational leadership, with the former signifying the majority of leadership models which focused on the relationship between leaders and followers. Transactional leadership focuses heavily on an exchange value for appropriate behaviour whereas transformational leadership is a process in which the leader engages with followers to heighten the motivation and moral awareness of both leaders and followers. It is thought that transformational leaders are able to influence the actions and values of subordinates through a combination of personality characteristics (dominance, a desire to influence, confidence and strong values) and behavioural traits (acts as strong role model, demonstrates competence, articulates goals, communicates high expectations and confidence and encourages individual motivation) (House, 1976).

While intuitively appealing, a number of criticisms of this approach have been noted. Tracey and Hinkin (1998) questioned the clarity of the concepts used to define transformational leadership and demonstrated some overlap between the dimensions used to measure the concept. The parameters of transformational leaders have also been suggested to overlap with other models of leadership, and Bryman (1992) specifically argued that transformational and charismatic leadership were often treated synonymously despite some models using charisma as only one component of charismatic leadership (e.g., Bass, 1985). Tejeda and colleagues (2001) disputed the validity of the measurement of transformational leadership and stated that the parameters used demonstrated a high correlation which suggested they were not distinct factors. Yukl (1999) questioned the overemphasis on leaders' ability to influence and pointed out that little attention had been given to the role of subordinates or informal social interaction in the literature on transformational leadership.

In addition to the various approaches described above, researchers have also explored the leadership style–gender relationship and the cultural dimensions of leadership in organizations. Over three decades ago, researchers started to investigate gender differences in leadership and suggested that women were generally more inclined to use democratic and transformational styles than men (e.g., Bartol and Butterfield, 1976; Eagly and Johnson, 1990). The effectiveness of leadership has also been assessed using male and female leaders as a comparison. Eagly et al. (1995) used meta-analysis to find that male and female leaders were equally effective, but that female leaders were most effective when in a leadership role that was congruent with expectations of their gender. This notion highlights the importance of culture in leadership studies and of gender stereotypes.

House and Javidan (2004) articulated nine dimensions which varied across national cultures; however, this research took no account of regional or local contexts and therefore represented a considerable generalization of the term 'culture'. However, one important contribution this research makes is the evidence to substantiate that different cultures have different expectations of the appropriate role and behaviour of men and women. In relation to leadership, the norms and values of a national culture can have a significant effect on what an individual or group considers appropriate for their male or female leader whereby different cultures may lend themselves to different leadership styles – and different accepted styles for men and women.

Overall, the literature on leadership is vast with the above discussions providing a general overview of the most common themes within the field. Despite growing interest within the academic community the leadership literature has also been fiercely criticized, with Bennis and Nanus (1985:) suggesting that 'never have so many laboured so long to say so little'. However, researchers have suggested some significance in the study of leadership behaviour and context in relation to organization change and the control of resources (Burns, 1978). That is, leaders can play a significant role in the control and influence of organizational actors as well as their goals and behaviour. Pettigrew (1987), drawing on the work of McCall and Lombardo (1978), recalls that leaders should be studied in natural settings using qualitative methodologies rather than the traditional quantitative obsession with dependent and independent variables in order to provide holistic accounts of actual leader behaviour. Crucial within the context of this thesis, therefore, is the attention paid to the role of leaders in the process of organization control to describe their 'approach' and involvement in the group. This qualitative approach is thus more concerned with perceptions of leadership style, traits and impacts and less with inferring causal relationships between these phenomena.

Leadership has also been of interest to those studying the management of sport and some mainstream leadership theory has been used to examine sport organizations, such as Hoye's (2006) use of leader–member exchange theory to study relationships in Australian voluntary sport organization boards. According to Maby and Brady (1996) it was the trait, behavioural and situational leadership theories that formed the basis of sport-related leadership theory which focused on athletics. Chelladurai and Carron (1981) provided a fundamental start to this area of sport leadership research with their 'multi-dimensional theory of sports leadership', which has subsequently been used in attempts to understand the dynamics of leadership in a sport-related setting (e.g., Carron et al., 1985; Chelladurai and Arnott, 1985; Chelladurai and Carron, 1981; Chelladurai and Saleh, 1980; Chelladurai et al. 1987; Robinson and Carron, 1982; Westre and Weiss, 1991).

It should be noted however that Chelladurai's work and much of the resulting studies are underpinned by organization behaviour rather than organization theory. Nonetheless, they provided a key impetus to the study of leadership in a sport setting. Gender and leadership have been the subject of scholarly investigation such as in the work of Theberge (1984), Hums and Sutton (1999), and Leberman and Palmer (2009). Other researchers have looked at the relationship between transformational leadership, culture and organization effectiveness (Weese, 1996).

Smart and Wolfe (2003) examined leadership and human resources in Major League Baseball. Their study provided evidence that leadership contributed very little to organization success when compared to human resources (i.e., player resources and skills). Smart et al. (2008), once again investigating Major League Baseball, extended this study by developing a more comprehensive operationalization of the leadership concept but still found limited evidence that leaders contributed significantly to the performance of the sport organization.

Research on leadership is fraught with difficulties in defining and measuring the concept. For all the studies that demonstrate the significance of leadership or elements of 'effective' leaders, there are an equal if not greater number that seem to contradict or challenge previous studies. Although it is a challenging concept it is also a popular one among researchers, perhaps because of the ease with which the concept can be conceptualized in order to be consistent with different perspectives and theories. This begs the question however of whether the concept is indeed a useful construct to assist in understanding sport organizations, or whether scholars would find greater utility in focusing on less ambiguous more specific elements of the leadership concept, such as skills/competencies, personality, or experience.

To understand leadership more fully, the reader may refer to the concepts of **power**, **control** and **context** that can be found elsewhere in this book.

leadership

FURTHER READING

For some further reading on this concept, we would recommend the following:

Chelladurai, P., Malloy, D., Imamura, H. and Yamagucki, Y. (1987) A cross-cultural study of preferred leadership in sports. *Canadian Journal of Sport Sciences*, 12: 106–110.

Hoye, R. (2006) Leadership within Australian voluntary sport organization boards. *Nonprofit Management and Leadership*, 16(3): 297–313.

Northouse, P.G. (2009) *Leadership: Theory and Practice*. London: Sage.

BIBLIOGRAPHY

Bartol, K.M. and Butterfield, D.A. (1976) Sex effects in evaluating leaders. *Journal of Applied Psychology*, 61: 446–454.

Bass, B.M. (1985) *Leadership and Performance Beyond Expectations*. New York: Free Press.

Bass, B.M. (1990) *Bass and Stogdill's Handbook of Leadership: A Survey of Theory and Research*. New York: Free Press.

Bennis, W. and Nanus, B. (1985) *Leaders: The Strategies for Taking Charge*. New York: Harper and Row.

Blake, R.R. and McCanse, A.A. (1991) *Leadership Dilemmas: Grid Solutions*. Houston, TX: Gulf Publishing Company.

Blake, R.R. and Mouton, J.S. (1964) *The Managerial Grid*. Houston, TX: Gulf Publishing Company.

Blake, R.R. and Mouton, J.S. (1978) *The New Managerial Grid*. Houston, TX: Gulf Publishing Company.

Blake, R.R. and Mouton, J.S. (1985) *The Managerial Grid III*. Houston, TX: Gulf Publishing Company.

Blanchard, K. (1985) *SLII: A Situational Approach to Managing People*. Escondido, CA: Blanchard Training and Development.

Blanchard, K., Zigarmi, P. and Zigarmi, D. (1985) *Leadership and the One Minute Manager: Increasing Effectiveness through Situational Leadership*. New York: William Morrow.

Bryman, A. (1992) *Charisma and Leadership in Organizations*. London: Sage.

Burns, J.M. (1978) *Leadership*. New York: Harper and Row.

Carron, A.V., Widmeyer, W.N. and Brawley, L.R. (1985) The development of an instrument to assess cohesion in sport teams: the group environment questionnaire. *Journal of Sport and Exercise Psychology*, 7(3): 244–266.

Chelladurai, P. and Arnott, M. (1985) Decision styles in coaching: preferences of basketball players. *Research Quarterly for Exercise and Sport*, 56: 15–24.

Chelladurai, P. and Carron, A.V. (1981) Applicability to youth sports of the leadership scale for sports. *Perceptual and Motor Skills*, 53(2): 361.

Chelladurai, P. and Saleh, S.D. (1978) Preferred leadership in sports. *Canadian Journal of Applied Sport Sciences*, 3: 85–92.

Chelladurai, P. and Saleh, S.D. (1980) Dimensions of leader behavior in sports: development of a leadership scale. *Journal of Sport Psychology*, 2: 34–45.

Chelladurai, P., Malloy, D., Imamura, H. and Yamagucki, Y. (1987) A cross-cultural study of preferred leadership in sports. *Canadian Journal of Sport Sciences*, 12: 106–110.

Conger, J.A. and Kanungo, R.N. (1987) *Charismatic Leadership*. San Francisco/London: Coastwise Consulting.

Conger, J.A. and Kanungo, R.N. (1988) *Charismatic Leadership: The Elusive Factor in Organizational Effectiveness*. San Francisco, CA: Jossey-Bass.

Dansereau, F., Graen, G.B. and Haga, W. (1975) A vertical dyad linkage approach to leadership in formal organizations. *Organizational Behaviour and Human Performance*, 13: 46–78.

key concepts in
sport management

Downton, J.V. (1973) *Rebel Leadership: Commitment and Charisma in a Revolutionary Process*. New York: Free Press.

Eagly, A.H. and Johnson, B.T. (1990) Gender and leadership style: a meta-analysis. *Psychological Bulletin*, 108(2): 233–256.

Eagly, A.H., Karau, S.J. and Makhijani, M.G. (1995) Gender and the effectiveness of leaders: a meta-analysis. *Psychological Bulletin*, 117: 125–145.

Fielder, F.E. (1964) A contingency model of leadership effectiveness. In L. Bekowitz (ed.), *Advances in Experimental Social Psychology*. New York: Academic Press.

Fiedler, F.E. (1967) *A Theory of Leadership Effectiveness*. New York: McGraw-Hill.

Fiedler, F.E. and Garcia, J.E. (1987) *New Approaches to Leadership: Cognitive Resources and Organizational Performance*. New York: Wiley.

Goldberg, L.R. (1990) An alternative 'description of personality': The big-five factor structure. *Journal of Personality and Social Psychology*, 59: 1216–1229.

Graen, G.B. (1976) Role-making processes within complex organisations. In M.D. Dunnette (ed.), *Handbook of Industrial Organizational Psychology*. Chicago, IL: Rand McNally.

Graen, G.B. and Cashman, J. (1975) A role-making model of leadership in formal organizations: a developmental approach. In J.G. Hunt and L.L. Larson (eds), *Leadership Frontiers*. Kent, OH: Kent State University Press.

Graen, G.B. and Uhl-Bien, M. (1995) Relationship-based approach to leadership: development of leader–member exchange (LMX) theory of leadership over 25 years: applying a multi-level, multi-domain perspective. *Leadership Quarterly*, 6(2): 219–247.

Hersey, P. and Blanchard, K.H. (1984) *The Situational Leader*. Escondido, CA: Center for Leadership Studies.

Hoffman, B.J. (2004) Great man or great myth? A meta-analytic investigation of the relationship between leader traits and leader effectiveness. *15th Annual International Society for the Study of Work Values Proceedings*.

House, R.J. (1976) A 1976 theory of charismatic leadership. In J.G Hunt and L.L. Larson (eds), *Leadership: The Cutting Edge*. Carbondale: Southern Illinois University Press.

House, R.J. and Javidan, M. (2004) Overview of GLOBE. In R.J. House, P.J. Hanges, M. Javidan, P.W. Dorfman, V. Gupta et al. (eds), *Culture, Leadership and Organizations: The GLOBE Study of 62 Societies*. Thousand Oaks, CA: Sage.

Hoye, R. (2006) Leadership within Australian voluntary sport organization boards. *Nonprofit Management and Leadership*, 16(3): 297–313.

Hums, M.A. and Sutton, W.A. (1999) Women working in the management of professional baseball: getting to first base? *Journal of Career Development*, 26(2): 147–158.

Jago, A.G. (1982) Leadership: perspectives in theory and research. *Management Science*, 28(3): 315–336.

Judge, T.A., Bono, J.E., Ilies, R. and Gerhardt, M.W. (2002) Personality and leadership: a qualitative and quantitative review. *Journal of Applied Psychology*, 87: 765–780.

Katz, R.L. (1955) Skills of an effective administrator. *Harvard Business Review*, 33(1): 33–42.

Kirkpatrick, S.A. and Locke, E.A. (1991) Leadership: do traits matter? *The Executive*, 5: 48–60.

Leberman, S. and Palmer, F. (2009) Motherhood, sport leadership and domain theory: experiences from New Zealand. *Journal of Sport Management*, 23: 305–334.

Liden, R.C., Wayne, S.J. and Stilwell, D. (1993) A longitudinal study on the early development of leader–member exchange. *Journal of Applied Psychology*, 78: 662–674.

Maby, R. and Brady, G. (1996) Sports-related leadership. *Journal of Leadership and Organization Studies*, 3(1): 131–137.

MacGregor Burns, J. (1978*) Leadership*. New York: Harper and Row.

Mann, R.D. (1959) A review of the relationship between personality and performance in small groups. *Psychological Bulletin*, 56: 241–270.

McCall, M.W. and Lombardo, M.M. (1978) *Leadership: Where Else Can We Go?* Durham, NC: Duke University Press.

McCrae, R.R. and Costa, P.T. (1987) Validation of the five factor model of personality across instruments and observers. *Journal of Personality and Social Psychology*, 52: 81–90.

Mumford, M.D., Zaccaro, S.J., Harding, F.D., Jacobs, T.O. and Fleishman, E.A. (2000) Leadership skills for a changing world: solving complex social problems. *Leadership Quarterly*, 11(1): 11–35.

Musumi, J. (1985) *The Behavioural Science of Leadership: An Interdisciplinary Japanese Research Programme*. Ann Arbor: University of Michigan Press.

Nadler, W. and Tushman, M. (1989) Organisational framebending. *Academy of Management Executive*, 3: 194–202.

Northouse, P.G. (2007) *Leadership: Theory and Practice*. London: Sage.

Pauchant, T.C. (1991) Transformational leadership: towards a more complex understanding of charisma in organizations. *Organization Studies*, 12: 507–527.

Pettigrew, A. (1987) Context and action in the transformation of the firm. *Journal of Management Studies*, 24(6): 650–670.

Robinson, T.T. and Carron, A.V. (1982) Personal and situational factors associated with dropping out versus maintaining participation in competitive sport. *JSTOR*, 4(4): 364–378.

Sashkin, M. (1988) The visionary leader. In J.A. Conger and R.N. Kanungo (eds), *Charismatic Leadership: The Elusive Factor in Organizational Effectiveness*. San Francisco, CA: Jossey-Bass. pp. 122–160.

Schriesheim, C.A., Castro, S.L., Zhou, X. And Yammarino, F.J. (2001) The folly of theorizing 'A' but testing 'B': a selective level-of-analysis review of the field and a detailed leader–member exchange illustration. *Leadership Quarterly*, 12: 515–551.

Smart D.L. and Wolfe, R.A. (2003) The contribution of leadership and human resources to organizational success: An empirical assessment of performance in Major League Baseball. *European Sport Management Quarterly*, 3(3): 165–188.

Smart, D.L. Winfree, J.A. and Wolfe, R.A. (2008) Major League Baseball managers: do they matter? *Journal of Sports Management*, 22(3): 303–321.

Smith, J.A. and Foti, R.J. (1998) A pattern approach to the study of leader emergence. *Leadership Quarterly*, 9(2): 147–160.

Stogdill, R.M. (1948) Personal factors associated with leadership: a survey of the literature. *Journal of Psychology*, 25: 35–71.

Stogdill, R.M. (1974) *Handbook of Leadership: A Survey of Theory and Research*. New York: Free Press.

Tejeda, M.J., Scandura, T.A. and Pillai, R. (2001) The MLQ revisited: psychometric properties and recommendations. *Leadership Quarterly*, 12: 31–52.

Theberge, M. (1984) Some evidence of the existence of a sexual double standard in mobility to leadership positions in sport. *International Review for the Sociology of Sport*, 19: 185–197.

Tracey, J.B. and Hinkin, T.R. (1998) Transformational leadership or effective managerial practices? *Group and Organization Management*, 23(3): 220–236.

Vecchio, R.P. and Boatwright, K.J. (2002) Preferences for idealized style of supervision. *Leadership Quarterly*, 13: 327–342.

Weese, J. (1996) Do leadership and organizational culture really matter? *Journal of Sport Management*, 10: 197–206.

Westley, F. and Mintzberg, H. (1989) Visionary leadership and strategic management. *Strategic Management Journal*, 10 (Special Issue): 17–32.

Westre, K.R. and Weiss, M.R. (1991) The relationship between perceived coaching behaviors and group cohesion in high school football. *The Sport Psychologist*, 5: 41–51.

Yammarino, F.J. (1993) Transformational leadership studies: Bernard Bass' leadership and performance beyond expectations. *Leadership Quarterly*, 4(3): 379–382.

Yukl, G.A. (1994) *Leadership in Organizations* (3rd edition). Englewood Cliffs, NJ: Prentice Hall.

Yukl, G.A. (1999) An evaluation of conceptual weaknesses in transformational and charismatic leadership theories. *Leadership Quarterly*, 10(2): 285–305.

Zaccaro, S.J., Kemp, C. and Bader, P. (2004) Leader traits and attributes. In J. Antonakis, A.T. Cianciolo and R.J. Sternberg (eds), *The Nature of Leadership*. Thousand Oaks, CA: Sage.

> Legacy is defined as those planned and unplanned, positive and negative, tangible and intangible benefits stemming from a sporting event over the short and long term.

Bid committees, promoters, and governments alike will seek to host **mega events** in order to benefit from the legacies these events can accrue despite the potential negative impacts such as the so-called white elephants (i.e., large empty stadiums, such as occurred after the 2008 Beijing Olympic Games), cost overruns (e.g., the 2004 Olympic Games in Athens), potential terrorist threats, and transportation nightmares (e.g., the 1996 Olympic Games in Atlanta) for example. In fact, many governments are now requesting information on the potential benefits within their hosting policies before they agree to support a bid (see for example Leopkey et al., 2010). In addition to all this, since 2002, cities wishing to host the Olympic Games have had to formally describe the potential legacies for their host community in their bid books.

Nevertheless, the literature has yet to agree on what legacy truly is, how to measure it, or how to maximize the potential legacies from an event. In the past, research has often focused on the economic impact of events (a form of legacy). However, the measurement of economic impact is fraught with difficulties and easily critiqued (cf., Crompton, 1995, 2004; Gratton et al., 2006; Lee and Taylor, 2005; Preuss, 2005). For example, should we count a new highway as a Games cost when it was in the community's plans – albeit fifteen years down the road? And what is the actual tourism money that was spent in the community that would not have been spent had the Games not been in that community? What exactly is the amount of money that was diverted from the community because people chose to not come there, or chose to spend their money elsewhere or on other activities? Moreover, legacy is more than the economic impact alone. Ritchie (1984) was one of the first to describe the range of possible impacts stemming from an event. He listed six potential impacts: economic (e.g., expenditures); tourism/commercial (e.g., awareness, reputation), physical (e.g., facilities, environment), socio-cultural (e.g., regional traditions), psychological (e.g., local pride), and political (e.g., political propaganda, image). Ritchie and Smith (1991) later found that the 1988 Calgary Winter Olympic Games did dramatically increase the level of awareness and modified the image of the city of Calgary, but there was decay thereafter and it was not obvious how the image/awareness translated into tourist receipts. Moreover, they also found that the yearly Calgary Stampede had a more enduring positive impact on the city than the 1988 Olympic Games.

What we see in Ritchie's (1984) classification is the argument for both tangible (e.g., economic, physical) and intangible (e.g., psychological, political) legacies. Koenig and Leopkey (2009) and de Moragas and colleagues (2003) indicated that intangible legacies can also lead to future tangible legacies. For example, skills learned by individuals as volunteers of an event can eventually lead them to help build future infrastructure. Dimanche (1997) also noted that the impacts of mega-events are both short and long term and may be different for each time period (e.g., negative in the short term, as in the case of the 1984 Louisiana World's Fair in New Orleans, but positive in the longer term). Dimanche provided the different types of impacts or legacies found within this setting: event participation (increased travel), infrastructure improvement (capacity and visitor satisfaction), community benefits (satisfaction), increased media coverage (awareness, tourism image), and increased tourism promotion. Toohey (2008) also examined short- and long-term legacies in her article on the 2000 Sydney Olympic Games.

Other researchers have focused on different aspects of legacy. For example, Chappelet (2008) was interested in the environmental aspect; Cashman (2006) highlighted informational/educational, cultural, and symbolic/historical legacies (see also Cashman and Hughes, 1998; Halbwirth and Toohey, 2001); Preuss (2007) examined the tourism legacy for the 2006 FIFA World Cup; Shipway (2007) noted health and social legacies; and Girginov and Hills (2008) were interested in the relationship between hosting Olympic Games and increasing sport participation in the host country. Related to this, Parent (2008) looked at sport development within mega events. She argued that mega sport events could be inscribed within the sports development literature as they demonstrate indigenous (stemming from the community), planned, and global types of development (cf. Mintzberg, 2006); they also demonstrated individual, interpersonal, institutional, and environmental change dynamics. Parent went on to explore three levels of sports development within mega sport events: individual, infrastructure, and policy/planning. Each type includes positive and negative impacts, and is associated with specific development types and change dynamics.

Finally, Jinxia and Mangan (2008) examined the potential planned and unplanned, tangible and intangible legacies associated with the 2008 Beijing Olympic Games. They found positive and negative tangible legacies (e.g., new buildings but also increased traffic congestion and pollution, and the changing economy towards a service economy but also a housing price boom) as well as intended and critical intangible legacies such as increased national pride, the increased openness of China to the rest of the world, a blending of the Olympic culture with Chinese traditional culture, an improved awareness of environmental priorities, and increased professional expertise in sport event management.

Preuss (2007: 86) incorporated the various aspects mentioned above into his definition of legacy as being 'all planned and unplanned, positive and negative, intangible and tangible structures created by and for a sport event that remain for a longer time than the event itself'.

Notwithstanding the fact that the term 'legacy' can have different meanings in different cultures and languages (see de Moragas et al., 2003, for more information), we can see that the literature is leaning towards a rather broad definition of legacy as anything which is left after an event (cf. Cashman, 2003). This perspective poses some difficulties for researchers wishing to analyse and measure legacy, as parameters and limitations are necessary so as to make a study on legacy practicable.

Moreover, this allows bid committees, promoters, and governments to focus only on the positive aspects of legacy, without addressing the potentially negative impacts (cf. Cashman, 2006). And yet these boundaries result in an inherently restricted or limited view of the context/legacies being studied.

Finally, one interesting perspective is that of Lenskyj (1996, 2000) who argues that losing a bidi actually provides more positive legacies (or perhaps less negative legacies) than winning the bid; i.e., she proposes that the social costs (for example, the displacement of low-income residents for new event buildings) incurred during the preparations for the event in question would outweigh the potential benefits, in addition to the fact that if international visibility is the key desired outcome for the host community, this can be achieved within the bidding phase.

To understand legacy more fully, the reader may refer to the concept of **mega events** that can be found elsewhere in this book.

FURTHER READING

For some further reading on this concept, we would recommend the following:

Cashman, R. (2003) What is 'Olympic legacy'? In M. de Moragas, C. Kennett and N. Puig (eds), *The Legacy of the Olympic Games 1984–2000*. Lausanne, Switzerland: International Olympic Committee. pp. 31–42.

Gratton, C. and Preuss, H. (2008) Maximizing Olympic impacts by building up legacies. *International Journal of the History of Sport*, 25(14): 1922–1938.

Ritchie, J.R.B. (1984) Assessing the impact of hallmark events: conceptual and research issues. *Journal of Travel Research*, 23(1): 2–11.

BIBLIOGRAPHY

Cashman, R. (2003) What is 'Olympic legacy'? In M. de Moragas, C. Kennett and N. Puig (eds), *The Legacy of the Olympic Games 1984–2000*. Lausanne, Switzerland: International Olympic Committee. pp. 31–42.

Cashman, R. (2006) *The Bitter-sweet Awakening: The Legacy of the Sydney 2000 Olympic Games*. Sydney: Walla Walla Press.

Cashman, R. and Hughes, A. (1998) *Staging the Olympics: The Event and its Impact*. Sydney, Australia: University of New South Wales Press.

Chappelet, J.L. (2008) Olympic environmental concerns as a legacy of the Winter Games. *International Journal of the History of Sport*, 25(14): 1884–1902.

Crompton, J.L. (1995) Economic impact analysis of sport facilities and events: eleven sources of misapplication. *Journal of Sport Management*, 9(1): 14–35.

Crompton, J.L. (2004) Beyond economic impact: an alternative rationale for the public subsidy of major league sports facilities. *Journal of Sport Management*, 18(1): 40–28.

de Moragas, M., Kennett, C. and Puig, N. (eds) (2003) *The Legacy of the Olympic Games 1984–2000*. Lausanne, Switzerland: International Olympic Committee.

Dimanche, F. (1997) Special events legacy: the 1984 Louisiana World's Fair in New Orleans. In P.E. Murphy (ed.), *Quality Management in Urban Tourism*. Chichester: Wiley.

Girginov, V. and Hills, L. (2008) A sustainable sports legacy: creating a link between the London Olympics and sports participation. *International Journal of the History of Sport*, 25(14): 2091–2116.

Gratton, C., Shibli, S. and Coleman, R. (2006) The economic impact of major sports events: a review of ten events in the UK. *The Sociological Review*, 54(s2): 41–58.

Halbwirth, S. and Toohey, K. (2001) The Olympic Games and knowledge management: a case study of the Sydney Organising Committee of the Olympic Games. *European Sport Management Quarterly*, 1(2): 91–111.

Jinxia, D. and Mangan, J.A. (2008) Beijing Olympics legacies: certain intentions and certain and uncertain outcomes. *International Journal of the History of Sport*, 25(14): 2019–2040.

Koenig, S. and Leopkey, B. (2009) *Sustainable Development in Canadian Sporting Events: An Analysis of Legacy and Sports Development*. Paper presented at the Administrative Sciences Association of Canada Conference, Niagara Falls, Canada.

Lee, C. and Taylor, T. (2005) Critical reflections on the economic impact assessment of a mega-event: the case of the 2002 FIFA World Cup. *Tourism Management*, 26: 595–603.

Lenskyj, H.J. (1996) When winners are losers: Toronto and Sydney bids for the summer Olympics. *Journal of Sport and Social Issues*, 20(4): 392–410.

Lenskyj, H.J. (2000) *Inside the Olympic Industry: Power, Politics and Activism*. Albany, NY: State University of New York Press.

Leopkey, B., Mutter, O. and Parent, M.M. (2010) Barriers and facilitators when hosting sporting events: exploring the Canadian and Swiss sport event hosting policies. *International Journal of Sport Policy*, 2(2): 113–134.

Parent, M.M. (2008) Mega sporting events and sports development. In V. Girginov (ed.), *Management of Sports Development*. London: Elsevier. pp. 147–163.

Preuss, H. (2005) The economic impact of visitors at major multi-sport events. *European Sport Management Quarterly*, 5(3): 281–301.

Preuss, H. (2007) FIFA World Cup 2006 and its legacy on tourism. In R. Conrady and M. Buck (eds), *Trends and Issues in Global Tourism 2007*. Berlin/Heidelberg, Germany: Springer. pp. 83–102.

Ritchie, J.R.B. (1984) Assessing the impact of hallmark events: conceptual and research issues. *Journal of Travel Research*, 23(1): 2–11.

Ritchie, J.R.B. and Smith, B.H. (1991) The impact of a mega-event on host region awareness: a longitudinal study. *Journal of Travel Research*, 30(1): 3–10.

Shipway, R. (2007) Sustainable legacies for the 2012 Olympic Games. *Journal of the Royal Society for the Promotion of Health*, 127(3): 119–124.

Toohey, K. (2008) The Sydney Olympics: striving for legacies – overcoming short-term disappointments and long-term deficiencies. *International Journal of the History of Sport*, 25(14): 1953–1971.

Media/Broadcasting

> *Media refers to forms of communication that are designed to inform and educate the public about issues of relevance and importance to society, and also to entertain them.*
>
> *Broadcasting refers to the transmission of information and entertainment, via television, radio or internet, which is deemed to be of interest or relevance to society.*

The broadcasting industry is part of and yet different from the 'media' which would include many different forms of communication through various printed media (e.g., a newspaper, magazine, book). There is a considerable amount of information available on the history and development of broadcasting and media generally, often focused on a particular country, such as the United States and its radio broadcasting industry (Albarran and Pitts, 2001; Leblebici et al., 1991) and television production in the UK (Doyle and Paterson, 2008). Other aspects of media and broadcasting that have been the focus of researchers include the development of media policy (Freedman ,2008), **corporate social responsibility (CSR)** in media industries (Gulyas, 2009), media **ethics** (Wilkins and Christians, 2009), broadcasting regulation (Salomon, 2008) and media markets (Gripsrud and Weibull, 2010). Many of these issues in broadcasting and media have also been investigated in the context of sport.

Sport media and broadcasting have had a significant impact on the management of sport over the last few decades. Rowe (2009) suggested that sport would be unrecognizable today without the media (but strongly argued that a continuing analysis of this relationship was needed, including the impact of sport *on* the media). These impacts have since been examined by researchers and include the social, cultural and economic effects upon the ways in which sport is represented, governed, managed and regarded as a social institution. Deloitte and Touche (2009), in their report *The Impact of Broadcasting on Sport in the UK*, examined the economic impacts of broadcasting on several sport organizations, including case studies of the England and Wales Cricket Board (ECB), the Ryder Cup, the Rugby Football Union (RFU), the Irish/Scottish and Welsh Football Associations, and England Netball. The report highlights the substantial portion of income that broadcasting represents for many sports in the UK and the challenges that this presents to sport organizations regarding their independence.

Aside from the impacts of media and broadcasting, there has been interest in the regulation of the broadcasting of professional sport and, in particular, the differences between (and effects of) the regulation of broadcast sports in Europe versus those in North America (see, for example, Hoehn and Lancefield, 2003). The authors found that there were common trends and differences in the quality, quantity, availability and price of televised sports throughout Europe and the USA. To understand these trends and differences, policy interventions through governments and regulatory authorities are examined for their impact on the organization and governance of sport.

Much of the literature on media/broadcasting in sport attributes the rapid commercialization of many sports to the revenue streams created by broadcasters' interest in sport as a product for mass consumption. Here the reader should refer to Szymanski (2006), who examined the 'economic evolution' of broadcasting in sport and its powerful influence on the increasing **demand** for sport. He discussed how broadcasting has transformed sport and how broadcasting has been influenced by the 'potential of sports' (2006: 428). However, many researchers have examined other aspects of the **commercialization** of sport through broadcasting, recognizing broadcasters as new and powerful sport **stakeholders**. Wolfe et al. (2002) used **network** theory to examine the relationships between national governing Bodies (NGBs), the media, and corporate sponsors. They pointed to the varying nature of these relationships over time and 'change drivers' (e.g., new technologies, regulation, new media and economic/social changes) as important for understanding the relevant power relationships, and discussed their implications for sport organizations in trying to manage commercialization (brought about through broadcasting stakeholders).

Researchers have also looked at the media coverage of sport, using content analysis of different forms of media – including newspaper and television. This area of research tends to be underpinned by approaches from sociology/media studies rather than an economics focus. Bishop (2003) examined the coverage of women's sport provided by 569 issues of the magazine *Sports Illustrated*, and reported that there was no significant increase in coverage when compared with an earlier and similar investigation by Reid and Soley (1979). Despite an increase in broadcasting, professional leagues and youth participation, the authors concluded that *SI* did not accurately reflect the growing popularity and status of women's sport. In a later article, Vincent et al. (2007) focused on the print media coverage of women tennis players in Britain. A further focus on tennis can be found in Crossman and colleagues' (2007) gender-based comparison of three national newspapers.

Research has also criticized how the media portray women, generally arguing that women are not promoted as athletic, powerful, or skilled. Rather, there tends to be a concentration on their sexual appearance and dependency on men, which serves to demean their contribution to sport (Lebel and Danylchuk, 2009; Rowe, 2004). Such critical reflection on how women are portrayed, and the implications of this portrayal on sport and society more generally, represent a significant development that should be followed up in the study of gender issues related to media/broadcasting and sport.

As a precursor to understanding economic or social issues related to the media/broadcasting and sport relationship, the reader should see Rowe's (2009) discussion of the power of media in society and in sport. Rowe provides a discussion of the relationship between media, sport and society, and questions the future of this relationship. Noting the influence of media on sport and the influence of media and sport on society, and considering the active role that the media have played in developing sport into the commercial product it is today, Rowe argues for the reinstatement of the 'social priorities' (p. 163) of sport culture through, primarily, a reform of the media 'on grounds of sporting and social equity' (p. 164). Whannel (2009) – also a prominent writer on sport and the media (especially television) – discussed the transformation both of sport and television by examining the Olympic Games, football, and mega events.

Overall, the literature on sport broadcasting and media has examined a variety of economic and social issues pertaining to sport. There has been extensive analysis of different types of media coverage to illustrate bias and inequality in how sport is portrayed in the media. The positive and negative impacts of the media on sport have been well documented. Future research may focus on the changing nature of the media and sport and on how technological changes impact on the management of sport and sport organizations.

To understand media and broadcasting more fully, the reader may refer to the concepts of **corporate social responsibility (CSR), commercialization, demand, networks, ethics** and **stakeholders** that can be found elsewhere in this book.

FURTHER READING

For some further reading on this concept, we would recommend the following:

Rowe, D. (2009) Power trip: sport and media. *International Journal of Sport Management and Marketing*, 6(2): 150–166.

Syzmanski, S. (2006) The economic evolution of sport and broadcasting. *Australian Economic Review*, 39(4): 428–434.

Wolfe, R., Meenaghan, T. and O'Sullivan, P. (2002) The sports network: insights into the shifting balance of power. *Journal of Business Research*, 55(7): 611–622.

BIBLIOGRAPHY

Albarran, A. and Pitts, G. (2001) *The Radio Broadcasting Industry*. Boston, MA: Allyn and Bacon.

Bishop, R. (2003) Missing in action: feature coverage of women's sports in *Sports Illustrated*. *Journal of Sport and Social Issues*, 27(2): 184–194.

Crossman, J., Vincent, J. and Speed, H. (2007) 'The times they are a-changing': gender comparisons in three national newspapers of the 2004 Wimbledon Championships. *International Review for the Sociology of Sport*, 42(1): 27–41.

Deloitte and Touche (2009) *The Impact of Broadcasting on Sport in the UK*. London: Deloitte LLP.

Doyle, G. and Paterson, R. (2008) Public policy and independent television production in the UK. *Journal of Media Business Studies*, 5(3): 17–33.

Freedman, Des (D.J.) (2008) *The Politics of Media Policy*. Cambridge: Polity.

Gripsrud, J. and Weibull, L. (2010) *Media, Markets and Public Spheres: European Media at the Crossroads*. Bristol: Intellect.

Gulyas, A. (2009) Corporate social responsibility in the British media industries: preliminary findings. *Media, Culture and Society*, 31(4): 657–668.

Hoehn, T. and Lancefield, D. (2003) Broadcasting and sport. *Oxford Review of Economic Policy*, 19(4): 552–568.

Lebel, K. and Danylchuk, K. (2009) Generation Y's perception of women's sport in the media. *International Journal of Sport Communication*, 2(2): 146–164.

Leblebici, H., Salancik, G.R., Copay, A. and King, T. (1991) Institutional change and the transformation of interorganizational fields: an organizational history of the U.S. radio broadcasting industry. *Administrative Science Quarterly*, 36(3): 333–363.

Reid, L.N. and Soley, L.C. (1979) *Sport Illustrated*'s coverage of women in sport. *Journalism Quarterly*, 56(4): 861–863.

Rowe, D. (2004) *Critical Readings: Sport, Culture and the Media*. Maidenhead: Open University Press.

Rowe, D. (2009) Power trip: sport and media. *International Journal of Sport Management and Marketing*, 6(2): 150–166.

Salomon, E. (2008) *Guidelines for Broadcasting Regulation*. Paris: CBA and UNESCO.

Szymanski, S. (2006) The economic evolution of sport and broadcasting. *Australian Economic Review*, 39(4): 428–434.

Vincent, J., Pedersen, P.M., Whisenant, W.A. and Massey, D. (2007) Analyzing the print media coverage of professional tennis players. *International Journal of Sports Marketing and Sponsorship*, 8(2): 141–158.

Whannel, G. (2009) Television and the transformation of sport. *The ANNALS of the American Academy of Political and Social Science*, 625: 205–218.

Wilkins, L. and Christians, C.G. (eds) (2009) *The Handbook of Mass Media Ethics*. Abingdon: Routledge.

Wolfe, R., Meenaghan, T. and O'Sullivan, P. (2002) The sports network: insights into the shifting balance of power. *Journal of Business Research*, 55(7): 611–622.

Mega Events

> *Mega sporting events are defined as those one-time sporting events of an international scale organized by a special 'authority' and yielding extremely high levels of media coverage and impacts (economic, tourism, infrastructure, etc.) for the host community because of the event's significance and/or size. The mega event is often accompanied by parallel activities such as festivals and/or cultural events.*

Over the last thirty years, mega sporting events have become a popular vehicle for obtaining political, cultural, and economic benefits for the hosting region: political benefits include increased international recognition of the host region and the propagation of certain political values held by the government and/or the local population; cultural benefits include the possible strengthening of local traditions and values; and economic benefits can include increased expenditures and employment within the region (Ritchie, 1984).

Major or large-scale sporting events can also be known as mega events if they have an international market and are organized by a special 'authority'. Examples include the Olympic Games, the World Cup of football, and the Super Bowl. Special events can be described as events having a 'regional' international or national market and are coordinated by various levels of government (e.g., a Formula 1 Racing Grand Prix or the Pan-American Games). Hallmark events have a national or regional appeal (e.g., any national sport championship), and community events a regional or local one (e.g., a minor municipal baseball tournament) (Hall, 1989).

There has been, however, some disagreement over the various terms previously described. For example, Hall (1992) described hallmark events as composed of mega events, special events, and community events. In turn, Getz (2005) saw hallmark events as being recurring events that provided the host community with a competitive advantage because of their significance (i.e., tradition, attractiveness, image, or publicity) and argued that mega events would yield 'extraordinarily high levels of tourism, media coverage, prestige or economic impact for the host community, venue or organization' (2005: 18) because of the event's significance and/or size. The mega event is often accompanied by parallel activities such as festivals. Thus, hallmark events and mega events may or may not be different. In addition,

key concepts in sport management

Jago and Shaw (1998) reviewed the literature on the event definition and concluded that an event can be ordinary or special; a special event can be minor, a festival, or major; and a major event is either a hallmark event or a mega event, where the hallmark event is tied to a specific place while the mega event is described as a one-time event on an international scale.

Together with high-profile sporting events, such as the Olympic Games, the Pan-American Games and the World Cup of football, smaller niche-market events have begun to emerge (such as the Journalist World Games, the World Masters Games, the West-Asian Games, the Winter World Transplant Games, the X Games, the World Air Games, the World Dwarf Games, the World Police and Firefighter Games, the Military World Games, the Muslim Women's Games, the World Peace Games, and the Francophonie Games).

Most books and articles on mega sporting events are intended for popular rather than academic consumption (e.g., Jennings, 2000; McGeoch, 1994; Pound, 2004). Research articles analysing mega sporting events have increased in numbers over the last decade and tend to focus on tourism (e.g., Liu, 2006; Toohey et al., 2003; Whitson and Macintosh, 1996), marketing/sponsorship/branding (e.g., Brown, 2000, 2002; Crompton, 1994; Ludwig and Karabetsos, 1999; Maguire et al., 2008; Parent and Séguin, 2008; Séguin and O'Reilly, 2008; Stipp, 1998; Stipp and Schiavone, 1996), economic impact (e.g., Crompton, 1995, 1999; Daniels and Norman, 2003; Gratton et al., 2000; Lee and Taylor, 2005; Preuss, 2005), political/municipal impacts (e.g., Burbank et al., 2001; Gratton and Henry, 2001; Gratton and Preuss, 2008; Hall, 1992; Horne and Manzenreite, 2004; Jones, 2001; Kim and Uysal, 2003; Porter, 1999; Ritchie and Smith, 1991), environmental impacts (e.g., Chappelet, 2008), or risk management/security issues (e.g., Chappelet, 2001; Leopkey and Parent, 2009; Taylor and Toohey, 2006).

Related to the study of impacts and previously discussed in this book is the concept of **legacy** associated with mega events. Legacy is both a practical and an academic concern. In practice, governments, the IOC, national sport governing Bodies and the public are interested in what sort of legacy hosting a mega event can leave and how this compares to the costs of doing so. Academics have been more sceptical of legacy and are currently debating both its meaning and the measurement of this term, thereby questioning the validity of much government evidence that mega events can and will provide lasting and positive legacies.

Studying mega sporting events means going beyond asking the usual questions about 'what type of event?' and 'what did the organizing committee do?' More precisely, it involves examining who was involved, what was required to organize a mega sporting event, what the dynamics were between the various stakeholders involved, what were the apparent and hidden processes and results of the organizing committee's actions, and so on. There are therefore many issues that remain to be studied as regards mega sporting events and work has now begun examining these organization theory questions. For example, Theodoraki (2001) provided a conceptual framework for studying Olympic Games organizing committees' (OCOGs) structural configurations using Mintzberg's configurations; Parent (2008) suggested three operational modes for, and 13 issue categories to be managed by, the organizing committees of major sporting events and their stakeholders; Parent and Deephouse (2007) characterized the **stakeholders** involved in major sporting events; and finally, Chappelet and Kübler-Mabbott (2008) described the International Olympic Committee's **governance** structure, placing this organization on the same level as other international non-governmental organizations such as the Red Cross and UNESCO.

To understand mega events more fully, the reader may refer to the concepts of **legacy**, **governance** and **stakeholders** that can be found elsewhere in this book.

FURTHER READING

For some further reading on this concept, we would recommend the following:

Getz, D. (2005) *Event Management and Event Tourism* (2nd edn). Elmsford, NY: Cognizant Communication Corp.

Parent, M.M. (2008) Evolution and issue patterns for major-sport-event organizing committees and their stakeholders. *Journal of Sport Management*, 22(2): 135–164.

Ritchie, J.R.B. (1984) Assessing the impact of hallmark events: conceptual and research issues. *Journal of Travel Research*, 23(1): 2–11.

BIBLIOGRAPHY

Brown, G. (2000) Emerging issues in Olympic sponsorship: implications for host cities. *Sport Management Review*, 3: 71–92.

Brown, G. (2002) Taking the pulse of Olympic sponsorship. *Event Management*, 7: 187–196.

Burbank, M.J., Andranovich, G.D. and Heying, C.H. (2001) *Olympic Dreams: The Impact of Mega-events on Local Politics*. London: Lynne Reiner.

Chappelet, J.-L. (2001) Risk management for large-scale events: the case of the Olympic Winter Games. *European Journal for Sport Management*, (Special Issue): 6–12.

Chappelet, J.-L. (2008) Olympic environmental concerns as a legacy of the Winter Games. *International Journal of the History of Sport*, 25(14): 1884–1902.

Chappelet, J.-L. and Kübler-Mabbott, B. (2008) *The International Olympic Committee and the Olympic System*. Abingdon: Routledge.

Crompton, J.L. (1994) Benefits and risks associated with sponsorship of major events. *Festival Management and Event Tourism*, 2: 65–74.

Crompton, J.L. (1995) Economic impact analysis of sport facilities and events: eleven sources of misapplication. *Journal of Sport Management*, 9(1): 14–35.

Crompton, J.L. (1999) The economic impact of sports tournaments and events. *Parks and Recreation*, 34(9): 142–150.

Daniels, M.J. and Norman, W.C. (2003) Estimating the economic impacts of seven regular sport tourism events. *Journal of Sport Tourism*, 8: 214–222.

Getz, D. (2005) *Event Management and Event Tourism* (2nd edn). Elmsford, NY: Cognizant Communication Corp.

Gratton, C. and Henry, I.P. (eds) (2001) *Sport in the City: The Role of Sport in Economic and Social Regeneration*. London: Routledge.

Gratton, C. and Preuss, H. (2008) Maximizing Olympic impacts by building up legacies. *International Journal of the History of Sport*, 25(14): 1922–1938.

Gratton, C., Dobson, N. and Shibli, S. (2000) The economic importance of major sports events: a case-study of six events. *Managing Leisure*, 5(1): 17–28.

Hall, C.M. (1989) The definition and analysis of hallmark tourist events. *GeoJournal*, 19(3): 263–68.

Hall, C.M. (1992) *Hallmark Tourist Events: Impacts, Management and Planning*. London: Belhaven.

Horne, J. and Manzenreiter, W. (2004) Accounting for mega-events: forecast and actual impacts of the 2002 Football World Cup finals on the host countries Japan/Korea. *International Review for the Sociology of Sport*, 39: 197–203.

Jago, L.K. and Shaw, R.N. (1998) Special events: a conceptual and definitional framework. *Festival Management and Event Tourism*, 5: 21–32.

Jennings, A. (2000) *The Great Olympic Swindle: When the World Wanted its Games Back*. London: Simon and Schuster.

Jones, C. (2001) Mega-events and host-region impacts: determining the true worth of the 1999 Rugby World Cup. *International Journal of Tourism Research*, 3: 241–251.

Kim, K. and Uysal, M. (2003) Perceived socio-economic impacts of festivals and events among organizers. *Journal of Hospitality and Leisure Marketing*, 10(3–4): 159–171.

Lee, C. and Taylor, T. (2005) Critical reflections on the economic impact assessment of a mega-event: the case of the 2002 FIFA World Cup. *Tourism Management*, 26: 595–603.

Leopkey, B. and Parent, M.M. (2009) Risk management issues in large-scale sporting events: a stakeholder perspective. *European Sport Management Quarterly*, 9(2): 187–208.

Liu, F.-M. (2006) Analysis on influential factors of Olympic tourism development. *Journal of Chengdu Sport University*, 32(2): 15–18.

Ludwig, S. and Karabetsos, J.D. (1999) Objectives and evaluation processes utilized by sponsors of the 1996 Olympic Games. *Sport Marketing Quarterly*, 8(1): 11–19.

Maguire, J., Barnard, S., Butler, K. and Golding, P. (2008) Olympic legacies in the IOC's 'Celebrate Humanity' campaign: ancient or modern? *International Journal of the History of Sport*, 25(14): 2041–2059.

McGeoch, R. (1994) *The Bid: How Australia won the 2000 Games*. Port Melbourne: William Heinemann Australia.

Parent, M.M. (2008) Evolution and issue patterns for major-sport-event organizing committees and their stakeholders. *Journal of Sport Management*, 22(2): 135–164.

Parent, M.M. and Deephouse, D.L. (2007) A case study of stakeholder identification and prioritization by managers. *Journal of Business Ethics*, 75(1): 1–23.

Parent, M.M. and Séguin, B. (2008) Toward a model of brand creation for international large-scale sporting events: the impact of leadership, context, and nature of the event. *Journal of Sport Management*, 22(5): 526–549.

Porter, P.K. (1999) Mega-sports events as municipal investments: a critique of impact analysis. In J. Fizel, E. Gustafson and L.Hadley (eds), *Sport Economics: Current Research*. Westport, CT: Praeger. pp. 61–74.

Pound, R.W. (2004) *Inside the Olympics: A Behind-the-Scenes Look at the Politics, the Scandals, and the Glory of the Games*. Mississauga, Canada: Wiley and Sons Canada Ltd.

Preuss, H. (2005) The economic impact of visitors at major multi-sport events. *European Sport Management Quarterly*, 5(3): 281–301.

Ritchie, J.R.B. (1984) Assessing the impact of hallmark events: conceptual and research issues. *Journal of Travel Research*, 23(1): 2–11.

Ritchie, J.R.B. and Smith, B.H. (1991) The impact of a mega-event on host region awareness: a longitudinal study. *Journal of Travel Research*, 30(1): 3–10.

Séguin, B. and O'Reilly, N.J. (2008) The Olympic brand, ambush marketing and clutter. *International Journal of Sport Management and Marketing*, 4(1): 62–84.

Stipp, H. (1998) The impact of Olympic sponsorship on corporate image. *International Journal of Advertising*, 17(1): 75–87.

Stipp, H. and Schiavone, N.P. (1996) Modeling the impact of Olympic sponsorship on corporate image. *Journal of Advertising Research*, 36(4): 22.

Taylor, T. and Toohey, K. (2006) Impacts of terrorism-related safety and security measures at a major sport event. *Event Management*, 9(4): 199–209.

Theodoraki, E. (2001) A conceptual framework for the study of structural configurations of organising committees for the Olympic Games (OCOGs). *European Journal For Sport Management*, 8 (Special issue): 106–124.

Toohey, K., Taylor, T. and Lee, C.K. (2003) The FIFA World Cup 2002: The effects of terrorism on sport tourists. *Journal of Sport Tourism*, 8(3): 167–185.

Whitson, D. and Macintosh, D. (1996) The global circus: international sport, tourism, and the marketing of cities. *Journal of Sport and Social Issues*, 20(3): 278–295.

Networks

> Networks are defined as a web of relationships between three or more actors who exchange tangible and/or intangible resources.

Networks are a web of relationships between more than two partners. These relationships are typically based on the exchange of resources such as knowledge, capital, or skills (cf. Child and Faulkner, 1998). Each partner or actor in a network is depicted as a node. These nodes are linked by formal or informal ties. Strategic alliances would therefore, for example, be considered a form of network (albeit a small one) but a network would not be seen as a strategic alliance, strictly speaking, as strategic alliances require organizational learning to be a part of the relationship, which is not a requirement for networks in general.

Being in a network provides the actor (e.g., organization) with increased access to resources, such as knowledge and skills, with greater flexibility, more production capacity, and decreased uncertainty. In order to do so, legitimacy must be built between actors and in the eyes of external groups (Child and Faulkner, 1998). Presenting a network as a good or special entity in itself, as the preferred organizational form, or as a profitable set of relationships, allows the actors in the network to gain this legitimacy (cf. Human and Provan, 2000).

Management research related to networks (network theory) can focus on structural or relational aspects at three different levels: individual actors, actor dyads, and the network as a whole. Research focusing on individual actors will typically present their characteristics: for example, organizations in a network will choose a potential partner based on information that is freely available to them (Child and Faulkner, 1998), on past reputation (Podolny, 1993) and status (Benjamin and Podolny, 1999; Podolny, 1994), or on partners' available resources.

These resources can be described in terms of forms of capital, with Bourdieu (1986) providing a good framework. More precisely, capital can be separated into four forms: economic, cultural, social, and symbolic. Economic capital is the traditional view of capital as financial resources. Cultural capital is an individual's (or an organization's) background, knowledge, qualifications, and cultural goods. Cultural capital can be embodied, objectified, or institutionalized. Social capital is the set of relationships or memberships within a given group that will facilitate resource access. Finally, symbolic capital is the legitimation of the other three forms of capital (Bourdieu, 1986). The more forms of capital a potential actor has, the more likely it is that they will be a desirable network partner.

In his study of the high-tech industry, Stuart (2000) found that firms with a technological overlap were more likely to form partnerships. In addition, high-prestige firms were more likely to form partnerships with others in distinct technological areas. Stuart also found a demographic component to partnership formations where partnership formation opportunities varied across technological positions and that network crowding and organizational prestige were structural factors underlying partnership formation.

In terms of research examining actor dyads, Granovetter (1973) looked at the strength of dyadic ties. The strength of a tie is defined as a combination of the amount of time, the emotional intensity, the intimacy, and the reciprocal services that characterize this tie. For example, the overlap in two business circles is predicted to be least when there is no tie, most when a tie is present and strong, and intermediate when the tie is present but weak. Stronger ties involve larger time commitments. The stronger the tie, the more similar the two actors are in various ways. Granovetter suggests that a weak tie should be called a bridge. This bridge is the line in a network that provides the only path between two nodes. Granovetter also suggested that different parts of a network could have different densities: an effective network would be the part where ties are strong and an extended network would include the weaker ties. Weak ties would be more likely to link members of various small groups than strong ones, which would tend to concentrate within particular groups. Strong ties would breed local cohesion but could lead to an overall fragmentation.

Granovetter (1985) went on to study the degree to which economic action was embedded in the structures of social relations. He found that actors did not behave or decide as atoms outside a social context, and nor did they adhere slavishly to a script written for them by the particular intersection of social categories that they happened to occupy. Their attempts at purposive action were instead embedded in concrete, ongoing systems of social relations. The embeddedness argument stresses the role of concrete relationships and the structures of such relations (networks) in generating trust and discouraging malfeasance. Business relations are mixed up with personal ones and this overlay may play a crucial role (e.g., power relations cannot be neglected). Many complexities between organizations are resolved by implicit or explicit power relations among the organizations. Granovetter argued that the detailed analysis of social structure was key to understanding how existing institutions arrived at their present state.

Uzzi (1997) further examined the issue of embeddedness and found that it allowed for economies of time and offered an alternative to the price system for allocating resources. Each organization satisfies rather than maximizes on price in embedded relationships. Organizations linked through embeddedness do not usually search for competitive prices; instead, they will negotiate key agreements afterwards. The unique expectations of reciprocity and the cooperative resource sharing of embedded ties generate investments that cannot be achieved through arm's length ties that are based on immediate gain. Embeddedness assists adaptation. Embedded firms continue to cooperate even after the end of the game is apparent. Embedded networks generate Pareto improvements – namely, the reallocation of resources that makes at least one person better off but does not make anyone worse off. Close personal ties heighten empathy which increases altruistic behaviour. A portfolio of social ties boosts risk taking.

Burt (2000) found that participation in, and control of, information diffusion underlies the social capital of structural holes. Social capital is a function of brokerage opportunities. Weaker connections between two groups in a network indicate a structural hole. There is a competitive advantage for those whose relationships span the holes; it is an opportunity to broker the flow of information between actors and control projects that brings together actors from opposite sides of the hole. Burt argues that structural holes separate non-redundant sources of information, sources that are more additive than overlapping. Redundancy can be determined through two indicators: cohesion and equivalence. Contingency factors, such as insiders/outsiders and network closure, affect the strength of association between social capital and performance.

In terms of research examining the network as a whole, Rowley (1997) presented structural conditions which would impact an organization's strategic responses: network density and organization centrality. Network density refers to the relative number (high or low) of dyadic ties in the network. Density is measured as the ratio of the number of existing ties over the number of total possible ties in the network. In turn, organization centrality is an organization's *degree* or number of direct ties, its *closeness* or independent access to others, and its *betweenness* or **control** over other actors (cf. Brass and Burkhardt, 1993). In addition to this, Burt (2000) argued that there were three kinds of networks: cliques, which are small, dense and non-hierarchical; entrepreneurial or broker networks, which are large, sparse and non-hierarchical; and hierarchical networks, which are large, sparse, and anchored on a central contact, and exist where social capital is borrowed.

In relation to network theory in research which has examined the management of sport, there have been a few articles dealing with the concept of networks. Chadwick (2000) noted the importance of organizations' network centrality or positioning and of promoting collaborative relationships as were found in the networks in the *European Journal for Sport Management* article entitled 'A research agenda for strategic collaboration in European club football'. Added to this, Turner and Westerbeek (2004) studied the network of relationships which were formed during the bidding process for a major sporting event in their article 'Network relationships in the bidding process for major sporting events'. The reader should also look at the work of Seippel (2008), Quatman and Chelladurai (2008) and Barnes et al. (2007), describe below, for some of the most recent work on network theory in the management of sport.

Quatman and Chelladurai (2008), for example, focus on exploring the various ways social network theory can be utilized in research on the management of sport.

In their discussion of ontological, epistemological and methodological perspectives related to network analysis, the authors draw on examples from the sport management literature to demonstrate the value of network analysis. They conclude by encouraging researchers using network theory to move beyond simply describing the relationships they discover to explaining how and why those relationships occurred. Seippel (2008) likewise used network theory to examine the role and influence of voluntary sport organizations in civil society. By examining data based on Norwegian surveys from 1982, 1990 and 2003, he demonstrated that sport organizations were influential owing to their size but also 'relatively weakly embedded and positioned within civil society' (2008: 1). He also showed that sport organizations were weakly embedded in the broader category of voluntary associations. Barnes and colleagues (2007) used their content analysis of Canadian Sport Policy documents to demonstrate that the administrative structure, the degree of network coupling, and the strength of ties between actors reflected low levels of integration in the network of sport providers. Their research suggested barriers to poor integration which moved beyond a simple lack of resources.

It is certainly the case that a network approach provides an interesting lens by which to study various sport management-related topics. As such we would urge the sport management research community to consider network theory as a possible theoretical lens.

To understand networks more fully, the reader may refer to the concept of **control** that can be found elsewhere in this book.

FURTHER READING

For some further reading on this concept, we would recommend the following:

Czarniawska-Joerges, B. and Herns, T. (2005) *Actor–Network Theory and Organizing*. Copenhagen: Copenhagen Business School Press.
Quatman, C. and Chelladurai, P. (2008) Social network theory and analysis: a complementary lens for enquiry. *Journal of Sport Management*, 22(3): 338–360.
Seippel, Ø. (2008) Sports in civil society: networks, social capital and influence. *European Sociological Review*, 24(1): 69–80.

BIBLIOGRAPHY

Barnes, M., Cousens, L. and MacLean, J. (2007) From silos to synergies: a network perspective of the Canadian sport system. *International Journal of Sport Management and Marketing*, 2(5–6): 555–571.
Benjamin, B.A. and Podolny, J.M. (1999) Status, quality, and social order in the California wine industry. *Administrative Science Quarterly*, 44: 563–589.
Bourdieu, P. (1986) The forms of capital. In J.G. Richardson (ed.), *Handbook of Theory and Research for the Sociology of Education*. New York: Greenwood. pp. 241–258.
Brass, D.J. and Burkhardt, M.E. (1993) Potential power and power use: an investigation of structure and behavior. *Academy of Management Journal*, 36: 441–470.
Burt, R.S. (2000) The network structure of social capital. *Research in Organizational Behaviour*, 22: 345–423.

Chadwick, S. (2000) A research agenda for strategic collaboration in European club football. *European Journal for Sport Management*, 7: 6–29.

Child, J. and Faulkner, D. (1998) *Strategies of Cooperation: Managing Alliances, Networks, and Joint Ventures*. New York: Oxford University Press.

Granovetter, M. (1973) The strength of weak ties. *American Journal of Sociology*, 78: 1360–1380.

Granovetter, M. (1985) Economic action and social structure: the problem of embeddedness. *American Journal of Sociology*, 91: 481–510.

Human, S.E. and Provan, K.G. (2000) Legitimacy building in the evolution of small-firm multilateral networks: a comparative study of success and demise. *Administrative Science Quarterly*, 45: 327–365.

Podolny, J.M. (1993) A status-based model of market competition. *American Journal of Sociology*, 98 (4): 829–872.

Podolny, J.M. (1994) Market uncertainty and the social character of economic exchange. *Administrative Science Quarterly*, 39: 458–483.

Quatman, C. and Chelladurai, P. (2008) Social network theory and analysis: a complementary lens for enquiry. *Journal of Sport Management*, 22(3): 338–360.

Rowley, T.J. (1997) Moving beyond dyadic ties: a network theory of stakeholder influences. *Academy of Management Review*, 22: 887–910.

Seippel, Ø. (2008) Sports in civil society: networks, social capital and influence. *European Sociological Review*, 24(1): 69–80.

Stuart, T.E. (2000) Interorganizational alliances and the performance of firms: a study of growth and innovation rates in a high-technology industry. *Strategic Management Journal*, 21: 791–811.

Turner, P. and Westerbeek, H.M. (2004) Network relationships in the bidding process for major sporting events. *International Journal of Sport Management*, 5: 335–356.

Uzzi, B. (1997) Social structure and competition in interfirm networks: the paradox of embeddedness. *Administrative Science Quarterly*, 42: 35–67.

Organizational Culture

> *Organizational culture involves the stories, ceremonies, language, values, beliefs, ways of operating and physical settings of an organization. It brings people back into organizations without paying attention to psychological measures.*

Organizational culture (sometimes called corporate culture) became popular when managers realized that Japanese companies which were successful operated differently from corporations in the West. While the culture of Japanese society is obviously different from the culture we find in Western societies, people who study organizations were concerned about the culture of the organizations that were found in those societies. While there is no universal definition of organizational culture, it involves shared stories, ceremonies, language, values, beliefs, ways of operating, and the physical settings of the organizations involved (cf. Lewis, 2002; Pettigrew, 1979; Schein, 1991; Wilkins, 1983). It is generally accepted in the management literature, however, that an organization needs a 'positive' organizational culture in order to perform well.

The organizational culture brings people back into organizations without resorting to psychological measures. Trice and Beyer (1984) suggest that rites, ceremonies, rituals, myths, sagas, legends, stories, folktales, symbols, language, gestures, physical settings and artefacts were all manifestations of an organization's culture. Smith (2009) focuses on stories as elements of an organization's culture but the arguments he put forward could equally well be applied to other aspects of culture which Trice and Beyer (1984) identify. Smith suggests that it was not so much the story but the way it was interpreted that contributed to the culture of an organization. He argued that the stories he referred to as minimally counter-intuitive were more likely to be found in the culture of an organization. The popular literature stresses the benefits of a strong culture which is engrained in an organization (referred to as a 'thick' culture) (cf. Deal and Kennedy, 1982; Peters and Waterman, 1982). This thick culture is thought to be advantageous to an organization that experiences little change, namely where it is in a stable environment. When an organization has a weaker culture (a 'thin' culture) it is easier to **change**. Culture can act as a substitute for formalization (see **structure**). Organizations are usually portrayed as having one culture, but Gregory (1983) – building on the ideas in anthropology – suggested that organizations, like societies, were multicultural: it would be the dominant culture which would often be more noticeable in an organization. Taormina (2009) likewise looked at the socialization process in organizations and its relationship to organizational culture, and stressed the multi-dimensional nature of an organization's culture, suggesting that this culture may be bureaucratic, innovative, or supportive.

An organization's culture must be created and managed. The creation of this culture is often held to be a result of the founders' ideas and activities (cf. Schein, 1983). The management of culture, according to Schein (1985), is the result of five activities. These are:

- What leaders pay attention to, measure, and attempt to control.
- The leader's reaction to critical incidents and organizational crises.
- The deliberate role modelling, teaching, and coaching done by leaders.
- The criteria for the allocation of rewards and status.
- The criteria used for recruitment, selection, promotion, retirement, and excommunication.

Lorsch (1986) suggests that an organization's culture can be changed and he suggested a number of stages to the change process. The first is an awareness of the need to change. This is followed by a period of confusion when new values interact with the old values and often a new leader will be appointed who may articulate a vision for the organization. The final stage is called experimentation. Here the company experiments with new aspects of the organization until a suitable culture is found. This culture may be reinforced by the actions that Schein (1985) discusses.

There are multiple general frameworks which can be used to measure the various dimensions of organizational culture, such as the Organizational Culture Inventory or OCI (Cooke and Rousseau, 1988), the Organizational Culture Profile or OCP (O'Reilly et al., 1991), and the Organizational Culture Assessment Instrument or OCAI (Cameron and Quinn, 1999). Culture has also been used as a 'perspective' from which to analyse other concepts such as **knowledge transfer** (KT), revealing obstacles in the KT process and the importance of culture both to organizations and to project teams (Ajmal and Koskinen, 2008). In fact, organizational culture has been shown to impact upon many other aspects of management such as **strategy** and **leadership** (see Baumgartner, 2009).

Organizational culture is a relatively new concept in sport management. Sport organizations are rife with the rites, ceremonies, rituals, myths, sagas, legends, stories, folktales, symbols, language, gestures, physical settings and artefacts that Trice and Beyer (1984) suggest make up the evidence for an organization's culture. Sport management researchers have been examining organizational culture in the fitness industry (e.g., MacIntosh and Doherty, 2008), state and federal organizations (e.g., Colyer, 2000; Smith and Shilbury, 2004), sporting events (e.g., McDonald, 1991), and campus recreation/intercollegiate athletics departments (e.g., Smart and Wolfe, 2000; Weese, 1995).

As MacIntosh and Doherty (2008) note, the need to examine industry-specific aspects of organizational culture means that further research is certainly needed on sport management generally and different types of organizations specifically (e.g., sporting goods). MacIntosh and Doherty (2010) propose a fitness industry-specific organizational culture framework called the Cultural Index for Fitness Organizations (CIFO). Their work suggests that the culture of the fitness industry is multi-dimensional and that the atmosphere of the industry was the factor most likely to lead to job satisfaction. 'Atmosphere' includes the notion that a workplace which is welcoming, friendly, upbeat, and somewhere that fitness staff can work, and both clients and staff can work out in a positive environment, is a key feature of fitness organizations.

Whether in sport or the broader management literature, organizational culture research requires a more varied methodology and one which truly accesses the 'internal' aspects of organizational life. As well as this, process-related research is needed in order to move beyond simply stating that organizational culture impacts on job satisfaction, the intention to leave, and performance, and proceed towards an understanding of how this actually occurs. This may be progressed further by focusing on culture as a mechanism of control or by concentrating on how culture controls individuals and groups within organizations. However, as we have indicated already, there is scope for more research on culture in sport organizations to build a more comprehensive picture of the range of cultures which exist (and why organization cultures vary) and management practices in managing cultures (and their effectiveness), as well as looking at how and why organization cultures are formed, changed, or prove resistant to change. Frontiera (2010) has already begun to address these issues in his examination of leadership and culture transformation in professional sport. And added to this, we can see similarities between the concept of culture and identity that are each focused on values. This may be a worthwhile relationship to explore in future research on organizational culture.

To understand organization culture more fully, the reader may refer to the concepts of **knowledge transfer**, **structure**, **strategy**, **leadership** and **change** that can be found elsewhere in this book.

FURTHER READING

For some further reading on this concept, we would recommend the following:

Frontiera, J. (2010) Leadership and organizational culture transformation in professional sport. *Journal of Leadership and Organizational Studies*, 17(1): 71–86.

Frost, P.J., Moore, L.F., Louis, M.R., Lundberg, C.C. and Martin, J. (eds) (1985) *Reframing Organizational Culture*. Beverly Hills, CA: Sage.

Kent, A. and Weese, J.W. (2000) Do effective organizations have better executive leadership and/ or organizational cultures? A study of selected sport organizations in Canada. *European Journal for Sport Management*, 7: 4–21.

BIBLIOGRAPHY

Ajmal, M.M. and Koskinen, K.U. (2008) Knowledge transfer in project-based organizations: an organizational culture perspective. *Project Management Journal*, 39(1): 7–15.

Baumgartner, R.J. (2009) Organizational culture and leadership: preconditions for the development of a sustainable corporation. *Sustainable Development*, 17(2): 102–13.

Cameron, K. and Quinn, R.E. (1999) *Diagnosing and Changing Organizational Culture: Based on the Competing Values Framework*. Reading, MA: Addison-Wesley.

Colyer, S. (2000) Organizational culture in selected Western Australian sport organizations. *Journal of Sport Management*, 14: 321–341.

Cooke, R.A. and Rousseau, D.M. (1988) Behavioral norms and expectations: a quantitative approach to the assessment of organizational culture. *Groups and Organizational Studies*, 13: 245–273.

Deal, T.E. and Kennedy, A.A. (1982) *Corporate Cultures: The Rites and Rituals of Corporate Life*. Reading, MA: Addison-Wesley.

Frontiera, J. (2010) Leadership and organizational culture transformation in professional sport. *Journal of Leadership and Organizational Studies*, 17(1): 71–86.

Gregory, K.L. (1983) Native-view paradigms: multiple cultures and culture conflicts in organizations. *Administrative Science Quarterly*, 28: 359–376.

Lewis, D. (2002) Five years on: the organizational culture saga revisited. *Leadership and Organization Development Journal*, 23: 280–287.

Lorsch, J. (1986) Managing culture: the invisible barrier to strategic change. *California Management Review*, 28: 95–109.

Macintosh E.W. and Doherty, A. (2008) Inside the Canadian fitness industry: development of a conceptual framework of organizational culture. *International Journal of Sport Management*, 9: 303–327.

Macintosh E.W. and Doherty, A. (2010) The influence of organizational culture on job satisfaction and intention to leave. *Sport Management Review*, 13: 106–117.

McDonald, P. (1991) The Los Angeles Olympic Organizing Committee: developing organizational culture in the short run. In P.J. Frost, L.F. Moore, M.R. Louis, C.C. Lundberg and J. Martin (eds), *Reframing Organizational Culture*. Beverly Hills, CA: Sage. pp. 26–38.

O'Reilly, C.A., III, Chatman, J. and Caldwell, D.F. (1991) People and organizational culture: a profile comparison approach to assessing person–organization fit. *Academy of Management Journal*, 34: 487–516.

Peters, T.J. and Waterman, R.H. (1982) *In Search of Excellence*. New York: Harper & Row.

Pettigrew, A.M. (1979) On studying organizational cultures. *Administrative Science Quarterly*, 24: 570–581.

Schein, E.H. (1983) The role of the founder in creating organizational culture. *Organizational Dynamics*, 12: 13–28.

Schein, E.H. (1985) *Organizational Culture and Leadership*. San Francisco, CA: Jossey-Bass.

Schein, E H. (1991) The role of the founder in the creation of organizational culture. In P.J. Frost, L.F. Moore, M.R. Louis, C.C. Lundberg and J. Martin (eds), *Reframing Organizational Culture*. Beverly Hills, CA: Sage. pp. 14–25.

Smart, J.C. and Wolfe, R.A. (2000) Examining sustainable competitive advantage in intercollegiate athletics: a resource-based view. *Journal of Sport Management*, 14: 133–153.

Smith, A. (2009) An exploration of counter-intuitive conceptual structures in organizational stories. *Journal of Sport Management*, 23: 483–510.

Smith, A. and Shilbury, D. (2004) Mapping cultural dimensions in Australian sporting organizations. *Sport Management Review*, 7: 133–165.

Taormina, R.J. (2009) Organizational socialization: the missing link between employee needs and organizational culture. *Journal of Managerial Psychology*, 24: 650–676.

Trice, H.M. and Beyer, J.M. (1984) Studying organizational cultures through rites and ceremonies. *Academy of Management Review*, 9: 653–669.

Weese, J.W. (1995) Leadership and organizational culture: an investigation of Big Ten and Mid-American conference campus recreation administrations. *Journal of Sport Management*, 10: 197–206.

Wilkins, A.L. (1983) The culture audit: a tool for understanding organizations. *Organizational Dynamics*, 12: 24–38.

Organizational Goals

> *Organizational goals are statements often developed by senior managers which communicate the reason(s) for a sport organization's existence and summarize the intended operations of that organization.*

Some of the first organizational theorists to critically discuss and define organizational goals were Simon (1964) and Cyert and March (1963). These authors usefully discussed the difference and relationship between organization goals and **decision making** in organizations. They noted that decisions were often taken within a range of constraints and not necessarily made solely in pursuit of goals. Simon (1964) also recognized that it was difficult not to discuss goals when talking about other aspects of organizations, such as strategy, individual behaviour, or structure. Many researchers have subsequently focused on organizational goals to understand other concepts such as organizations (Mohr, 1973), organizational performance (Smith et al., 1990), and **conflict** (Cohen, 1984).

Goals are important in all organizations for two principal reasons. First, all organizations exist for a reason; if an organization does not have a reason to exist then there is no need for it. Goals are statements that summarize and articulate the rationale for an organization's existence. Second, goals provide guidelines for managers and other employees in such areas as decision making, performance appraisal, the reduction of uncertainty, the direction and motivation of employees, and organizational legitimacy. Organizations usually have several different types of goals, each of which performs a particular function. Some goals may overlap. For example, official goals are usually non-operative while short-term goals are usually operative.

Official goals are representative of the general functions of the organization as found in the constitution, annual reports, and public statements by key executives. Official goals, or mission statements as they are frequently called, are often subjective and usually not measurable; they express the values of the organization and give it legitimacy with stakeholders; they describe the reason(s) for the organization's being; and serve as the reason(s) for employees and members to identify with the organization. While official goals exemplify what an organization says it wants to achieve, operative goals tell us what the organization is actually trying to achieve. Operational goals can be measured objectively: they may be official but are most likely to be operative. Operational goals may be developed through a process known as Management by Objectives (MBO). A non-operational goal is one that cannot be measured objectively. Official goals, or mission statements, are usually non-operational.

Long-term goals are those that an organization would like to achieve over a relatively lengthy period of time, e.g., within a season or a period of years. Short-term goals are set for a relatively brief period of time. **Organizations** formulate overall goals. They may be official or operative, operational or non-operational, long term or short term. However, departments or sub-units within an organization may also formulate their own goals. Department and sub-unit goals should not be seen as ends in themselves but as a means to achieving the organization's **strategy** (Daft, 2009). The concept of organizational goals is important in organization theory and in the design and **effectiveness** of organizations (see, e.g., Daft, 2009).

Although they did not solely focus on goals, the research by Kikulus et al. (1992) demonstrated the significance of goals in sport organizations and their role in understanding change and change management. In fact, giving explicit attention to goals in research on the management of sport is rare. One exception to this was Trail and Chelladurai's (2000) article which examined goal perception in athletics. Examining different stakeholder groups, the author's perceptions of goals differed most significantly in respect to gender and faculty/student sub-group status. MBO has frequently been suggested as a means of goal-setting for sport organizations (cf. Jensen, 1983; Kelly, 1991; VanderZwaag, 1984).

Implicit attention on goals or an examination of goals in relation to other concepts is more common in research on the management of sport. In research on organization **performance**, reference is often made to if and how goals are achieved as these serve as a performance indicator (Covell et al., 2007). In research on **sport for development**, the focus is often on how sport can help achieve the goals of other organizations (Beutler, 2008).

Overall, the concept of goals is often referred to in research on many other concepts, within the mainstream business and management literature, and in the literature on the management of sport. This suggests the importance of considering how goals impact on our research questions about other concepts such as strategy or decision making. Those of us interested in research on organizational goals should clarify what type of goals are important in the organizations investigated and consider how these goals relate to what the current literature suggests about goals in organizations generally and in sport organizations specifically.

To understand organizational goals more fully, the reader may refer to the concepts of **performance management**, **sport development**, **sport organization**, **strategy**, **conflict**, **effectiveness** and **decision making** that can be found elsewhere in this book.

FURTHER READING

For some further reading on this concept, we would recommend the following:

Beutler, I. (2008) Sport serving development and peace: achieving the goals of the United Nations through sport. *Sport in Society*, 11(4): 359–369.

Daft, R.L. (2009) *Organization Theory and Design*. Belmont, CA: Cengage Learning.

Trail, G. and Chelladurai, P. (2000) Perceptions of goals and processes of intercollegiate athletics: a case study. *Journal of Sport Management*, 14(2): 154–178

BIBLIOGRAPHY

Beutler, I. (2008) Sport serving development and peace: achieving the goals of the United Nations through sport. *Sport in Society*, 11(4): 359–369.

Cohen, M.D. (1984) Conflict and complexity: goal diversity and organizational search effectiveness. *The American Political Science Review*, 78(2): 435–451.

Covell, D., Walker, S. and Siciliano, J. (2007) *Managing Sports Organizations: Responsibility for Performance*. Oxford: Butterworth-Heinemann, Elsevier.

Cyert, R.M. and March, J.G. (1963) *A Behavioral Theory of the Firm*. Englewood Cliffs, NJ: Prentice-Hall.

Daft, R.L. (2009) *Organization Theory and Design*. Belmont, CA: Cengage Learning.

Jensen, C.R. (1983) *Administrative Management of Physical Education and Athletic Programs*. Philadelphia, PA: Lea and Febiger.

Kelly, T.W. (1991) Performance evaluation. In R.L. Boucher and W.J. Weese (eds), *Management of Recreational Sports in Higher Education*. Carmel, IN: Benchmark Press. pp. 153–165.

Kikulus, L.M., Slack, T. and Hininys, C.R. (1992) Institutionally specific design archetypes: A framework for understanding change in national sport organizations. *International Review for the Sociology of Sport*, 27(4): 343–369.

Mohr, L.B. (1973) On the concept of organizational goal. *The American Political Science Review*, 67(2): 470–481.

Simon, H.A. (1964) On the concept of organizational goal. *Administrative Science Quarterly*, 9(1): 1–22.

Smith, K.G., Locke, E.A. and Barry, D. (1990) Goal setting, planning, and organizational performance: an experimental simulation. *Organization Behavior and Human Decision Processes*, 46(1): 118–134.

Trail, G. and Chelladurai, P. (2000) Perceptions of goals and processes of intercollegiate athletics: a case study. *Journal of Sport Management*, 14: 154–178.

VanderZwaag, H.J. (1984) *Sport Management in Schools and Colleges*. New York: Wiley.

Performance Management

> *Performance management is the measurement and evaluation of the use of resources (human, financial, organizational) that leads managers to taking corrective action in line with strategic objectives to ensure the optimum efficient and effective operation of an organization.*

Performance management is an ill-defined body of literature. Research on the performance of organizations is underpinned by a variety of disciplines such as economics, finance and human resource management, but is primarily an 'operations' issue within organizations. It can however also be 'strategic' in nature. The performance of staff, departments and the organization as a whole is usually measured against previously identified **goals**/objectives. It is the manager's role to continuously monitor this process of goal setting and achievement to ensure the organization is progressing in the right direction and at the right pace.

Performance management is also a tool for motivation and the career progression of staff and can reduce unwanted **conflict** that arises when there is uncertainty, ambiguity and a lack of transparency in organizational operations. Models of managing performance have been developed by researchers (e.g., Total Quality Management, Balanced Scorecards, Stakeholder Approach to Strategic Performance Management) in order to help practitioners manage all aspects of performance and to not rely solely on financial measures. And added to this, performance management is part of the function of **control** within organizations, allowing managers to influence employee behaviour through rewards and sanctions. We now discuss the concept of performance management in a little more detail using these themes of operations, human resources and control to show some of the research that has been conducted on this concept.

As an operations issue, one of the most widely discussed frameworks for performance management is the Balanced Scorecard. Kaplan and Norton (1996) developed this tool as a means for **strategy** implementation. Of course, as with most research, there are criticisms of the balance scorecard as a strategic management system. Other models that serve to challenge the balanced scorecard include 'performance dashboards' (Eckerson, 2011). Eckerson defines performance dashboards as such:

> A performance dashboard is more than just a screen with fancy performance graphics on it: It is a full-fledged business information system that is built on a business intelligence and data integration infrastructure. A performance dashboard is very

different from plain dashboards or scorecards. The latter are simply visual display mechanisms to deliver performance information in a user-friendly way whereas performance dashboards knit together the data, applications, and rules that drive what users see on their screens.

(2011: xiv)

Human resources have long been recognized as important for contributing to or detracting from the performance of organizations (Becker and Gerhart, 1996). Not surprisingly there has been a body of literature that focuses on how human resource management (HRM) could create value and a strategic advantage for organizations (see Lado and Wilson, 1994; Pfeffer, 1994) and how best to manage human resources to have a positive impact on organization performance (Amit and Shoemaker, 1993; Gerhart et al., 1996; Meyer et al., 1993; Pfeffer, 1994). The debates around HRM and performance still continue and consist of both theoretical and empirical discussions which the reader can more fully explore in Guest (2001, 2011) and Paauwe (2009).

Performance management as a form of organization control focuses on management's role in measuring, evaluating, and adjusting the performance of resources within organizations. Otley (1999) proposed a framework for analysing management control systems that was structured around five central issues:

- Objectives;
- Strategies and plans for the achievement of objectives;
- Target setting;
- Incentive and reward structures;
- Information feedback loops.

Subsequent research focuses on various aspects of control in pursuit of managing performance. Tuomela (2005) discussed 'levers of control' in a case study 'introducing a new performance management system'; Parekh et al. (2002) applied control theory to help achieve service level objectives within a performance management system; and Merchant and Van der Stede (2007) took a broad look at management control systems and their performance management function, including a consideration of ethical issues and how context could influence management control systems.

Studies on performance management in sport have mainly concentrated on national governing bodies or professional sport. Bayle and Robinson (2007) developed a framework for examining the performance of national sport governing bodies. This work recognizes that performance could be defined in economic, financial, organizational, or social terms, and acknowledged the studies mentioned above, as well as work by Bayle and Madella (2002), Wolfe et al. (2002), Frisby (1986) and Madella (1998), as having contributed to this body of knowledge. Bayle and Robinson (2007) provide a succinct review of literature pertaining to organizational performance which will give newcomers to the subjects discussed a grounding in the general and sport-specific research in this field. In their attempt to discuss the factors which explain why some national governing bodies in France performed better than others, the authors also addressed the factors which they believed inhibit performance rather than just the factors which facilitated optimum performance. Their work was concerned with the **effectiveness** of organizations more so than the efficiency, yet addressed the issue in terms of 'performance', and so the reader needs to be aware of the similarities between these concepts when forming research questions.

Barros (2006) conducted a performance evaluation of the English Premier Football League using data envelopment analysis (DEA). He evaluated best practices in the management of sport as well as financial measures. Using a different model of analysis Barros and Leach (2006) also analysed the English FA Premier League, defining performance in terms of efficiency. They identified the price of labour, the price of capital players, the price of capital stadiums, points gained, attendance, and turnover as playing a major role in football efficiency. A number of other studies have also assessed the relative contribution of leadership to organizational performance in sport; e.g., field managers in baseball (Porter and Scully, 1982; Kahn, 1993; Jacobs and Singell, 1993; Smart and Wolfe, 2003) and coaches in soccer (Dawson and Dobson, 2002; Dawson et al., 2000), intercollegiate athletics (Smart and Wolfe, 2000), and basketball (Fizel and D'Itri, 1999). Although not an academic study, the reader may be interested in Sir Clive Woodward's book *Winning* (Hodder and Stoughton, 2004) in which he describes his methods with the England 2003 World Cup-winning RU team.

Overall we can see that performance management is a concept with eclectic origins which has been approached by mainstream management and sport management scholars from a wide variety of definitions. In fact, research on performance management is found in three separate bodies of literature: operations, human resources, and management control. To date there has been little critical review of these different views of performance management. A systematic review which would help to provide an analysis, and where possible a synthesis, of the definitions, approaches and methods used in studying this concept could identify where gaps in knowledge exist and help fuel further study. This in turn would enable sport managers to gain a greater understanding of how the performance of their organizations could be effectively managed and how the techniques for the management of performance differ in various types of sport organizations and different sectors within those organizations. Moving beyond this, research to look at which contextual factors influence performance management would also be useful.

To understand performance management more fully, the reader may refer to the concepts of **organizational goals**, **conflict**, **control**, **strategy**, and **efficiency/ effectiveness** that can be found elsewhere in this book.

FURTHER READING

For some further reading on this concept, we would recommend the following:

Barros, C. (2006). Performance evaluation of the English Premier Football League with data envelopment analysis. *Applied Economics*, 38(12): 1449–1458.

Bayle, E. and Robinson, L. (2007) A framework for understanding the performance of national governing bodies of sport. *European Sport Management Quarterly*, 7(3): 249–268.

Gerrard, B. (2005) A resource-utilization model of organizational efficiency in professional sports teams. *Journal of Sport Management*, 19(2): 143–169.

Guest, D.E. (2011) Human resource management and performance: still searching for some answers. *Human Resource Management Journal*, 21(1): 3–13.

BIBLIOGRAPHY

Amit, R. and Shoemaker, J.H. (1993) Strategic assets and organizational rents. *Strategic Management Journal*, 14: 33–46.

Barros, C. (2006). Performance evaluation of the English Premier Football League with data envelopment analysis. *Applied Economics*, 38(12): 1449–1458.

Barros, C.P. and Leach, S. (2006) Analyzing the performance of the English F.A. Premier League with an Econometric Frontier model. *Journal of Sports Economics*, 7(4): 391–407.

Bayle, E. and Madella, A. (2002) Development of a taxonomy of performance for national sport organizations. *European Journal of Sport Science*, 2(2): 1–21.

Bayle, E. and Robinson, L. (2007) A framework for understanding the performance of national governing bodies of sport. *European Sport Management Quarterly*, 7(3): 249–268.

Becker, B. and Gerhart, B. (1996) The impact of human resource management on organizational performance: progress and prospects. *Academy of Management Journal*, 39(4): 779–801.

Dawson, P. and Dobson, S. (2002) Managerial efficiency and human capital: an application to English Association Football. *Managerial and Decision Economics*, 23: 471–486.

Dawson, P., Dobson, S. and Gerrard, B. (2000) Estimating coach efficiency in professional team sports: evidence from English Association Football. *Scottish Journal of Political Economy*, 47: 399–421.

Eckerson, W.W. (2011) *Performance Dashboards: Measuring, Monitoring, and Managing Your Business*. Hoboken, NJ: John Wiley & Sons.

Fizel, J.L. and D'Itri, M.P. (1999) Firing and hiring of managers: does efficiency matter? *Journal of Management*, 25(4): 567–585.

Frisby, W. (1986) The organizational structure and effectiveness of voluntary organizations: the case of Canadian sport governing bodies. *Journal of Park and Recreation Administration*, 4(3): 61–74.

Gerhart, B., Trevor, C. and Graham, M. (1996) New directions in employee compensation research. In G.R. Ferris (ed.), *Research in Personnel and Human Resource Management*, 14: 143–203. Greenwich, CT: JAI Press.

Gerrard, B. (2005) A resource-utilization model of organizational efficiency in professional sports teams. *Journal of Sport Management*, 19(2): 143–169.

Guest, D.E. (2001) Human resource management and performance: a review and research agenda. *International Journal of Human Resource Management*, 8(3): 263–276.

Guest, D.E. (2011) Human resource management and performance: still searching for some answers. *Human Resource Management Journal*, 21(1): 3–13.

Jacobs, D. and Singell, L. (1993) Leadership and organizational performance: isolating links between managers and collective success. *Social Science Research*, 22(2): 165–189.

Kahn, L. (1993) Free agency, long-term contracts and compensation in Major League Baseball: estimates from panel data. *Review of Economics and Statistics*, 75(1): 157–164.

Kaplan, R.S. and Norton, D.P. (1996) *The Balanced Scorecard*. Boston, MA: Harvard Business School Press.

Lado, A.A. and Wilson, M.C. (1994) Human resource systems and sustained competitive advantage: a competency based perspective. *Academy of Management Review*, 19: 699–727.

Madella, A. (1998) La performance di successo delle organizzazioni Spunti di riflessione per gestireefficacemente le societa di atletica leggera. [The organizational performance of the Italian Athletics Federation.] *Atleticastudi*, 1: 2–3.

Merchant, K.A. and Van der Stede, W.A. (2007) *Management Control Systems: Performance Measurement, Evaluation and Incentives*. Cambridge: Pearson.

Meyer, A.D., Tsui, A.S. and Hinings, C.R. (1993) Guest co-editors' introduction: configurational approaches to organizational analysis. *Academy of Management Journal*, 36: 1175–1195.

Otley, D. (1999) Performance management: a framework for management control system research. *Management Accounting Research*, 10(4): 363–382.

Paauwe, J. (2009) HRM and performance: achievements, methodological issues and prospects. *Journal of Management Studies*, 46(1): 129–142.

Parekh, S., Gandhi, N., Hellerstein, J., Tilbury, D., Jayram, T. and Bigus, J. (2002) Using control theory to achieve service level objectives in performance management. *Real-Time Systems*, 23(1–2): 127–141.

Pfeffer, J. (1994) *Competitive Advantage through People*. Boston, MA: Harvard Business School Press.

Porter P.K. and Scully G.W. (1982) Measuring managerial efficiency: the case of baseball. *Southern Economic Journal*, 48: 642–650.

Smart, D. and Wolfe, R. (2003) The contribution of leadership and human resources to organizational success: an empirical assessment of performance in Major League Baseball. *European Sport Management Quarterly*, 3: 165–188.

Tuomela, T.-S. (2005) The interplay of different levers of control: a case study of introducing a new performance masurement system. *Management Accounting Research*, 16(3): 293–320.

Wolfe, R., Hoeber, L. and Babiak, K. (2002) Perceptions of the effectiveness of sport organizations: the case of intercollegiate athletics. *European Sport Management Quarterly*, 2: 135–156.

Power

> *Power is the ability to influence the behaviour or ideas of one or more people.*

The study of power in organizations has had a long and rich history. Much of the research on organizational power during the 1960s and 1970s was underpinned by a narrow interpretation of Weber (1947, 1956), where power was conceptualized as exercised through rational decision-making processes in the context of organizational hierarchical interpretations of the external environment (Mumby, 2001). However, criticisms of this view highlighted that power can also be exercised in non-decision-making situations (Bachrach and Baratz, 1963). For example, power is exercised in situations where an individual (or possibly a group) limits the range of issues considered for discussion and subsequent decision making, such as a manager setting the agenda for a meeting, thereby limiting the issues to be discussed.

Lukes (1974) extends the ideas of Bachrach and Baratz (1963) further with his three-dimensional view of power. The 'one-dimensional' view of power focused on observable conflict and decision making, where an individual could be seen (in a meeting or interpersonal interaction) to influence the behaviour/action of another. Lukes' (1974) second dimension of power (an extension of the first) is an example of the elitist subjectivist view whereby power is exerted in non-decision-making situations when decisions are prevented from being taken on (potential) issues over observable conflicts (Bachrach and Baratz, 1963). And finally, Lukes'

(1974) third dimension of power, a radical view, is when power is exerted through social forces and institutional practices, shaping the individual's bias and opinions without that person necessarily expressing any knowledge. Here, the radical view provides a valuable criticism of the decision/non-decision views which see power as inherently related to conflict (Robson and Cooper, 1989).

Giddens (1989), Knights and Wilmott (1985), and Robson and Cooper (1989) have criticized the radical view for its preoccupation with the problem of 'objective' interests: namely, that the third dimension assumes people will act against their objective interests, failing (subjectively) to appreciate what those objective interests are. The radical view presented by Lukes clearly suggests an important role for socialization and identification in the exercise of power (Cheney, 1983), in that power is most effectively exercised when actors internalize and identify with the interests and norms of dominant groups (this is often accomplished through rhetoric) (Mumby, 2001).

The objectivist perception of power sees the legitimation of self-interest as part of the successful use and abuse of power, whereby the term 'power' becomes synonymous with 'authority' (Robson and Cooper, 1989). While this view has been commended for its recognition that power is an expandable property of social systems within which members of society interact (Giddens, 1984), it has also been criticized for its similarity to subjectivist views, which intrinsically relate power to interests (congruent interests in functionalism and conflictual interests in subjectivism) (Oliga, 1989). The Marxian structuralist conception of power is possessive and negative in that it sees power as a result of institutional structures (Oliga, 1989) and as the ability of a social class to recognize its objective interests (Poulantzas, 1973) and use power to further its own sectional motivations (Oliga, 1989).

There are several relational perspectives of power which theorize about the nature of forces thought to be essential (structures and agents) for the relations of power (Oliga, 1989). Perceptions of power in micro-politics concentrate on the exercise of power in specific conditions or in everyday situations rather than on the global focus of Marxist or functional theories. Foucault's (1972, 1977, 1980) conception of power was discussed by Minson (1980) as a contestation of the Marxist view. Foucault believed power was diffused throughout society and tied in closely with practical knowledge, which he referred to as 'disciplinary power' (Oliga, 1989). Therefore, power can be exercised efficiently and effectively through its invisibility (Oliga, 1989), whereby knowledge of an individual is apparent but the power (effects of their knowledge) is unnoticed by the subject (Robson and Cooper, 1989).

Power and negative relationism can be seen in Giddens' (1976) notion of the 'dialectic of control' which emphasizes the relational nature of power by suggesting that, for example, to exert power over another person or group requires some form of compliance from that person or group. This means that the powerful are never completely autonomous from the powerless and that the powerless always possess some element of power over the powerful (Oliga, 1989). In organizations this could mean that subordinates are never totally dependent on hierarchical superiors if it is accepted that they have choices and will actively participate in social interaction: for example, groups within organizations can go on strike or stage other protests such as hunger strikes or 'work to rule' (performing minimal contractual duties only).

The main criticism of this conception is of course that it presents a view of power which is necessarily conflictual and relational, leaving a one-sided view that does not consider agent identity-securing motives. This leads to the positive relational view of power as presented by Knights and Wilmott (1985) which highlights that 'it is the social practices and self-understandings of subordinates, no less than those of the powerful, that sustain and reproduce the very structures of domination in society' (cf. Fay, 1987: 120).

The rational agency view of power conceives of power as positive and inextricably linked to action. Giddens (1984) suggested that power, implicated in action and logically prior to subjectivity, was exercised in everyday social interaction. Otherwise, 'an agent ceases to be such if he or she loses the capability to "make a difference", that is, to exercise some sort of power' (Giddens, 1984: 14). The main criticism of this view is simply that it relates to the individual level of analysis and does not consider, as does the contingent relationist view, the social level of analysis as well. The contingent relationist view attempts to avoid the weaknesses of previously mentioned conceptions while utilizing the strengths of those views, attempting to provide a critical and more comprehensive conceptualization of the concept of power. Therefore, power is seen as potentially having both positive and negative affects and so can be exploitative and oppressive, or empowering, transformative, and synergistic (Oliga, 1989).

However, the approach is critical of situations characterized by structures of domination and denies that power is inherently positive or inherently oppressive. The structural forces of power are grounded in and constituted by agents' understandings (Oliga, 1989). From reviewing these different conceptions of power, the problematic and contestable nature of the concept is evident. However, the underlying assumptions and both the strengths and weaknesses of each perspective are clear, which enables some understanding of the concept and its centrality to social enquiry and an investigation of organization **control**. That is, the different perspectives reveal how power can be recognized throughout society and in organizations, suggesting that more than one 'level' or type of power can operate simultaneously.

Power can be exerted by individuals and groups. Over time, institutions and social structures may be perceived as powerful and therefore able to enable/constrain individual actors and groups. Slack and Parent (2006) discuss individual sources of power (legitimate, reward, coercive, referent, and expert) and suggested that power could be evident in organizations as a result of structural arrangements rather than a characteristic of an individual person. Power can exist and influence without an individual or group consciousness of how that power impacts upon them. It is at this juncture that we can begin to see the relationship and distinction between power and control. Power, enacted through an institutional force or individual resource, can facilitate the control of actors or situations. In turn, the control of individuals or situations can also signify the accumulation of power.

Given the difficulties in observing power in sport organizations, it is not surprising that there have been relatively few studies which have focused on the concept. Sport organizations are also often seen as being free from power situations; however, sport organizations, like other organizations, can exhibit power struggles. However, some exceptions include Henry (2001), calling for more recognition and focus on the dimensions of power on sport **policy** research; Fink et al. (2001), who examine power in Division IA intercollegiate athletic organizations; and Wolfe and colleagues (2002), who developed a model demonstrating the role of power in a sport network. More recent work by Crompton et al. (2003) examined power in community structures as a source of influence in public investment in major league facilities. Byers and colleagues (2007) also considered how various perspectives of power could contribute to understanding the control of voluntary sport organizations.

However, the concept of power is often integral to studies whose primary focus is another concept such as **decision making** and gender in **sport organizations**. Hovden (2006) examines gender distribution in the upper echelons of Norwegian sport organizations and discussed the role of symbolic power (Bourdieu, 1995) in preventing gender being recognized as a policy issue that needed to be addressed. In research focused on understanding organizational change, Amis et al. (2004) identify the important role of power in determining how disagreements were resolved in the process of change. Their work proposed a key role for interests, power and capacity in shaping the change process.

Overall there is considerable theoretical and empirical research on the concept of power. In research on the management of sport, there is still considerable scope for the analysis of different forms of power and how these are manifest in sport organizations. A significant consideration for anyone interested in doing research on power in or between sport organizations is the perspective/definition of power adopted along with a clear rationale for the chosen perspective (i.e., how a contribution to the field is achieved through the work/definition) given the plethora of perspectives which can be found in the mainstream literature.

To understand power more fully, the reader may refer to the concepts of **control**, **sport policy**, **decision making** and **sport organization** that can be found elsewhere in this book.

FURTHER READING

For some further reading on this concept, we would recommend the following:

Byers, T., Henry, I. and Slack, T. (2007) Understanding control in voluntary sport organizations. In M.M. Parent and T. Slack (eds), *International Perspectives on the Management of Sport*. London: Elsevier.

Clegg, S. (2009) *The Sage Handbook of Power*. London: Sage.

Knights, D. and Wilmott, H. (1985) Power and identity in theory and practice. *Sociological Review*, 33(1): 22–46.

Wolfe, R., Meenaghan, T. and O'Sullivan, P. (2002) The sports network: insights into the shifting balance of power. *Journal of Business Research*, 55(7): 611–622.

BIBLIOGRAPHY

Amis, J., Slack, T. and Hinings, C.R. (2004) Strategic change and the role of interests, power and organizational capacity. *Journal of Sport Management*, 18: 158–198.

Bachrach, P. and Baratz, M.S. (1963) Decisions and non-decisions: an analytical framework. *American Political Science Review*, 57: 641–651.

Bourdieu, P. (1995) Structure, habitus, practices. In *The Polity Reader in Social Theory*. Cambridge: Polity Press.

Byers, T., Henry, I. and Slack, T. (2007) Understanding control in voluntary sport organizations. In M.M. Parent and T. Slack (eds), *International Perspectives on the Management of Sport*. London: Elsevier.

Cheney, G. (1983) On the various and changing meanings of organizational membership: a field study of organizational identification. *Communication Monographs*, 50: 342–362.

Crompton, J.L., Howard, D.R. and Var, T. (2003) Financing major league facilities: status, evolution and conflicting forces. *Journal of Sport Management*, 17(2): 156–184.

Fay, B. (1987) *Critical Social Science*. Oxford: Polity.

Fink, J.S., Pastore, D.L. and Reimer, H.A. (2001) Do differences make a difference? Managing diversity in division IA collegiate athletics. *Journal of Sport Management*, 15(1): 10–51.

Foucault, M. (1972) The *Archaeology of Knowledge*. London: Tavistock.

Foucault, M. (1977) *Discipline and Punish: The Birth of the Prison*. London: Penguin.

Foucault, M. (1980) Truth and power. In C. Gordon (ed.), *Michel Foucault*. New York: Pantheon.

Giddens, A. (1976) *New Rules of Sociological Method*. London: Hutchinson.

Giddens, A. (1984) *The Constitution of Society*. London: Polity.

Giddens, A. (1989) A reply to my critics. In D. Held and J.B. Thompson (eds), *Social Theory of Modern Societies: Anthony Giddens and His Critics*. Cambridge: Cambridge University Press. pp. 249–301.

Henry, I.P. (2001) *The Politics of Leisure Policy*. London: Palgrave.

Hovden, J. (2006) The gender order as a policy issue: a study of Norwegian sports organizations. *Nordic Journal of Women's Studies*, 14(1): 41–53.

Knights, D. and Wilmott, H. (1985) Power and identity in theory and practice. *Sociological Review*, 33(1): 22–46.

Lukes, S. (1974) *Power: A Radical View*. London: Macmillan.

Minson, J. (1980) Strategies for socialists? Foucault's conception of power. *Economy and Society*, 9 (1): 1–43.

Mumby, D.K. (2001) Power and politics. In F. Jablin and L.L. Putnam (eds), *The Handbook of Organizational Communication*. Thousand Oaks, CA: Sage. pp. 585–623.

Oliga, J.C. (1989) *Power, Ideology and Control*. London: Plenum.

Poulantzas, N. (1973) *Political Power and Social Classes*. London: New Left Books.

Robson, K. and Cooper, D.J. (1989) Power and management control. In W.F. Chua, T. Lowe and T. Puxty (eds), *Critical Perspectives in Management Control*. London: Macmillan.

Ross, E.A. (1901) *Social Control*. New York: Macmillan.

Slack, T. and Parent, M.M. (2006) *Understanding Sport Organizations: The Application of Organization Theory* (2nd edn). Champaign, IL: Human Kinetics.

Weber, M. (1947) *The Theory of Social and Economic Organization*. New York: The Free Press.

Weber, M. (1956) *The Protestant Ethic and the Spirit of Capitalism*. London: Allen and Unwin.

Wolfe, R., Meenaghan, T. and O'Sullivan, P. (2002) The sports network: insights into the shifting balance of power. *Journal of Business Research*, 55(7): 611–622.

Quality is a subjective concept which is related to the level of satisfaction a person perceives along a number of dimensions in relation to a product or service.

The concept of quality has received much attention from researchers focused on service organizations both within and outside of the sport industry and can primarily be found in a body of literature known as 'operations management' and 'sport operations management'. The concept has also been examined in relation to 'customer satisfaction', and anyone doing research on one of or both of these subjects should be careful to differentiate between the two. Meanwhile researchers have debated how to define quality, and a variety of perspectives exist, such as those suggested by Garvin (1984):

the transcendent approach;

the manufacturing-based approach;

the user-based approach;

the product-based approach;

the value-based approach.

The transcendent approach defines quality as 'of the highest standard' where quality is innately excellent in nature. An example would be a newly built sports stadium with the latest technological and architectural innovations, compared to a local community-centre sports ground; according to this view, the stadium would be classed a 'quality' facility and the community centre as being of inferior quality. The manufacturing-based approach views quality as conformance to some specification; this approach to quality would suggest that as long as a service or product met the original specifications of its design, it would be considered high quality. The user-based approach deems quality to exist if a service/product meets the requirements of the customer/user; that is, the service/or product is 'fit for purpose'. This perspective does not consider price or value to be important in assessing the quality of a product or service. Arguably, it confuses quality with satisfaction, where satisfaction will exist when customer expectations have been met. The product-based approach is quantitatively defined, where more (or in some cases less) equals better quality and measurable characteristics are of the greatest importance. Finally, the value-based approach takes 'cost' into consideration by viewing a product of quality as something that provides value for money; this is a subjective judgment performed by a customer.

In trying to define and measure service quality Parasuraman et al. (1985, 1988) were influential in facilitating the debate and criticism of a universal model that is applicable in all sectors and **contexts**. Their model is known as SERVQUAL and measured service quality across five dimensions: reliability, responsiveness, empathy, assurance, and tangibles. The model was influential in subsequent research in sport and leisure services which sought to use a similar methodology in identifying the elements of a service which were important to customers when evaluating quality, and as a result, their satisfaction with a product or service. MacKay and Crompton (1990) developed REQUAL after their examination of leisure and recreation services; Kim and Kim (1995), researching Korean sports clubs, developed QUESC, which was a scale including eleven dimensions of service quality;

and McDonald et al. (1995) likewise developed TEAMQUAL to assess service quality in professional sports. The CERM developed by Howat and colleagues (1996) focused on Australian leisure clubs.

The different types of services subject to this examination of quality factors included public sector leisure and recreation services (Backman and Veldkamp, 1995; MacKay and Crompton, 1990; Robinson, 2003; Wright et al., 1992); sports clubs (Kim and Kim, 1995; Papadimitriou and Karteroliotis, 2002); professional sport (McDonald et al., 1995); and sport tourism (Thwaites, 1999). Theodorakis et al. (2001) also examined the relationship between service quality and the customer satisfaction of spectators of professional sports.

There has also been some research focused on service quality at sport events (e.g., Bitner, 1992; Kelley and Turley, 2001). For a further discussion of these and other related studies, the reader should see Byers (2004). In addition, Tsitskari et al. (2006) provided a literature review on the evaluation of service quality in sport-related services and suggested that the construct varies considerably when considered in different countries and service sectors.

Some recent literature which has continued the debate about defining service quality and its relationship with customer satisfaction includes Javadein et al. (2008), who extended the debate by also focusing on the relationship of quality to satisfaction, customer loyalty/commitment and trust, and Koo et al. (2009), who examined the causal effects between service quality and customer satisfaction in minor league baseball.

The concept of quality has also recently been studied in relation to brand loyalty (Alexandris et al., 2008), economic success (Kim and Lough, 2007), and internationalization (Abdi et al., 2008). Alexandris et al. (2008) provided an empirical examination of the influence of brand associations on the development of brand loyalty and the role of service quality on the development of brand associations. Using a 25-item questionnaire to measure service quality and a factor analysis of 165 members of a fitness club, the research suggested eight brand association factors (popularity, management, logo, escape, vicarious achievement, nostalgia, pride and affect). Five of these factors significantly contributed toward the prediction of loyalty and the service quality dimensions predicted significant variances in all eight brand associations. The authors then discuss the implications of their study for developing marketing strategies.

Research on service quality is not theoretically rich yet it does provide a good topic for undergraduate students to examine, because the nature of quality and the implications of customer perceptions of quality seem to vary across different organizations/business types. The concept of quality has been conceptualized and operationalized by many researchers and so students can easily locate and review this work in order to inform a newly designed study. For postgraduate students, a more critical review of this literature would be useful and some innovation in conceptualizing and operationalizing the concept through new methods/methodologies would be most welcome. The concept is of course very interesting to practitioners as well, as the research in this field has clear and direct implications for those managing sport-related services in health and fitness, professional sport, or sport clubs.

Research on the concept of quality is slowly moving beyond discussions solely focused on the functional importance and measurement of quality in sport services. Kwak and Kang (2009) drew on the notion of 'symbolic pressure' from the generic marketing literature and suggested that their model could be useful in predicting sport fans' perceptions of purchase decisions on team-licensed merchandise.

To understand quality more fully, the reader may refer to the concept of **context** that can be found elsewhere in this book.

FURTHER READING

For some further reading on this concept, we would recommend the following:

Koo, G., Hardin, R., McClung, S., Taejin, J., Cronin, J., Vorhees, C. and Bourdeau, B. (2009) Examination of the causal effects between the dimensions of service quality and spectator satisfaction in minor league baseball. *International Journal of Sport Marketing and Sponsorship*, 11(1): 46–59.

Kwak, D.H. and Kang, J.H. (2009) Symbolic purchase in sport: the roles of self-image congruence and perceived quality. *Management Decision*, 47(1): 85–99.

Parasuraman, A., Zeithaml, V.A. and Berry, L.L. (1988) SERVQUAL: a multiple item scale for measuring consumer perceptions of service quality. *Journal of Retailing*, 64(1): 14–40.

Theodorakis, N., Kambitsis, C., Laios, A. and Koustelios, A. (2001) Relationship between measures of service quality and satisfaction of spectators in professional sports. *Managing Service Quality*, 11(6): 431–438.

BIBLIOGRAPHY

Abdi, S.N.A., Awan, H.N. and Bhatti, M.I. (2008) Is quality management a prime requisite for globalization? *Quality and Quantity*, 42(6): 821–833.

Alexandris, K., Douka, S., Papadopoulos, P. and Kaltsatou, A. (2008) Testing the role of service quality on the development of brand associations and brand loyalty. *Managing Service Quality*, 18(3): 239–254.

Backman, S.J. and Veldkamp, C. (1995) Examination of the relationship between service quality and user loyalty. *Journal of Park and Recreation Administration*, 13(2): 29–41.

Bitner, M.J. (1992) Servicescapes: the impact of physical surroundings on customer and employees. *Journal of Marketing*, 56(21): 57–72.

Byers, T. (2004) Managing operations, quality and performance. In J. Beech and S. Chadwick (eds). *The Business of Sport Management*. Harlow: Pearson Education Ltd.

Garvin, D. (1984) What does 'product quality' really mean? *Sloan Management Review*, Fall: 22–44.

Howat, G., Crilley, G., Absher., J. and Milne, I. (1996) Measuring customer service quality in recreation and parks. *Australian Parks and Recreation*, Summer: 77–89.

Javadein, S., Khanlari, A. and Estiri, M. (2008) Customer loyalty in the sport services industry: the role of service quality, customer satisfaction, commitment and trust. *International Journal of Human Sciences*, 5(2): 1–19.

Kelley, S.W. and Turley, L.W. (2001) Consumer perceptions of service quality attributes at sporting events. *Journal of Business Research*, 54(2): 161–166.

Kim, D. and Kim, S.Y. (1995) QUESC: an instrument for assessing the service quality of sport centres in Korea. *Journal of Sport Management*, 9: 208–220.

Kim, H.D. and Lough, N. (2007) An investigation into relationships among constructs of service quality, customer satisfaction and repurchase intension in Korean private golf courses. *ICHPER-SD Journal of Research*, 2(1): 14–22.

key concepts in sport management

Koo, G., Hardin, R., McClung, S., Taejin, J., Cronin, J., Vorhees, C. and Bourdeau, B. (2009) Examination of the causal effects between the dimensions of service quality and spectator satisfaction in minor league baseball. *International Journal of Sport Marketing and Sponsorship*, 11(1): 46–59.

Kwak, D.H. and Kang, J.H. (2009) Symbolic purchase in sport: the roles of self-image congruence and perceived quality. *Management Decision*, 47(1): 85–99.

McDonald, M., Sutton, W.A. and Milne, G.R. (1995) TEAMQUAL™: measuring service quality in professional team sports. *Sport Marketing Quarterly*, 4(2): 9–15.

MacKay, K.J. and Crompton, J.L. (1990) Measuring the quality of recreation services. *Journal of Park and Recreation Administration*, 8: 47–56.

Papadimitriou, D. and Karteroliotis, K. (2000) The service quality expectations in private sport and fitness centres: a re-examination of the factor structure. *Sport Marketing Quarterly*, 9: 157–64.

Parasuraman, A., Zeithaml, V.A. and Berry, L.L. (1985) A conceptual model of service quality and its implications for future research. *Journal of Marketing*, 49(4): 41–50.

Parasuraman, A., Zeithaml, V.A. and Berry, L.L. (1988) SERVQUAL: a multiple item scale for measuring consumer perceptions of service quality. *Journal of Retailing*, 64(1): 14–40.

Robinson, L. (2003) Committed to quality: the use of quality schemes in UK public leisure services. *Managing Service Quality*, 13(3): 247–255.

Theodorakis, N., Kambitsis, C., Laios, A. and Koustelios, A. (2001) Relationship between measures of service quality and satisfaction of spectators in professional sports. *Managing Service Quality*, 11(6): 431–438.

Thwaites, D. (1999) Closing the gaps: service quality in sport tourism. *Journal of Services Marketing*, 13(6): 500–516.

Tsitskari, E., Tsiotras, D. and Tsiotras, G. (2006) Measuring service quality in sport services. *Total Quality Management and Business Excellence*, 17: 623–631.

Wright, B.A., Duray, N. and Goodale, T. (1992) Assessing perceptions of recreation center service quality: an application of recent advancements in service quality research. *Journal of Park and Recreation Administration*, 10(3): 33–47.

Sponsorship

Sponsorship is a business relationship whereby one or more partners provide financial or other support in return for some effort that aims to assist that partner to meet their business objectives.

Most sport organizations, teams, events, and individual athletes will seek sponsorship in order to provide financial or in-kind support for their activities. At the Olympic level large corporations such as Coca-Cola, McDonald's and Visa will support the Games. At the community level organizations such as local restaurants or automobile service stations may sponsor sporting activities (cf. Gardner and Shuman, 1988; Slack and Bentz, 1996). It is impossible to determine the value of the sponsorship market, as it is difficult to calculate the value of smaller sponsorships in money and goods. However, the market is indeed big and it has been suggested that it reaches billions of dollars (Fenton, 2009). It is only necessary to look at major sporting events or elite athletes to realize how much money is gained via sponsorship. Market research reports have tried to value the sponsorship market and provide some indication of its market size, issues, and global nature (Key Note, 2009). Other reports cover specific countries and individual sports (Mintel, 2009).

Sponsorship is often seen as an exchange where the entity doing the sponsoring gives money or goods and in return is associated with the purity and image of the sport or the group of sporting events. Milne and McDonald (1999) entitled their book on **sport marketing**, in which they include a chapter on sponsorship, *Sport Marketing: Managing the Exchange Process*, while Slack and Amis (2004), writing about sponsorship, quote Alvesson and Willmott's (1996) commentary on marketing in general and how they noted 'the idea that marketing transactions such as sponsorship are based on *exchange* obscures, or at least fails to address, the social relations of inequality that privilege or exclude participation in marketized transactions' (emphasis in original). This exchange fails to take account of the fact that some sports are more able to profit from the exchange than others. It also fails to account for the fact that some sport entities, usually individual athletes, may not live up to their responsibilities in that exchange. Ben Johnson's drug scandal, the alleged drug taking of athletes such as baseball's Barry Bonds and other players, as well as cycling's Lance Armstrong, and the alleged marital infidelity of athletes like Tiger Woods are all examples of this type of breakdown. Some sponsorship agreements will now have a morals clause included as a result.

To the best of our knowledge there has been little investigation focused on how moral violations or **corruption** can influence an individual athlete's sponsorship earnings; i.e., does the sponsorship just continue, is it terminated, or is it simply phased out over a period of time? A recent exception to this was Westberg et al.'s (2008a) research exploring the effects of player transgressions (committed by team members in professional sport) on sport organizations' relationship with their sponsors. Their research resulted in a model of player transgression and response for the management of sponsor relationships and suggestions for future research were also made. Similarly, Westberg and colleagues (2008b) discussed the impact of their research on developing public relations strategy in sport organizations and on managing the sponsorship relationship. As discussed previously, Gorse and Chadwick (2010) have also done some work to clarify the role of corruption in the sponsorship relationship.

Sport has undoubtedly benefited from its association with sponsorship (Slack and Amis, 2004). Games receive the support they need, charities gain funds when the sponsoring entity requires funding to the charity as part of the sponsorship agreement, teams are able to purchase much needed equipment, television stations show sport which would not normally be seen, and individual athletes no longer have to rely on state funding and instead will receive funds that make them celebrities. However, sponsorship changes the way sport is experienced and practised. As a result of sponsorship, sportsmen and -women will often have to take part even when they may be injured and events will be arranged to coincide with television schedules. Sponsors require exposure and they will want to increase the size of their viewing audience, either live or on television. Consequently they will require elite athletes and teams to participate. In addition to this only the more visible and higher-profile sports will receive funding from sponsorship, and particularly hard hit in this regard are women's sport and female athletes (Rowe, 2009). Research has also examined why there is disparity between the investment in men's and women's sponsorship (Lough, 1996; Shaw and Amis, 2001)

An association with sponsorship may serve to legitimate some of the so-called sin products (tobacco, alcohol, and gambling). The literature is mixed on whether or not sponsorship increases the involvement with such products (cf. Davies, 2009). In some countries tobacco sponsorship is banned and there are currently calls for alcohol sponsorship to be banned (see e.g., *New Scientist*, 2009). Davies (2009), for example, presented evidence to suggest that alcohol sponsorship encouraged young boys to drink excessively but discouraged young girls away from a culture of alcohol, and based on evidence from research on tobacco sponsorship and consumer behaviour, suggested alternative sponsorship advertisements (involving low-alcohol or non-alcoholic products) rather than strict bans as being more effective in changing cultures.

Sponsorship also changes the way sport is experienced. Sponsors want close contests and association football, rugby, cricket, and rowing are just some of the sports that have changed their format to provide what is seen as a more exciting contest (and thus they meet the needs of sponsors). As stated above, the development of sport has benefited considerably from sponsorship money. However, while this has been the case, fans may be disadvantaged by the involvement of sporting entities in sponsorship: they do not have a choice in the products that are involved in sponsorship and are subject to such advertising whether they use a product or not. The only option available to fans is to not purchase the sponsor's product, though in some cases this may be difficult as the product is the only one available at the sporting venue (this may be part of the sponsorship arrangement) or it may have a particular association with the sponsorship. In several countries the money corporations spend on sponsorship is tax-deductible while the cash that fans spend on sport is subject to taxation. As acknowledged, sport has benefited considerably from the sponsorship it receives; however, in any work on sponsorship it is important to examine both sides of the relationship. Sponsorship does indeed change the way sport is practised and experienced by the participants. For a review of the literature on sponsorship (and a case study proposing a 'network approach' to developing sponsorship arrangements), the reader may wish to consult Olkkonen (2001). Following on from that, Wallizer (2003) provides a review of the international sponsorship literature.

To understand sponsorship more fully, the reader may refer to the concepts of **corruption** and **sport marketing** that can be found elsewhere in this book.

FURTHER READING

For some further reading on this concept, we would recommend the following:

Fenton, W. (2009) The global sponsorship market. *Journal of Sponsorship*, 2(2): 120–130.

Lough, N.L. (1996) Factors affecting corporate sponsorship of women's sport. *Sport Marketing Quaterly*, 5(2): 11–19.

Rowe, D. (2009) Power trip: sport and the media. *International Journal of Sport Management and Marketing*, 6(2): 150–166.

Shaw, S. and Amis, J. (2001) Image and investment: sponsorship and women's sport. *Journal of Sport Management*, 15(3): 219–246.

BIBLIOGRAPHY

Alvesson, M. and Willmott, H. (1996) *Making Sense of Management*. London: Sage.

Davies, F. (2009) An investigation into the effects of sporting involvement and alcohol sponsorship on underage drinking. *International Journal of Sports Marketing and Sponsorship*, 11(1): 25–45.

Fenton, W. (2009) The global sponsorship market. *Journal of Sponsorship*, 2(2): 120–130.

Gardner, M.P. and Shuman, P. (1988) Sponsorship and small business. *Journal of Small Business Management*, 26: 44–52.

Gorse, S. and Chadwick, S. (2010) Conceptualising corruption in sport: implications for sponsorship programmes. *The European Business Review*, July/August, 2010: 40–45.

Key Note (2009) *Sport Sponsorship*. Middlesex: Key Note.

Lough, N.L. (1996) Factors affecting corporate sponsorship of women's sport. *Sport Marketing Quarterly*, 5(2): 11–19.

Milne, G. and McDonald, M. (1999) *Sport Marketing: Managing the Exchange Process*. Sudbury, MA: Jones and Bartlett.

Mintel (2009) *Sport Sponsorship: UK*. London: Mintel.

New Scientist (2009) Alcohol and sport are unhappy bedfellows. Accessed online at http://www.newscientist.com/article/mg20427344.500-alcohol-and-sport-are-unhappy-bedfellows.html

Olkkonen, M. (2001) Case study: the network approach to international sport sponsorship arrangements. *Journal of Business and Industrial Marketing*, 16(4): 309–329.

Rowe, D. (2009) Power trip: sport and the media. *International Journal of Sport Management and Marketing*, 6(2): 150–166.

Shaw, S. and Amis, J. (2001) Image and investment: sponsorship and women's sport. *Journal of Sport Management*, 15(3): 219–246.

Slack, T. and Amis, J. (2004) Money for nothing and your cheques for free? A critical perspective on sport sponsorship. In T. Slack (ed.), *The Commercialization of Sport*. London: Routledge. pp. 269–286.

Slack, T. and Bentz, L. (1996) Small businesses and sport sponsorship. *Managing Leisure*, 1: 175–184.

Wallizer., B. (2003) An international review of sponsorship research: extension and update. *International Journal of Advertising*, 22: 5–40.

Westberg., K., Stavros, C. and Wilson, B. (2008a) An examination of the impact of player transgressions on sponsorship b2b relationships. *International Journal of Sports Marketing and Sponsorship*, 9(2): 125–134.

Westberg, K., Stavros, C. and Wilson, B. (2008b) Player transgressions and the management of the sport-sponsor relationship. *Public Relations Review*, 34(2): 99–107.

Sport Development (and Sport for Development, Development through Sport)

Sport development and sport for development/development through sport differ in that they focus either on sport itself or use sport as a tool for the development of targeted communities. Regardless, the approach is typically a positive one, looking at both process and progress.

Sports development is typically defined in a rather broad way. For example, it can refer to the activities performed to enable participation for those already in sport and to encourage participation for those not yet in sport. It can also refer to recreational participation or elite performance and the development and support of elite athletes. It can include the pathways and structures needed for people to progress in sport and also be conceptualized as an activity that is focused on the service inputs (e.g., the facilities) and opportunities created, as well as service outcome and benefit maximization (see Houlihan and White, 2002). Houlihan and Green (2008) compare elite sport development across nine countries, through an examination of the systems, structures and public policy of the countries which serve to develop the high-performance athlete. The focus is on policy development, which is considered a key element of sport development.

In contrast, Girginov (2008a) argues that sports development can be conceptualized as a vision (with social, political, and economic objectives), a process for social change (subjective perceptions of development), and delivery/practice (who does what and how). This definition offers a holistic vision of sport development and helps to define its multi-faceted nature.

The move from sport development to 'sport for development' (S4D) has been attributed in part to the Olympic speed skating champion Johann Olav Koss and his Olympic Aid programme in the mid-1990s (Kidd, 2008). S4D and development through sport are seen today when national and international bodies (sport organizations, governments, non-governmental organizations or NGOs, etc.) use sport as a tool or 'vehicle for broad, sustainable social development, especially in the most disadvantaged communities in the world' (Kidd, 2008: 370). For example, the United Nations, UNICEF, the International Olympic Committee, and Commonwealth Games Canada all have S4D programmes and projects. Kidd nevertheless notes that, internationally, this movement is being termed Sport for Development and Peace (SDP). Darnell (2007: 560) remarks that the international development-through-sport movement usually operates in one of two discursive frameworks that are distinct yet also overlap: sport/play being universal and integrating social practices; and the northern 'First World' being the benevolent deliverer of aid, expertise, and/or goods/services to the southern 'Third World'. Darnell uses the Right to Play (www.righttoplay.com) as an example of such international development through sport projects and argues that 'encounters and experiences within development through sport serve in the (re) construction of particular knowledge' (2007: 560), in this case, race and ethnicity-related issues.

With the notable exception of Houlihan and White (2002), Girginov (2008a) argues that sports development has been predominantly focused on practice, for example, their link with the United Nation's Millennium Development Goals. Girginov further notes that there are six main **stakeholders** who can act as 'developers' and each will have different visions and management approaches: international organizations, governments, sports federations, non-governmental organizations, research institutes, and the sporting goods industry.

Regardless of the definition, the connotation is a positive one for development and – in contrast to change which can be positive or negative – it is about progress (Girginov, 2008a; Powell, 1995). From the 1960s to the late 1990s, Houlihan and

White (2002) note that the emphasis has varied from a focus on the social objectives and seeing sport as a tool for human development (i.e., development *through* sport) to a focus on sport itself (i.e., the development *of* sport). Changes in governments and government policy have resulted in sport development changing the focus from Sport For All, to facility development, to talent identification programmes (Houlihan and White, 2002). However, the current focus for most international programmes and projects seems to rest on S4D/development through sport (cf. Kidd, 2008), while countries (e.g., Canada with its Long-Term Athlete Development (LTAD) programme) are focusing on sports development.

In a review of four local authorities and four national sport governing bodies, Houlihan and White (2002) found that organizations were generally successful in being innovative and in service development, despite environmental (government) instability, uncertainty, and policy changes. Nevertheless, the evolution of sports development has been fragmented, leading to a variety of definitions as well as a tension between the development of sport and (community) development through sport. This has been due in part to the various stakeholders creating coalitions and competing against each other for the limited resources instead of working together towards a common overall goal (Houlihan and White, 2002).

While Girginov (2008a) harks back to the Victorian era, Houlihan and White (2002) argue that sport development has its origins as a legitimate sub-area of the broader field of sport policy in the mid-1960s for governments in relation to spending decisions. Given this, it is not surprising that research related to sport development and its variants is much more popular in the sociology of sport and sport policy than sport management research. A good example of this would be Green's (2004) study which examined the changing elite sport development policies in Canada and the United Kingdom and related asymmetries of power. In addition to this, Guest (2009) examined the historical diffusion of development through the sport practices of the Olympic Movement within Africa, whereas Coalter (2010) looked at the politics (policy rhetoric) within S4D programmes and organizations. He found a number of dangers in the rhetoric and warned that research and evaluation should be focused on local programme development instead of legitimizing the international organizations doing the programmes.

Nevertheless, research on sport development has been burgeoning within sport management, including notably the various chapters within Girginov's (2008b) book. Girginov discusses the management of sports development as having three interrelated aspects: normative, analytical, and process-oriented. A series of authors then discuss sports development within one of the three perspectives of vision, the process of social **change**, and the delivery process. For example, Hylton and Bramham (2008) present models of sports development (vision), whereas Parent (2008) examines the link between the sports development process of change and mega events (the process of social change) and Burnett (2008) examines the monitoring and evaluation of sports development (the delivery process).

Added to this, Skinner and colleagues (2008) examine development through sport and provide implications for sport managers, including having them undertake continual education that will help them develop their skills and knowledge relative to delivering sport programmes which will foster positive **change** and community development. Skinner et al. also warn that a proper evaluation (tools) of programmes and ensuring sustainability should be key concerns for sport managers. Finally, they note that development through sport provides a wide range of positive community relationships and networks, which thereby foster social capital. Hayhurst and Frisby (2010) also examined tensions within (elite sport) partnerships between Canadian and Swiss S4D NGOs. They found three key tensions: competing values; gaining legitimacy; and resource dependency.

Houlihan and White (2002) note that the future evolution of sports development was dependent on four trends:

1 'greater acknowledgement and impact of equity issues' (p. 209), related gender, disability, class, ethnicity, and age;
2 'consolidation of the commercialization of sport' (p. 212), that is, the greater professionalization of sport, and the use of commercialization as an increasingly important source of funding;
3 'decline in deference towards voluntarism and amateurism in sports clubs and governing bodies' (p. 212); and
4 'a substantial change in the way people connect with public services' (p. 213), that is, increasing marginality of the services and scepticism of the state's role, in this case, within sport.

A more critical view of sport for development (specifically, peace and reconciliation) is eloquently presented by Sugden (2010). This research suggests the circumstances under which sport can positively influence social justice and human rights in fragmented societies such as those of South Africa, Northern Ireland, and Israel. Finally, the popularity of sports development and S4D can be seen in the topic-specific conferences which are emerging. For example, the Sport Matters Group hosts an annual Sport for Development Gathering (the latest edition being hosted jointly with the University of Ottawa's Research Centre for Sport in Canadian Society in June 2010). The International Platform on Sport and Development (www.sportanddev.org) promotes a multitude of conferences and events related to S4D, including the International Sport for Development and Peace Association's (ISDPA) Power of Sport Summit (last hosted in Boston, in the USA, in June 2010). In the United Kingdom, there is also the National Association for Sports Development (NASD).

To understand sport development more fully, the reader may refer to the concepts of **stakeholders**, and **change** that can be found elsewhere in this book.

FURTHER READING

For some further reading on this concept, we would recommend the following:

Bloyce, D., Smith, A., Mead, R. and Morris, J. (2008) 'Playing the game (plan)': a figurational analysis of organisational change in sports development in England. *European Sport Management Quarterly*, 8(4): 359–378.

Girginov, V. (ed.) (2008) *Management of Sports Development*. Oxford: Butterworth-Heinemann.

Li, M., MacIntosh, E. and Brave, G. (2011) *International Sport Management*. Champaign, IL: Human Kinetics.

Sugden, J. (2010) Critical left-realism and sport interventions in divided societies. *International Review for the Sociology of Sport*, 45(3): 258–272.

BIBLIOGRAPHY

Burnett, C. (2008) Accounting for sports development. In V. Girginov (ed.), *Management of Sports Development*. Oxford: Butterworth-Heinemann. pp. 259–275.

Coalter, F. (2010) The politics of sport-for-development: limited focus programmes and broad gauge problems? *International Review for the Sociology of Sport*, 45(3): 295–314.

Darnell, S.C. (2007) Playing with race: right to play and the production of whiteness in 'Development through Sport'. *Sport in Society*, 10(4): 560–579.

Girginov, V. (2008a) Management of sports development as an emerging field and profession. In V. Girginov (ed.), *Management of Sports Development*. Oxford: Butterworth-Heinemann. pp. 3–37.

Girginov, V. (ed.) (2008b) *Management of Sports Development*. Oxford: Butterworth-Heinemann.

Green, M. (2004) Power, policy, and political priorities: elite sport development in Canada and the United Kingdom. *Sociology of Sport Journal*, 21(4): 376–396.

Guest, A.M. (2009) The diffusion of development-through-sport: analysing the history and practice of the Olympic Movement's grassroots outreach to Africa. *Sport in Society*, 12(10): 1336–1352.

Hayhurst, L.M.C. and Frisby, W. (2010) Inevitable tensions: Swiss and Canadian Sport for Development NGO perspectives on partnerships with high performance sport. *European Sport Management Quarterly*, 10(1): 75–96.

Houlihan, B. and Green, M. (2008) *Comparitive Elite Sport Development: Systems, Structures and Public Policy*. Oxford: Butterworth-Heinemann.

Houlihan, B. and White, A. (2002) *The Politics of Sports Development: Development of Sport or Development through Sport?* London: Routledge.

Hylton, K. and Bramham, P. (2008) Models of sports development. In V. Girginov (ed.), *Management of Sports Development*. Oxford: Butterworth-Heinemann. pp. 41–58.

Kidd, B. (2008) A new social movement: sport for development and peace. *Sport in Society*, 11(4): 370–380.

Parent, M.M. (2008) Mega sporting events and sports development. In V. Girginov (ed.), *Management of Sports Development*. Oxford: Butterworth-Heinemann. pp. 147–163.

Powell, M. (1995) Culture: intervention or solidarity? *Development in Practice*, 5(3): 196–206.

Skinner, J., Zakus, D.H. and Cowell, J. (2008) Development through sport: building social capital in disadvantaged communities. *Sport Management Review*, 11(3): 253–275.

Sugden, J. (2010) Critical left-realism and sport interventions in divided societies. *International Review for the Sociology of Sport*, 45(3): 258–272.

Sport Funding and Finance

Sport funding refers specifically to how sport organizations seek and receive funds to support their operations such as fundraising, government grants, sponsorship and voluntary sector trusts. Sport finance is a larger body of literature and subject area that covers a wide range of financial issues related to sport, such as investment, financial statement analysis and performance measurement.

We combine the terms 'funding' and 'finance' in this concept because the literature related to this area uses both terms. The concepts have been used interchangeably but can also be differentiated in the same way we have done with the above definitions. We take them as separate concepts here and discuss their differences while also recognizing where they may overlap. Sport finance is a broader concept that refers to a large subject area with a more developed and diverse body of literature. We deal firstly with the concept of sport funding and then move on to look at sport finance. Sport funding is a concept that is central to all levels (i.e., local, regional, national and international) of managing sport. The concept is of concern not just to large, professional, commercial sport organizations but also to small, voluntary sport clubs, individual athletes, and those who participate in sport (and provide sport services/facilities) at a recreational level. There are many questions surrounding this concept which have been addressed through books and journals, including: Where does funding for sport come from? How can funds for sport business/stadia be raised? Where can we get funds for our sport club to support competition, travel and equipment? And how do I gain necessary funds as an athlete to help me progress in a professional sports career? These questions have been addressed in the literature on sport funding and their answers help us understand the breadth of this concept and its related literature.

Eastwood (2000) explains that funding for sport comes from three sectors: public, private, and voluntary. Gaining access to these funds as an individual, voluntary sport club, or a commercial sports business/stadium is unique to each group and also to each sector from which funds are sought and for the type of organization seeking the funds. Generally, the public sector funds sport organizations and projects which will help them achieve wider government objectives, such as increased social inclusion, decreased crime, increased health, and/or an increase in social/cultural capital. Government organizations such as the Sports Council (UK) only fund voluntary, non-profit organizations such as sports clubs or other governmental organizations such as local councils, to in turn distribute funds appropriately to local sport. Access to voluntary sector funds is granted by demonstrating that the sport club/organization has the same values/goals as the trust/voluntary organization (e.g., Youth sport trust, a local Airport Trust) from which it seeks funding. Funding comes from the private sector in the form of **sponsorship**, donations, banks and/or fundraising events. Access to funds from these types of organizations requires the development of business relationships and a focus on how the relationship is of benefit to the private sector organization.

Eastwood (2000) focuses on sport funding for clubs and other such organizations. There has been limited research on funding issues in voluntary sport clubs and organizations but the reader may see Edwards et al,'s (2009) article on provincial sport organizations in Canada, or Garrett (2004). Edwards, Mason and Washington (2009) discussed how provincial sport organizations in Canada managed pressures from their institutional environment that focused on how funding was distributed from the national governing body, Sport Canada. Their research is interesting as it moves beyond describing what funding arrangements exist within the organizations to exploring the management and organizational implications of financial pressures. Garrett (2004) likewise provided some insight into how sport clubs were responding to National Lottery money distributed by Sport England. The evidence suggested the willingness and ability of clubs to fully meet funding conditions were variable.

Stewart (2007) provides a good overview and introduction to the issues surrounding funding and finance for sport. From the commercial context of sport as a business through to discussing the financial planning, management and evaluation of sport, the text offers a valuable insight into where funds may come from and how they should be managed. There are also specific chapters on funding in professional sport leagues and the challenges for managers of the professional sport product.

In addition to this there has been a significant interest in funding issues related to professional sport and specifically the stadia required for a professional sport team (Brown and Paul, 2002; Groothius et al., 2004; Long, 2005; Owen and Polley, 2006; Wilson and Pomfret, 2009). Brown and colleagues (2006) discussed the use of 'public funds for private benefit' through an examination of the relationship between public stadium funding and ticket prices in the NFL (National Football League), noting the rising trend for the construction of sport stadia in the USA's municipal districts. They also pointed out that the public funding for stadia has been decreasing and, as such, stadium managers would have to seek revenue from other sources, such as increasing ticket prices. The result of this study suggested that a 10 per cent increase in public funds translated into only a 42 cent decrease in ticket prices. Sports facilities in other contexts, such as those in Canadian universities, have also been forced to seek funding from sources other than government (see Lenskji, 2004). A more recent article by Dale (2009) argues that there is little economic or social justification for the use of public funds for professional sport facilities.

Aside from financing stadia, there has been global concern over the financing of professional sport teams, leagues, and mega sporting events. Miller (2007) discussed the determinants of sport franchise values, examining Major League Baseball teams, and found that franchise values were higher in teams who owned their own stadia, regardless of how their finance was acquired. While a team playing in its own stadium had a higher franchise value, the difference in franchise values between playing in a team-owned versus a publicly-owned stadium does not offset the cost of constructing the stadium in question. Rosenstraub (2006) examined the use of sports facilities for urban redevelopment and how funding from public and private sources may be used, while Rosenstraub et al. (2009) discussed the justification of public spending on sport facilities through measuring intangible elements.

Sport funding and finance are essential concepts for managers of sport organizations to grasp whether those organizations are small local sport clubs, provincial/regional organizations, or professional sport franchises. Research has examined how sport organizations can access funds from the external environment as well as the impacts of financial pressures on the management practices in sport organizations. Finance issues that are internal to a sport organization may include ticket pricing, the use of sponsorship, keeping financial records, and financial planning. As external financial pressures are continually evolving, there is always some scope for research to examine how sport organizations are managing those challenges and the impacts of sport organizations on their environments given the financial pressures they face.

To understand sport funding and finance more fully, the reader may refer to the concept of **sponsorship** that can be found elsewhere in this book.

FURTHER READING

For some further reading on this concept, we would recommend the following:

Garrett, R. (2004) The response of voluntary sports clubs to Sport England's Lottery funding: cases of compliance, change and resistance. *Managing Leisure*, 9(1): 13–29.
Rosenstraub, M., Swindell, D. and Tsvetkova, S. (2009) Justifying public investments in sports: measuring the intangibles. *Journal of Tourism*, 9(2): 133–159.
Stewart, B. (2007) *Sport Funding and Finance*. London: Elsevier.

BIBLIOGRAPHY

Brown, C. and Paul, D.M. (2002) The political scorecard of professional sports facility referendums in the United States, 1984–2000. *Journal of Sport and Social Issues*, 26(3): 248–267.
Brown, M.T., Rascher, D.A. and Ward, W.M. (2006) The use of public funds for private benefit: an examination of the relationship between public stadium funding and ticket prices in the National Football League. *International Journal of Sport Finance*, 1(2): 109–118.
Dale, M. (2009) Reflections on public funding for professional sports. *Journal of the Philosophy of Sport*, 36(1): 22–39.
Eastwood, N. (2000) *The Sports Funding Guide*. London: Directory of Social Change.
Edwards, J.R., Mason, D.S. and Washington, M. (2009) Institutional pressures, government funding and provincial sport organizations. *International Journal of Sport Management and Marketing*, 6(2): 128–149.
Garrett, R. (2004) The response of voluntary sports clubs to Sport England's Lottery funding: cases of compliance, change and resistance. *Managing Leisure*, 9(1): 13–29.
Groothius, P.A., Johnson, B.K. and Whitehead, J.C. (2004) Public funding of professional sports stadiums: public choice or civic pride? *Eastern Economic Journal*, 30(4): 515–526.
Lenskji, H. (2004) Funding Canadian university sport facilities. *Journal of Sport and Social Issues*, 28(4): 379–396.
LeRoux, K. (2009) Managing stakeholder demands: balancing responsiveness to clients and funding agents in non-profit social service organizations. *Administration and Society*, 41: 158–184.
Long, J.G. (2005) Full count: the real cost of public funding for Major League sports facilities. *Journal of Sports Economics*, 6(2): 119–143.
Miller, P. (2007) Private financing and sports franchise values: the case of Major League Baseball. *Journal of Sports Economics*, 8(5): 449–467.
Owen, J.G. and Polley, W.J. (2006) Cities and professional sports teams: a dynamic bargaining model. *International Journal of Sport Finance*, 2(2): 64–78.
Rosenstraub, M. (2006) Sports facilities and urban redevelopment: private and public benefits and a prescription for a healthier future. *International Journal of Sport Finance*, 1(4): 212–226.
Rosenstraub, M., Swindell, D. and Tsvetkova, S. (2009) Justifying public investments in sports: measuring the intangibles. *Journal of Tourism*, 9(2): 133–159.
Stewart, B. (2007) *Sport Funding and Finance*. London: Elsevier.
Wilson, J.K. and Pomfret, R. (2009) Government subsidies for professional team sports in Australia. *Australian Economic Review*, 42(3): 264–275.

Sport Law

> Sport law is a broad term used to describe the legal issues, legislation, and rulings affecting amateur and professional sport, athletes, managers and organizations.

Sport law is a subject discipline which has had increasing significance to the management of sport over the past two decades, mainly due to the increased commercialization and professionalization of the sport industry. The nature and sources of laws as they relate to the management of sport have also changed significantly in recent years. Sport governing bodies are considered the 'regulators' of sport. However, even international governing bodies do not operate outside of national and supra-national laws and so recent years have seen sport events, contests, player contracts and disputes resolved/managed through the legal system and not solely through their respective governing bodies. Gardiner and colleagues (2001, 2006) provided a thorough discussion of most major issues in and applications of sports law, but students and practitioners should also access a greater diversity of sources in order to keep abreast of changes in the law as applied to sport and to identify where research is needed. Gardiner et al. (2001, 2006) also discussed five aspects of sports law: the social context; the national, European, and international governance of sport; the commercial regulation of sport; the regulation of the workplace in sport; and safety issues in sport.

Sport is governed by the rules ('laws') of national and international governing bodies (although as mentioned above, these are created within and must comply with national law). There are laws for athletes as well for referees and umpires who must **control** and discipline play or a game, and added to these there are administrative rules to ensure the fair and sensible organization/control of a sport. In the event of a failure of these laws, as set by the governing bodies, national law can be enforced (e.g., employment law). However, this simple observation is constantly challenged and addressed in the literature.

Some key concepts receiving much attention from academics and sports law practitioners include dispute resolution (Carli, 2009; Blackshaw, Siekmann and Soek, 2006), contracts (Earle and Groome, 2009), the regulation/**governance** of sport (Hums et al., 2009) and intellectual property (McKelvey and Mooreman, 2007), and mediation and arbitration (Blackshaw, 2009). The significance of sports law is being increasingly recognized as it is thought to have implications for the development of general international, comparative and national law, as well as dispute resolution (Mitten and Opie, 2010).

The reader should note the variety of **contexts** in which sports law and/or the law in relation to sport is studied, such as professional sport (see Kim and Parlow, 2009). Authors may also combine their interest in an issue with a specific sport to provide a clear focus on the implications of law as it is applied to sports contexts. Minan (2008) discussed negligence in golf, for example. The context within which sports law is studied is quite important as regulatory/legal frameworks and processes will differ from country to country.

Increasingly there is some debate around the use of 'international sports law' or 'global sports law' (see Foster, 2003, for a clarification of these terms). The term 'comparative sports law' has been used to indicate sports law literature that compares the legal frameworks and practices of different countries with specific reference to sports law issues. Kaburakis (2008) examined the differences between European Union (EU) and United States (US) competition and labour law as it is applied to sport in their analysis of the different systems of sport governance in each country. He argues that the two systems may not be as philosophically/culturally different as has been historically believed and that sport needs politics to survive. A significant development has been the creation of the Court of Arbitration for Sport (CAS) and the reader is directed to Blackshaw et al. (2006) for an interesting discussion of CAS from 1984 to 2004.

The subject of sport law and research related to the law as it is applied to sport is rapidly developing across the globe. Sports law is significant in amateur and professional sporting contexts primarily owing to the increasing commercialization and professionalization of sport at all levels and also due to an increasingly litigious society. There is a need for more research on the management implications of sport's legal environment and for empirical studies of how sport managers monitor and are affected by changes and developments in sports law.

To understand sport law more fully, the reader may refer to the concepts of **context**, **control** and **governance** that can be found elsewhere in this book.

FURTHER READING

For some further reading on this concept, we would recommend the following:

Foster, K. (2003) Is there a global sports law? *Entertainment Law*, 2(1): 1–18.

Gardiner, S., James, M., O'Leary, J., Welch, R., Blackshaw, I., Boyles, S. and Caiger, A. (2006) *Sports Law* (3rd edition). Australia: Cavendish.

Mitten, M. and Opie, H. (2010) 'Sports law': implications for the development of international, comparative and national and global dispute resolution. *Tulane Law Review*, 85(2): 269–322.

BIBLIOGRAPHY

Blackshaw, I. (2009) *Sport, Mediation and Arbitration*. The Hague: TMC Asser Press.

Blackshaw, I.S., Siekmann, R.C.R. and Soek, J.W. (eds) (2006) *The Court of Arbitration for Sport 1984–2004*. The Hague: TMC Asser Press.

Carli, M. (2009) Sports, sponsorship and arbitration: legal and regulatory issues. *Journal of Sponsorship*, 2(4): 387–397.

Earle, R. and Groome, K. (2009) Managing sponsorship contracts through the recession: an English law perspective. *Journal of Sponsorship*, 2(3): 281–291.

Foster, K. (2003) Is there a global sports law? *Entertainment Law*, 2(1): 1–18.

Gardiner, S., James, M., O'Leary, J., Welch, R., Blackshaw, I., Boyles, S. and Caiger, A. (2001) *Sports Law*. London: Cavendish.

Gardiner, S., James, M., O'Leary, J., Welch, R., Blackshaw, I., Boyles, S. and Caiger, A. (2006) *Sports Law* (3rd edition). London: Cavendish.

Hums, M.A., Moorman, A.M. and Wolf, E.A. (2009) The inclusion of the Paralympics in the Olympic and Amateur Sports Act. *Journal of Sport and Social Issues*, 27(3): 261–275.

Kaburakis, A. (2008) The US and EU systems of sport governance: commercialized vs socio-cultural model – competition and labour law. *International Sports Law Journal*, 3(4): 108–127.

Kim, J.Y. and Parlow, M.J. (2009) Off-court misbehavior: sports leagues and private punishment. *Journal of Criminal Law and Criminology*, 99(3): 573–597.

McKelvey, S. and Mooreman, A. (2007) Bush-whacked: a legal analysis of the unauthorized use of sport organizations' intellectual property in political campaign advertising. *Journal of Sport Management*, 21: 79–102.

Minan, J.H. (2008) *The Little Green Book of Golf Law*. Illinois: The American Bar Association.

Mitten, M. and Opie, H. (2010) 'Sports law': implications for the development of international, comparative and national and global dispute resolution. *Tulane Law Review*, 85(2): 269–322.

Sport Marketing

> *Sport marketing is the process and activities involved when informing potential and existing consumers about sport products and services with the intention of influencing consumer behaviour to purchase, engage with, or develop loyalty to that product, service, or brand.*

With the growth of the sport industry and the development of sport as a business, sport marketing has become increasingly important to many different **stakeholders** within sport. The concept holds relevance for voluntary as well as public sector sport organizations, sport business owners, individual athletes, and professional sport teams/leagues. Mullins et al. (2007) provided an excellent introduction to the subject area known as sport marketing by identifying the unique nature of marketing sport (products and services) as well as the obstacles to successful marketing in the sports industry. They offered the following definition of sport marketing:

> Sport marketing consists of all activities designed to meet the needs and wants of sport consumers through exchange processes. Sport marketing has developed two major thrusts: the marketing of sport products and services directly to consumers of sport, and the marketing of other consumer and industrial products or services through the use of sport promotions. (2007: 11)

Sport marketing can also be thought of as a business function that is composed of several interrelated elements including product development and management, promotion, pricing, and customer relations (Sullivan, 2004). Understanding customers is essential to the sport marketing function, including understanding the 'sports fan' (Hunt et al., 1999).

Shilbury and colleagues (2009) provide some discussion of marketing, sport marketing, and the 'strategic sport marketing process'. They went into considerable detail regarding the development of sport marketing and **strategy**, including television and media considerations, **sponsorship** (and an evaluation of same), and the **control** and implementation of this strategy. While the above-mentioned textbooks provide valuable introductions to sport marketing and strategic sport marketing, researchers, students and sport practitioners should also be aware that there are a wide variety of journals which contain contemporary and more specific debates and techniques related to sport marketing.

A key concept within sport marketing, and increasingly the focus for marketing and sport marketing journals, is sponsorship, and we have covered this as a separate concept. Related to sponsorship and increasingly important in sport marketing is ambush marketing. The term was first used during the 1984 Los Angeles Olympic Games to describe the marketing practices of non-sponsoring companies such as Kodak (Sandler and Shani, 1989). McKelvey and Grady (2008) discussed in more detail the transformation of the concept of ambush marketing from being an 'undermining' of official sponsors at major events to activities which seek to associate the non-sponsor with the event and confuse spectators as to who is the official sponsor. Debates around the ethical and legal characteristics of ambushing have also taken place in the literature and have helped to inform definitions of the concept (see Crow and Hoek, 2003; Glengarry, 2007; Hoek and Gendall, 2002; Meenaghan, 1994; Payne, 1993).

Through discussing definitions of ambush marketing and why/how companies engage in ambushing, McKelvey and Grady (2008) present ideas for sponsorship programme protection strategies and the nature of the events for which these strategies may be successful. Chadwick and Burton (2009) also investigate ambush marketing in sponsorship by exploring the strategies used by rights holders and sponsors to protect against ambush marketers, noting the increase in proactive management using counter-ambush strategies.

Trade/practitioner publications have discussed the prominence of ambush marketing at major sporting events (**mega events**) and the significant benefits to companies who engage in 'ambushing' (see Balfour and Tschang, 2008; Madden, 2007). There is also some interest among academics in measuring the effects of ambush marketing on brand recall among consumers (Portlock and Rose, 2009). Preuss et al.'s (2008) empirical work on ambush marketing in China uses a five-point categorization to distinguish between various methods of ambushing (examining the commercials used by corporations during CCTV5 coverage) at the 2004 Olympic Games in Athens. The research also discusses the cultural implications of ambushing and perceptions of this activity in China.

Another key research topic within sport marketing is concerned with 'brands'. Authors have examined brand recognition (Seguin et al., 2008), brand loyalty (Gladden and Funk, 2004), the impact of scandals on brands (Hughes and Shank, 2008), the development of successful brands (Chadwick and Burton, 2008), celebrity athlete brands (Hsu and McDonald, 2002), and most recently brand equity (Suckow, 2009). Brands in relation to ambush marketing have also been of interest (Seguin and O'Reilly, 2008). The concept of brands has been researched in a wide variety of contexts and those interested in sports brands should also consider the more generic literature on branding. We suggest this because it is incorrect to assume that branding issues in sport are any different from the development of successful brands in other contexts, and therefore reading both non-sport- and sport-related research on branding allows researchers to build stronger theoretical constructs and meaning for their research. In this way, they may also be able to make a contribution to the sport management literature and to the wider field of sport marketing and brand management. We now turn to look at some of the non-sport-related 'branding' literature to show its relevance to the concept of sport marketing and sports brands.

Laroche and Parsa (2000) examine brand management in hospitality, providing in-depth insights into research within the context of the hospitality industry and revealing the unique attributes of this industry which affect the management of brands. Boyle (2007) provides a conceptual model of brand 'co-creation' and discussed the nature of brands and implications for managers generally, without reference to a particular sector. Schmitt and Rogers (2008) presents an edited volume of 19 papers examining new concepts and contextual factors affecting brand design and management. These are just some examples of the broad array of conceptual and empirical, generic, and sector-specific work that has been done on branding. Their relevance to sport marketing and sport brands is that they are all about the fundamental concept of marketing and therefore need to be considered when doing research on specific areas such as 'co-creation' or brand design in order to fully inform thinking on brands in the context of sport.

Research on sport marketing is generally of a very pragmatic nature, with the aim of better understanding the function of sport marketing or to improve the marketing of sport products and services. Examples of contemporary issues of interest to researchers include ambush marketing, brands, and sport consumer behaviour.

To understand sport marketing more fully, the reader may refer to the concepts of **strategy, sponsorship, stakeholders, mega events** and **control** that can be found elsewhere in this book.

FURTHER READING

For some further reading on this concept, we would recommend the following:

Burton, N. and Chadwick, S. (2009) Ambush marketing in sport: an analysis of sponsorship protection means and counter-ambush measures. *Journal of Sponsorship*, 2(4): 303–315.
Mullins, B.J., Hardy, S. and Sutton, W.A. (2007) *Sport Marketing*. Champaign, IL: Human Kinetics.
Seguin, B., Richelieu, A. and O'Reilly, N. (2008) Leveraging the Olympic brand through the reconciliation of corporate and consumers' brand perceptions. *International Journal of Sport Management and Marketing*, 3(1/2): 78–99.
Shilbury, D., Westerbeek, H., Quick, S. and Funk, D. (2009) *Strategic Sport Marketing* (3rd edition). Australia: Allen and Unwin.

BIBLIOGRAPHY

Balfour, F. and Tschang, C.C. (2008) Ambush in Beijing. *Business Week*, 4076: 54–55.
Boyle, E. (2007) A process model of brand cocreation: brand management and research implications. *Journal of Product and Brand Management*, 16(2): 122–131.
Chadwick, S. and Burton, N. (2008) From Beckham to Ronaldo: assessing the nature of football player brands. *Journal of Sponsorship*, 1(4): 307–317.
Crow, J. and Hoek, J. (2003) Ambush marketing: a critical review and some practical advice. *Marketing Bulletin*, 14 (1): 1–14.
Gladden, J.M. and Funk, D.C. (2004) Understanding brand loyalty in professional sport: examining the link between brand associations and brand loyalty. In S.R. Rosner and K.L. Shropshire (eds), *The Business of Sports*. London: Jones and Bartlett. pp. 194–198.

Glengarry, J. (2007) Rugby World Cup legislation threatens our civil rights. *The New Zealand Herald*, 18 April. Retrieved 16 May, 2007, from http:www.nzherald.co.nz/topic/story.cfm?c_id=247andobjected=10434725

Hoek, J. and Gendall, P. (2002) Ambush marketing: more than just a commercial irritant? *Entertainment Law*, 1(2): 72–91.

Hsu, C. and McDonald, D. (2002) An examination on multiple celebrity endorsers in advertising. *Journal of Product and Brand Management*, 11(1): 19–29.

Hughes, S.F. and Shank, M.D. (2008) Assessing the impact of NCAA scandals: an exploratory analysis. *International Journal of Sport Management and Marketing*, 3(1/2): 78–99.

Hunt, K., Bristol, T. and Bashaw, R. (1999) A conceptual approach to classifying sports fans. *Journal of Services Marketing*, 13(6): 439–452.

Laroche, M. and Parsa, H.G. (2000) Brand management in hospitality: an empirical test of the Brisoux-Laroche model. *Journal of Hospitality and Tourism Research*, 24(2): 199–222.

Madden, N. (2007) Ambush marketing could hit a new high at Beijing Olympics. *Advertising Age*, 78(29): 22.

McKelvey, S. and Grady, J. (2008) Sponsorship programme protection strategies for special sport events: are event organizers outmanoeuvring ambush marketers? *Journal of Sport Management*, 22(5): 550–586.

Meenaghan, T. (1994) Point of view: ambush marketing: immoral or imaginative practice? *Journal of Advertising Research*, 34(5): 77–88.

Mullins, B.J., Hardy, S. and Sutton, W.A. (2007) *Sport Marketing*. Champaign, IL: Human Kinetics.

Payne, M. (1993) A talk by IOC market chief Michael R. Payne. *The Sport Marketing Letter*, 4.

Portlock, A. and Rose, S. (2009) Effects of ambush marketing: UK consumer brand recall and attitudes to official sponsors and non-sponsors associated with the FIFA World Cup 2006. *International Journal of Sports Marketing and Sponsorship*, 10(4): 271–286.

Preuss, H., Germeinder, K. and Seguin, B. (2008) Ambush marketing in China: counterbalancing Olympic sponsorship efforts. *Asian Business and Management*, 7(2): 243–263.

Sandler, D.M. and Shani, D. (1989) Olympic sponsorship vs ambush marketing: who gets the gold? *Journal of Advertising Research*, 29: 9–14.

Schmitt, B.H. and Rogers, D.L. (2008) *Handbook on Brand and Experience Management*. Cheltenham: Edward Elgar.

Seguin, B. and O'Reilly, N.J. (2008) The Olympic brand, ambush marketing and clutter. *International Journal of Sport Management and Marketing*, 4(1): 62–84.

Seguin, B., Richelieu, A. and O'Reilly, N. (2008) Leveraging the Olympic brand through the reconciliation of corporate and consumers' brand perceptions. *International Journal of Sport Management and Marketing*, 3(1/2): 78–99.

Shilbury, D., Westerbeek, H., Quick, S. and Funk, D. (2009) *Strategic Sport Marketing* (3rd edition). Australia: Allen and Unwin.

Suckow, C. (2009) Literature on brand equity in professional team sport: a German perspective on ice hockey. *International Journal of Sport Management and Marketing*, 5(1/2): 211–225.

Sullivan, M. (2004) Sport marketing. In J. Beech and S. Chadwick (eds), *The Business of Sport Management*. Harlow: Pearson Education.

Sport Organization

A sport organization is a group of people who are working together to accomplish goal(s) related to providing some sport-related product and/or service.

In conducting any research within the field of the management of sport, it is important to clearly define what is and is not considered a 'sport' organization. Slack and Parent (2006: 5) describe a sport organization as 'a social entity involved in the sport industry; it is goal-directed, with a consciously structured activity system and a relatively identifiable boundary'. Unlike other concepts in this book where we examine the mainstream literature and then the sport management literature, given the concept in question is 'sport organization', we have briefly addressed this first and now move to look at the concept of organization more generally and suggest how this can be useful to those studying sport organizations specifically. Organizations have been defined by many authors, which has been helpful in identifying aspects of management which require consideration and investigation. Therefore new conceptions of what constitutes an 'organization' can lead to new insights and possibilities for future research.

Rollinson (2002) describes an organization as a social entity created and maintained by individuals for a purpose, and including some structured and coordinated effort toward **organizational goals**. Robbins et al. (2003) suggested that an organization is simply people's deliberate cooperation in order to accomplish an agreed goal or goals. Earlier attempts at defining an organization by Bowman and Jarrett (1996) and Keuning (1998) also mentioned common goals and implied rationality in how individuals cooperate in attaining those goals, and with structure and hierarchy as key components in organizations. Therefore, if we consider that a sport organization can be formally structured (as in Rollinson's (2000) definition) or it can be more loosely defined as individuals working toward some common goal without a specified formal **structure** (as in Robbins et al., 2003), then a variety of small, medium and large-sized sport organizations can be examined. This is crucial in research on the management of sport as there is great variability in the size of organizations in our field and it is widely accepted (which you can see by reading about the concepts in this book) that organization strategy, control and other functions can vary depending on the size of such organizations.

Morgan (1997) introduced a variety of different ways in which to view organizations through the use of metaphors. He used metaphors of organizations as brains, machines, organisms, cultures and political systems, instruments of domination, psychic prisons and flux/transformations. Slack (1993) examines these concepts and explores 'organizations as machines' as the dominant perception of sport organizations in the literature before moving on to reveal how the other 'images' may contribute to a better understanding of sport organizations and produce more effective managers. Aside from looking at sport organizations from different perspectives, or using different metaphors to highlight new ill-understood aspects of these organizations, research has generally focused on either the formal or informal elements of these organizations.

The formal elements of sport organizations include the structure, written policy and **strategy** of the organization. The informal issues include less tangible elements such as **organization culture**, **leadership**, **power** and **control**. In fact, all of the concepts in this book will help the reader understand sport organizations and how they operate. One concept we have not included as 'key' but which is very important in understanding all organizations is gender. We have not included it as a key concept as we feel it is better suited to be discussed within the **context** of organizations (see Alvesson and Billing, 2009, for an overview) rather than more generally as a separate concept. This is because gender is a concept that has been used to provide alternative perspectives on many of the concepts in this book, and the way it has been incorporated into research on the management of sport has changed considerably over time (Sibson, 2010).

Sibson (2010: 379) suggests that liberal feminist approaches to examining gender have resulted in research that is focused on 'increasing women's involvement by developing women's skill-sets, removing any existing structural barriers and valuing the differences between men and women' (see, for example, Aitchison, 2000; Cunningham and Sagas, 2008; Hargreaves, 1994; Shaw and Frisby, 2006; Talbot, 2002). However, whilst the benefits of this work have been noted by researchers, Sibson and others (e.g., Shaw and Frisby, 2006) suggest that a poststructuralist view of gender is needed to challenge the taken-for-granted 'structures, practices, discourses and values' (Sibson, 2010: 380) that are prevalent in sport organizations in order to improve equality in the operation of sport organizations.

In summary, this entire book is about sport organizations and every concept is relevant to understanding the organization and management of sport. We can think of research on sport organizations as being focused on formal or informal elements or a combination of both, such as understanding the control of sport organizations, which requires an examination of structural/administrative controls and informal social controls. The research on sport organizations is therefore vast and diverse but we can recognize that the aim of this body of work has been either to validate existing theories of (sport) organizations or to generate new theory on how organizations operate. Those interested in doing research on sport organizations may consider which of these objectives best reflects the purpose of their work and how the testing of existing theory or the generation of new theory serves to contribute to the existing sport management literature. It is crucial to the development of knowledge on the management of sport to understand and challenge why we undertake the research we do and who may benefit from our efforts.

To understand sport organizations more fully, the reader may refer to the concepts of **organizational goals**, **context** and **structure** that can be found elsewhere in this book.

FURTHER READING

For some further reading on this concept, we would recommend the following:

Alvesson, M. and Billing, Y. (2009) *Understanding Gender and Organizations*. London: Sage.

Slack, T. and Parent, M.M. (2006) *Understanding Sport Organizations: The Application of Organization Theory*. Champaign, IL: Human Kinetics.

Talbot, M. (2002) Playing with patriarchy: the gendered dynamics of sports organizations. In S. Scraton and A. Flintoff (eds), *Gender and Sport: A Reader*. London: Routledge. pp. 277–291.

BIBLIOGRAPHY

Aitchison, C. (2000) Women in leisure services: managing the social-cultural nexus of gender equity. *Managing Leisure,* 5(4): 181–191.

Alvesson, M. and Billing, Y. (2009) *Understanding Gender and Organizations.* London: Sage.

Bowman, C. and Jarrett, M. (1996) *Management in Practice: A Framework for Managing Organisational Change.* London: Butterworth-Heinemann.

Cunningham, G.B. and Sagas, M. (2008) Gender and sex diversity in sport organizations: introduction to a special issue. *Sex Roles,* 58: 3–9.

Hargreaves, J.A. (1994) *Sporting Females: Critical Issues in the History and Sociology of Women's Sports.* London: Routledge.

Keuning, D. (1998) *Management: A Contemporary Approach.* London: Pitman.

Morgan, G. (1997) *Images of Organization.* London: Sage.

Robbins, S.P., Coulter, M. and Stuart-Kotze, R. (2003) *Management.* Englewood Cliffs, NJ: Prentice-Hall.

Rollinson, D. (1998) *Organization Behaviour and Analysis* (1st edn.). Harlow: Pearson Education.

Rollinson, D. (2002) *Organization Behaviour and Analysis* (2nd edn.). Harlow: Pearson Education.

Shaw, S. and Frisby, W. (2006) Can gender equity be more equitable? Promoting an alternative frame for sport management research, education, and practice. *Journal of Sport Management,* 20(4): 483–509.

Sibson, R. (2010) 'I was banging my head against a brick wall': exclusionary power and the gendering of sport organizations. *Journal of Sport Management,* 24: 379–399.

Slack, T. (1993) Morgan and the metaphors: implications for sport management research. *Journal of Sport Management,* 7: 189–193.

Slack, T. and Parent, M.M. (2006) *Understanding Sport Organizations: The Application of Organization Theory,* 2nd edition. London: Human Kinetics.

Talbot, M. (2002) Playing with patriarchy: the gendered dynamics of sports organizations. In S. Scraton and A. Flintoff (eds), *Gender and Sport: A Reader.* London: Routledge. pp. 277–291.

Sport Participation

> *The trend has been to define sport participation according to its two components, sport and participation, where sport is seen (usually) as a competitive activity involving two or more participants and participation must be done regularly either actively and/or passively.*

Sport participation's definition is dependent on how one defines sport. For example, many researchers (e.g., Berger et al., 2008; Bloom et al., 2005; Curtis et al., 2003; Girginov et al., 2009) see sport as being a competitive activity involving two or more participants, and without the use of a motorized vehicle as the primary determinant of performance outcome (Sport Canada, 1998). Other researchers (e.g., Alexandris and Carroll, 1997; Alexandris and Stodolska, 2004; Hinrichs et al., 2010; Park, 2004) take a broader view and include both leisure and recreational activities (e.g., walking, cycling). There have also been studies examining sport participation, where sport is specified as being alternative, extreme, or 'active', such as in the case of motocross. For example, Yong Jae and colleagues (2008) found that participants were motivated to participate in motocross by risk taking and fun/excitement. They also found differences based on gender and experience level. In turn, participation can be defined as either active or passive, but should be done regularly (whether daily, weekly, or monthly).

Many studies have examined the factors (facilitators, constraints) affecting sport participation. In their review of the literature, Berger et al. (2008) note that such factors typically fall within socio-individual characteristics (e.g., ethnicity, gender, and age), psychological predispositions (e.g., motivation), socio-cultural influences (e.g., family support, the household's socio-economic status), and situational/ environmental factors (e.g., availability of transportation, an urban *vs*. a rural setting). For example, Alexandris and Carroll (1997) found that sport participation in Greece depended on status, relaxation, and intellectual, social, competition/achievement, and health/fitness motivations. Alexandris and Stodolska (2004) describe certain sport participation constraints, including psychological and time constraints, a lack of knowledge, and a lack of interest-related constraints. Martin (1997) added that college students who continued to participate in sport did so because of self-fulfilment, whereas typically students who stopped did so because of other com-mitments (i.e., a lack of time).

Certain researchers are interested in a particular subset of the population and one popular area of study is youth sport participation. Examples here include Baxter-Jones and Maffulli (2003) and Hoyle and Leff (1997), who examine parental influ-ence on youth sport participation, and Berger et al. (2008), who used Canada's General Social Survey to examine factors affecting youth participation. They found household context, gender, community context, self-perceptions, and competing behaviours all impacted on youth sport participation. Berger et al.'s article paints a picture where youth are faced with stress, social role conflict, and a susceptibility to external influences, which impact on their participation in sport. In addition to this, participation in sport must itself compete with technology (TV, internet, social networking, etc.) for young people's attention. Park (2004) further explored the impact of the internet on their sport participation.

Others are interested in adult sport participation, such as is the case for Alexandris and colleagues (Alexandris and Carroll, 1997; Alexandris and Stodolska, 2004). However, we can also find researchers who are interested in the link between peo-ple's sport participation in their youth and its impact later in life (see for example Baker et al., 2010; Curtis et al., 1999; Dionigi, 2002). High school sport participation seems to positively impact on participation later in life (Curtis et al., 1999) and older adults' participation in competitive sport seems to be a significant strategy for these individuals 'adapting to later life, and provides a context for them to express youth-fulness and negotiate meanings of older age' (Dionigi, 2002: 4).

Still others are particularly interested in the relationship between gender and/or sexuality and sport participation. Klausen (1996: 111) took a historical perspective in examining the participation of Scandinavian women in sport, finding that women's role in sports seems to be related to accessing sport itself as well as the locus of decision making. This access was found to be dependent on government and **sport organizations**' policies. Likewise, Elling and Janssens (2009) examine sport participation according to gender and sexuality in a Dutch study. Their findings included sport as challenging but also confirming gays' and lesbians' stereotypical sport participation images, and these images or mappings then influenced the sport participation 'biographies of men and women with different sexual identifications' (2009: 71).

Added to this, some researchers are interested in studying individuals with disabilities and their sport participation. For example, Taub et al. (1999) examined how participation in sport and physical activity can be a strategy to reduce the stigma often associated with a person having a disability. Sport participation has also been linked to other concepts and examined for potential impacts. The following provides a sample of such studies:

- *Socio-economic benefits of sport participation:* Bloom et al. (2005) argue that participating in sport impacted on people (health/wellbeing, social networks, etc.), communities (e.g., social capital and cohesion), the economy (e.g., job creation), and also shaped Canadians' national and cultural identities (e.g., national pride). Vail (2007) added that a sport organization which takes a community development approach facilitates an increase in sport participation in a given community.
- *Sport events and sport participation:* using a process-oriented approach, Girginov and Hills (2008) examine the link between hosting an Olympic Games and increasing sport participation as a **legacy**. They argued that sport participation, as an event legacy, must be constructed – it is not just given – and found that 'the role of sports participation legacy has been to compensate for the propensities of Olympic growth' (2008: 2091).
- *Health and happiness:* Chin-Hsung et al. (2010) examine the relationship between sport participation time, health and happiness – finding that there was a stronger relationship between sport participation time and happiness than between sport participation time and health. As well as this, when examining these relationships within six different life stages, they found that the sport participation–happiness relationship was more positive for those classified as young and elderly, as opposed to those who were considered middle aged.
- *Self-esteem:* Slutzky and Simpkins (2009) examine the impact of children's team *vs.* individual sport participation on self-esteem, finding that children who participated in team sports typically had higher self-esteem.
- *Suicide:* frequent and vigorous sport participation may help decrease suicidality and a feeling of hopelessness in male adolescents while a low sport participation level in adolescent females actually increases suicidality and hopelessness (Taliaferro et al., 2008).
- *Violence:* contrary to popular belief, participating in (club) organized sport does not decrease the incidence of violence in male adolescents (Mutz and Baur, 2009).

- *Academic achievement:* Fox and colleagues (2010) support the relationship between sport participation and a higher grade-point average (GPA), but also went further by stating that:
  - o for high school girls, physical activity as well as sport team participation (independently) helped increase GPA;
  - o for high school boys, sport team participation helped increase GPA;
  - o for middle school girls and boys, physical activity with sport team participation (together) helped increase GPA.

Research, as can be seen above, has used a variety of perspectives, including managerial/ marketing, psychological, sociological and medical, although the management perspective may be lagging behind other perspectives, especially the psychological view. We also find certain differences between countries, which is perhaps the reason for a proliferation of research on sport participation in a variety of countries, such as: Canada (e.g., Sport Canada, 1998; Vail, 2007), the United Kingdom (e.g., Goretzki et al., 2008; Gratton et al., 2008), Australia (e.g., Dollman and Lewis, 2010), Greece (e.g., Alexandris et al., 1999), Taiwan (e.g., Tsai, 2009), Malaysia (e.g., Yusof and Omar-Fauzee, 2003), Belgium (e.g., Scheerder et al., 2005), the Netherlands (e.g., Elling and Janssens, 2009), Germany (e.g., Hinrichs et al., 2010), Norway (e.g., Skille, 2005), Poland (e.g., Jung, 2004), and Hungary (e.g., Perényi, 2010). Clearly, there is a need for meta-analyses to be undertaken.

To understand sport participation more fully, the reader may refer to the concepts of **sport organization** and **legacy** that can be found elsewhere in this book.

FURTHER READING

For some further reading on this concept, we would recommend the following:

MacLean, J. and Hamm, S. (2008) Values and sport participation: comparing participant groups, age, and gender. *Journal of Sport Behavior,* 31(4): 352–367.

Vander Kloet, M., O'Reilly, N. and Berger, I. (2007) Adolescent, adolescent culture, sport and physical activity: a literature review and implications for future research. *Journal of Adolescent Sports,* 2(2): 14–23.

BIBLIOGRAPHY

Alexandris, K. and Carroll, B. (1997) Motives for recreational sport participation in Greece: implications for planning and provision of sport services. *European Physical Education Review,* 3(2): 129–143.

Alexandris, K. and Stodolska, M. (2004) The influence of perceived constraints on the attitudes towards recreational sport participation. *Loisir and société,* 27(1): 197–217.

Alexandris, K., Carroll, B. and Alexandris, K. (1999) Constraints on recreational sport participation in adults in Greece: implications for providing and managing sport services. *Journal of Sport Management,* 13(4): 317–332.

Baker, J., Fraser-Thomas, J., Dionigi, R.A. and Horton, S. (2010) Sport participation and positive development in older persons. *European Reviews of Aging and Physical Activity,* 7(1): 3–12.

Baxter-Jones, A.D.G. and Maffulli, N. (2003) Parental influence on sport participation in elite young athletes. *Journal of Sports Medicine and Physical Fitness*, 43: 250–255.

Berger, I.E., O'Reilly, N., Parent, M.M., Séguin, B. and Hernandez, T. (2008) Determinants of sport participation among Canadian adolescents. *Sport Management Review*, 11: 277–307.

Bloom, M., Grant, M. and Watt, D. (2005) *Strengthening Canada: The Socio-economic Benefits of Sport Participation in Canada*. Ottawa: The Conference Board of Canada.

Chin-Hsung, K., Po-Yang, H. and Yu-Te Tom, K. (2010) Are you healthy and happy? Does sport participation matter? A study of the inter-relationships between sport participation, perceived health and perceived happiness at six life stages. *World Leisure Journal*, 52(1): 61–67.

Curtis, J., McTeer, W. and White, P. (1999) Exploring effects of school sport experiences on sport participation in later life. *Sociology of Sport Journal*, 16(4): 348–365.

Curtis, J., McTeer, W. and White, P. (2003) Do high school athletes earn more pay? Youth sport participation and earnings as an adult. *Sociology of Sport Journal*, 20(1): 60–76.

Dionigi, R. (2002) Leisure and identity management in later life: understanding competitive sport participation among older adults. *World Leisure Journal*, 44(3): 4–15.

Dollman, J. and Lewis, N.R. (2010) The impact of socioeconomic position on sport participation among South Australian youth. *Journal of Science and Medicine in Sport*, 13(3): 318–322.

Elling, A. and Janssens, J. (2009) Sexuality as a structural principle in sport participation. *International Review for the Sociology of Sport*, 44(1): 71–86.

Fox, C.K., Barr-Anderson, D., Neumark-Sztainer, D. and Wall, M. (2010) Physical activity and sports team participation: associations with academic outcomes in middle school and high school students. *Journal of School Health*, 80(1): 31–37.

Girginov, V. and Hills, L. (2008) A sustainable sports legacy: creating a link between the London Olympics and sports participation. *International Journal of the History of Sport*, 25(14): 2091–2116.

Girginov, V., Taks, M., Boucher, B., Martyn, S., Holman, M. and Dixon, J. (2009) Canadian national sport organizations' use of the Web for relationship marketing in promoting sport participation. *International Journal of Sport Communication*, 2(2): 164–184.

Goretzki, J., Esser, A. and Claydon, R. (2008) *Increasing Participation in Sport Research Debrief*. London: Sport England. Retrieved from http://www.sportengland.org/research/understanding_participation.aspx

Gratton, C., Kokolakakis, T. and Panagouleas, T. (2008) *An econometric model of the determination of sports participation in England*. Paper presented at the 16th European Association for Sport Management Conference, Bayreuth/Heidelberg, Germany.

Hinrichs, T., Trampisch, U., Burghaus, I., Endres, H., Klaaeszetten-Mielke, R., Moschny, A., et al. (2010) Correlates of sport participation among community-dwelling elderly people in Germany: a cross-sectional study. *European Reviews of Aging and Physical Activity*, 7(2): 105–115.

Hoyle, R.H. and Leff, S.S. (1997) The role of parental involvement in youth sport participation and performance. *Adolescence*, 32(125): 233–243.

Jung, B. (2004) The evolution of leisure and sport participation in Poland. *International Journal of the History of Sport*, 21(5): 727–741.

Klausen, K.K. (1996) Women and sport in Scandinavia: policy, participation and representation. *Scandinavian Political Studies*, 19(2): 111–131.

Martin, D.E. (1997) Interscholastic sport participation: reasons for maintaining or terminating participation. *Journal of Sport Behavior*, 20(1): 94–104.

Mutz, M. and Baur, J.R. (2009) The role of sports for violence prevention: sport club participation and violent behaviour among adolescents. *International Journal of Sport Policy*, 1(3): 305–321.

Park, S.-H. (2004) Constraints to recreational sport participation for adolescents exposed to Internet-related delinquency: developing marketing strategies for increasing sport participation. *International Journal of Applied Sports Sciences*, 16(1): 41–54.

Perényi, S. (2010) The relation between sport participation and the value preferences of Hungarian youth. *Sport in Society*, 13(6): 984–1000.

Scheerder, J., Taks, M., Vanreusel, B. and Renson, R. (2005) Social changes in youth sports participation styles 1969–1999: the case of Flanders (Belgium). *Sport, Education and Society*, 10(3): 321–341.

Skille, E.A. (2005) Individuality or cultural reproduction? Adolescents' sport participation in Norway: alternative versus conventional sports. *International Review for the Sociology of Sport*, 40(3): 307–320; 393–394; 396; 399; 402.

Slutzky, C.B. and Simpkins, S.D. (2009) The link between children's sport participation and self-esteem: exploring the mediating role of sport self-concept. *Psychology of Sport and Exercise*, 10(3): 381–389.

Sport Canada (1998) Sport participation in Canada. Retrieved 5 September 2010, from http://www.pch.gc.ca/pgm/sc/info-fact/1998-psc-spc/pdf/SPINC-all.pdf

Taliaferro, L.A., Rienzo, B.A., Miller, M.D., Pigg, R.M., Jr and Dodd, V.J. (2008) High school youth and suicide risk: exploring protection afforded through physical activity and sport participation. *Journal of School Health*, 78(10): 545–553.

Taub, D.E., Blinde, E.M. and Greer, K.R. (1999) Stigma management through participation in sport and physical activity: experiences of male college students with physical disabilities. *Human Relations*, 52(11): 1469–1483.

Tsai, C.-T.L. (2009) Media systems and their effects on women's sport participation in Taiwan. *Sport, Education and Society*, 14(1): 37–53.

Vail, S.E. (2007) Community development and sport participation. *Journal of Sport Management*, 21(4): 571–596.

Yong Jae, K., Hyewon, P. and Claussen, C.L. (2008) Action sports participation: consumer motivation. *International Journal of Sports Marketing and Sponsorship*, 9(2): 111–124.

Yusof, A. and Omar-Fauzee, M.S. (2003) Sport: perceptions of Malaysian college students about sport participation constraints. *Journal of the International Council for Health, Physical Education, Recreation, Sport and Dance*, 39(1): 32–36.

Sport Policy

> *Sport policy refers to the formal rules and regulations of a sport organization (or government) which are intended to guide employee actions.*

A sport policy is an outline of the direction a sport should take, according to makers of a policy. Policies are developed by national governments and sport organizations in order to guide sport in some desired direction. A sport organization's policy or government policy related to sport can therefore have a significant impact on the **governance** of that organization. Policy is akin to **strategy**. In private sector organizations the tendency is to talk about strategy. In public organizations we refer to policy. Nearly every national, provincial, state, and county organization will have a policy which will guide its direction and activities, although, as we show below, research on sport policy has mainly focused on national-level policy making as a process; comparative studies of sport policy in different countries; and the implementation of government policy through the sport system. A key driver for research on sport policy is the increasing involvement and interest of governments in sporting matters. Governments recognize sport's ability to achieve broader government objectives related to health, social wellbeing, crime, and other related issues that are of concern to modern society (Houlihan, 1997). For this reason, governments have become more involved in funding sport and creating national-level policies which impact on sport. One issue they are particularly focused on is how **sport participation** can influence the health and social capital of people, thereby reducing national health-care costs as well as crime and anti-social behaviour (see Nicholson et al., 2011). Similarly, governments are concerned with how volunteering (see the concept **voluntary**) can benefit the wider society and individuals (e.g., Commission on the Future of Volunteering, 2008).

Sport's policy-making process is examined in a number of different countries which has led to the comparison of these processes and discussions around how policy influences sport performance. Chalip and colleagues (1996) looked at the policy process in several different countries. Chalip (1996) also used critical policy analysis to examine the case of New Zealand. Piggin et al. (2009) also looked at sport policy in New Zealand, building on the work of Michel Foucault and showing how sources of knowledge were used in policy making. They argued that despite the claim by policy makers that 'evidence-based' knowledge founded on positivism was used, policy makers relied on a wider source of knowledge. Enjolras and Waldahl (2007) examine how public policy was made in Norway and discussed the relevance of three theoretical approaches (corporatism, policy communities and clientelism) to explain policy making in the Norwegian context. Their research highlighted some of the important changes which had been taking place in the policy-making process.

Henry et al. (2005) present a four-fold classification of sport policy. The first of these they label *Seeking Similarities*. Here policy is assessed by measures of participation or policy commitment. They suggest that research by Szalai (1972), Jones' (1989) work on European Countries, and Gratton's (1999) analysis of European states, as well as Rodgers' (1978) review of policy systems in European states, are all examples of this type of work. The second classification termed *Describing Difference*, is a more qualitative approach, and involved describing individual policy initiatives and the interactions between those initiatives. Henry et al. cited three studies that used this approach. They suggest that work by Henry and Nassis (1999), Houlihan (1997), and Paramio Salcines (1999) are examples of this approach.

The third approach was termed *Theorizing the Trans-national* and was related to issues of globalization. In many ways this was one of the newer approaches to policy studies since it did not focus on the nation-state. In this approach, policy initiatives were shaped by the interaction of the global context in which policy was produced. Henry et al. (2005) again cited three studies which were examples of this approach. First they cited Maguire's (1999) work but also noted that he primarily dealt with issues of sociology. The second and third examples were work by Henry and his students: Dulac and Henry (2001) and Henry and Uchiumi (2001).

Both studies addressed issues which moved beyond the nation-state. The fourth approach was termed *Defining Discourse*. In this approach, policy ws seen as discourse and looked at the way policy was shaped by language. As Henry et al. (2005) pointed out, this approach had not been used in relation to sport policy.

In the mid-1980s Sport Canada, a directorate of the federal government responsible for sport, initiated the Quadrennial Planning Programme (QPP). While not expressed as a policy the QPP provided direction to the national **sport organization** on how they should structure themselves in order to win medals at major international sport competitions. Kikulis et al. (1995) found that in order to make a complete transition to an organization that was run by professionals assisted by volunteers, which is what the QPP advocated, the decision-making structure of these organizations would have to change. In part in reaction to the QPP, Sport Canada initiated a programme for domestic sport. Again, while not expressed as a policy, the programme gave some direction to national sport organizations on how they should be structured in order to develop their domestic sport programmes. Thibault et al. (1993) suggested that the direction an organization took as regards domestic sport would be determined by its programme attractiveness and its competitive position. Programme attractiveness would be measured by a sport's fundability, its client base, its volunteer appeal, and its support group appeal. Competitive position would be measured by sports equipment cost and affiliation fees. Using these two dimensions they constructed a 2×2 matrix. A sport's domestic direction was determined by where it fell on the matrix. Sports that had a strong competitive position and high programme attractiveness were referred to as 'enhancers' and included such sports as rugby and volleyball. A sport which had a weak competitive position and high programme attractiveness was referred to as a 'refiner' and this category included such sports as figure skating and tennis. A sport which had a strong competitive position and low programme attractiveness was termed an 'innovator' and this included such sports as cycling and field hockey. A sport which was low on both programme attractiveness and competitive position was termed an 'explorer' and this category included sports such as equestrian events and yachting.

In one of the few studies that sought to explain the policy-making process in organizations below a national level, Pitter (2009) looked at the province of Nova Scotia, Canada, focusing on the politics of recreational sport, as well as environmental and health policy. He argued that the policy created by the Nova Scotia government wass under attack from what was termed 'the Kieran Pathways Society', an organization that supported an active transportation system within the province.

Harris and colleagues (2009) examined whether government policy could be delivered through voluntary sport organizations in six counties in eastern England. Measuring the perception of club members about government expectations for sport clubs to serve public policy, and considering the current pressures faced by clubs, the research cast doubt upon the feasibility of such a sport policy. Skille (2008) focused on developing a theoretical framework for the implementation of policy by sport clubs. He presented an alternative framework that focused on the implementation of policy which considered the local context.

As Henry et al. (2005) noted, despite the appearance in recent years of a number of texts dealing explicitly with comparative (and transnational) analysis in the field of sport and leisure policy and management (cf. Bramham et al., 1993; Chalip et al., 1996; Houlihan, 1997), there is still considerable scope for research on sport policy. As governments become increasingly involved in shaping the sport delivery system through **sport funding** and the policy-making process, research focused on how this is affecting sport organizations over time is needed. This research may focus on whether government intervention affects efficiency, or changes structures and cultures or decision making within sport organizations, as well as document the implications this may have for those managing or aspiring to manage within the sport industry. As clubs come under increasing pressure to professionalize, it will be interesting to see if their approach to government becomes more proactive and professional in turn so that they might take a more active role in influencing government policy and seek to control this uncertain element of their environment.

To understand policy more fully, the reader may refer to the concepts of **strategy**, **governance**, **voluntary**, **sport participation**, **sport funding and finance** and **sport organization**.

FURTHER READING

For some further reading on this concept, we would recommend the following:

Enjolras, B. and Waldahl, R.H. (2007) Policy-making in sport: the Norwegian case. *International Review for the Sociology of Sport*, 42: 201–216.
Henry, I., Amar, M., Al-Tauqi, M. and Lee, P.C. (2005) A typology of approaches to comparative analysis of sports policy. *Journal of Sport Management*, 19: 480–496.
Nicholson, M., Hoye, R. and Houlihan, B. (2011) *Participation in Sport: International Policy Perspectives*. Abingdon: Routledge.
Skille, E. (2008) Understanding sport clubs as sport policy implementers: a theoretical framework for the analysis of the implementation of central sport policy through local and voluntary sport organizations. *International Review for the Sociology of Sport*, 43: 181–200.

BIBLIOGRAPHY

Bramham, E., Henry, I., Mommaas, H. and Van der Poel, H. (eds) (1993) *Leisure Policies in Europe*. Wallingford: CAB International.
Chalip, L. (1996) Critical policy analysis: the illustrative case of New Zealand sport policy development. *Journal of Sport Management*, 10: 310–324.
Chalip, L., Johnson, A. and Stachura, L. (1996) *National Sports Policies: An International Handbook*. London: Greenwood.
Commission on the Future of Volunteering (2008) *Manifesto for Change*. Volunteering England, www.volcomm.org.uk
Dulac, C. and Henry, I. (2001) Sport and social regulation in the city: the cases of Grenoble and Sheffield. *Society and Leisure/Loisir et société*, 24(1): 47–76.
Enjolras, B. and Waldahl, R.H. (2007) Policy-making in sport: the Norwegian case. *International Review for the Sociology of Sport*, 42: 201–216.

Gratton, C. (1999) *COMPASS 1999: A project seeking the coordinated monitoring of participation in sports in Europe*. UK Sport and Italian Olympic Committee. London: UK Sport.

Harris, S., Mori, K. and Collins, M. (2009) Great expectations: voluntary sports clubs and their role in delivering national policy for English sport. *Voluntas*, 20(4): 405–423.

Henry, I. and Nassis, E. (1999) Sport, policy and clientelism in contemporary Greece. *International Review for the Sociology of Sport*, 34(1): 43–58.

Henry, I. and Uchiumi, K. (2001) Political ideology, modernity and sports policy: a comparative analysis of sports policy in Britain and Japan. *Hitotsubashi Journal of Social Sciences*, 33(2): 161–185.

Henry, I., Amar, M., Al-Tauqi, M. and Lee, P.C. (2005) A typology of approaches to comparative analysis of sports policy. *Journal of Sport Management*, 19: 480–496.

Houlihan, B. (1997) *Sport, Policy, and Politics: A Comparative Analysis*. London: Routledge.

Jones, H. (1989) *The Economic Impact and Importance of Sport: A European Study*. Strasbourg: Council of Europe.

Kikulis, L., Slack, T. and Hinings, C.R. (1995) Does decision making make a difference? Patterns of change within Canadian national sport organizations. *Journal of Sport Management*, 9: 273–299.

Maguire, J. (1999) *Global Sport: Identities,Societies, Civilizations*. Oxford: Polity.

Nicholson, M., Hoye, R. and Houlihan, B. (2011) *Participation in Sport: International Policy Perspectives*. Abingdon: Routledge.

Paramio Salcines, J. (1999) Leisure, culture and urban regeneration strategies in Britain and Spain. Unpublished doctoral dissertation, Loughborough University, Loughborough, UK.

Piggin, J., Jackson, S.J. and Lewis, M. (2009) Knowledge, power and politics: contesting 'evidence-based' national sport policy. *International Review for the Sociology of Sport*, 44: 87–101.

Pitter, R. (2009) Finding the Kieran Way: recreational sport, health, and environmental policy in Nova Scotia. *Journal of Sport and Social Issues*, 33: 331–351.

Rodgers, B. (1978) *Rationalising Sports Policies: Sport in its Social Context: International Comparisons*. Strasbourg: Council of Europe.

Skille, E. (2008) Understanding sport clubs as sport policy implementers: a theoretical framework for the analysis of the implementation of central sport policy through local and voluntary sport organizations. *International Review for the Sociology of Sport*, 43: 181–200.

Skirstad, B. and Felde, K. (1996) Sports policy in Norway. In L. Chalip, A. Johnson and L. Stachura (eds), *National Sport Policies: An International Handbook*. London: Greenwood.

Szalai, A. (ed.) (1972) *The Use of Time*. The Hague: Mouton.

Thibault, L., Slack, T. and Hinings, C.R. (1993) A framework for the analysis of strategy in voluntary sport organizations. *Journal of Sport Management*, 7: 25–43.

Sport Tourism

The current trend in sport tourism is to associate its definition to (sport) event tourism, although a definition of sport(s) tourism necessarily includes a reflection on the concepts of sport and tourism, as well as an interaction between activities, people, and places.

As Deery et al. (2004: 235) stated, the concept of sport tourism 'is fraught by definitional issues'. Beyond trying to define the terms 'sport' and 'tourism', the main issue is one of broadness *vs.* focus in defining the concept of sport tourism. That is, should all tourists who happen to undertake some sport or see sport (either actively or passively) be considered sport tourists or should the term be reserved for tourists who proactively travel to go and see or be part of a specific event? For example, in her introduction to a special issue on sport tourism in the *Journal of Sport Management*, Heather Gibson (2003) suggested that there were three types of sport tourism: travel to actively participate in sport; travel to watch sport; travel to a nostalgia-related sport attraction/place (e.g., sports halls of fame, former Olympic Games stadia and other famous facilities, sports-themed cruises). In contrast, Deery et al. argued that sport tourism was 'essentially event tourism and, as such, it is governed by the issues that effect [*sic*] events and event management' (2004: 235). They pointed out that tourists' travel motivations were central to the discussion, whereby the degree to which sport drives the reason for the travel and the actual tourism experience (i.e., you happen to take part in a sport event *vs.* you are going to a destination precisely in order to take part in that sport event) determines whether or not we are discussing tourism sport *vs.* sport tourism (see also Crompton, 1979; Faulkner et al., 1998; Gammon and Robinson, 2003).

Deery et al. (2004) suggest a more focused definition because of the need for effective market segmentation (i.e., the importance of a consumer motivation approach). Moreover, they built an argument for the 'sport' in sport tourism being competitive sport, not recreation or leisure. As such, they also proposed that sport tourism must be event related; focused on competitive sport; inclusive of both active and passive participants; able to find the motivation to participate in sport tourism as being intentional; and inclusive of the specific outcomes of sport tourism for the individual, community, and state/nation.

Getz (1997, 1998, 2005) would likely agree with Deery et al.'s view as he typically uses the term 'tourism' with event and sport. He sees event tourism as a destination development and **marketing** strategy, which has as its goal a realization of the full economic benefits of an event using the perspective that tourists are potential customers. In this perspective, events become attractions, animators, image makers, and catalysts, and are associated with place marketing (Getz, 2005).

Chalip and colleagues (2003) would also agree with Deery et al.'s argument and Getz's perspective as they focus on the effect of an event's media (advertising and telecast), as well as destination advertising, on the destination's image and people's intention to visit, thus demonstrating event tourism and tourists as a consumer approach to the subject. Chalip et al. found that the destination advertising, event telecast, and event advertising 'each affected different dimensions of destination image' (2003: 214). As well as this, the destination's image impacted on the intention to visit. Interestingly, the effects of the different relationship results varied according to the targeted market (United States *vs.* New Zealand). Of note here is that Chalip and Leyns (2002) argued for the leveraging of the event for local businesses, which was seen as an impact in Deery et al.'s (2004) definition of sport tourism.

However, Fairley (2003) seemed to take the broader definitional approach to sport tourism in the same special issue of the *Journal of Sport Management* as Gibson (2003). Fairley examined fan travel behaviour, particularly nostalgia sport tourism. She identified five themes for nostalgia sport tourism – 'nostalgia as motive; norms and rituals as objects of nostalgia; best experience as object of nostalgia; nostalgia as a basis for trip suggestions; and nostalgia through socialization' (2003: 284). She suggested that group-based nostalgia played a more important role in fan travel behaviour than other forms.

This is in line with Weed's (2005) contention that the concept of sport tourism is too narrow and must be presented as sports tourism, that is, a 'synergistic phenomenon that is more than the simple combination of sport and tourism', and should include all forms of sporting activity (formal/informal, competitive/recreational, active/vicarious/passive) as well as other people (co-travellers, hosts, etc.) in order for participants to be able to experience a feeling of *communitas*. Weed also suggested that sports tourism should be defined as a social, economic and cultural phenomenon that stems from the unique interaction of activity (i.e., sports), people, and place (see Weed, 2005; Weed and Bull, 2004).

Weed's (2005) article provided a 'state of the field' overview of the concepts, issues and epistemologies surrounding sport tourism research. The key conceptual aspects discussed included the definitional aspects (as noted above), the heterogeneous nature of sports tourism, and the conceptualisation of sports tourism. In this vein, Higham and Hinch (2003) suggested that sport, space and time were three interrelated parts within a system of sport tourism. Here, sport's core elements included rules, competition and play. In turn, sport included space (or travel distance and location), place, and environment. Finally, time was defined according to the short, medium or long term. Hinch and Higham (2001, 2005) also provided a clear conceptualization of sport as a tourism attraction, noting the complexity and heterogeneity of the phenomenon.

Weed (2005) made some suggestions for various issues worth pursuing when doing sports tourism research, issues which would significantly contribute to the literature. He noted the need to understand: the social, economic, and cultural aspects of sports tourism; the sports tourism participation experiences, activities, people, and places; and the interaction between these activities, people, and places. To this end, Yoon et al. (2000) presented some characteristics and behaviours of festival/event tourists. They found that in contrast to other types of tourists, festival/event tourists were more likely 'to begin their trips during the summer months and to participate in a wide array of recreation activities on these trips' (2000: 33). In addition, the planning for these trips would also be typically done earlier, the length of time of the travel would tend to be longer and more money would tend to be spent by these tourists than other types of tourists. Nevertheless, more needed to be done on this issue.

However, this does not represent sufficient information. As Weed (2005) pointed out, there is a need to understand the positive aspects of these experiences and the reasons for these. This could then be related to the how and why of generated impacts and possible **policy** and any managerial implications. The impacts should be examined in greater detail as well. Work by Holger Preuss (2005) advanced the state of knowledge in terms of economic impact by providing a sophisticated model for this topic. As well as this, Costa and Chalip (2005) offered leveraging strategies based on the local interaction of activity, people, and place, which thereby informed local policy and practice. A word of caution on policy is warranted here. Weed (2003) noted that integrating sport and tourism policies may not be possible at the national level but could be done at the regional level in the United Kingdom. In making this assessment, he used six suggested influences – ideology, definitions, regional contexts, government policy, organizational culture and structure, and individuals. Of course, this assessment would need to be validated in other countries which have different structures.

Sport tourism is arguably one key **legacy** and/or positive outcome of hosting a major sporting event or **mega event**. Again, a caveat should be issued here. While certain tourists may come to a destination to see or be part of a given event, others may avoid the destination because of the increased crowds and transportation/accommodation issues, and residents of the host destination leaving because of the increased crowds and 'hassle'. Ritchie and Smith (1991) also cautioned that while annual sporting events were better for increasing the level of awareness and modified image of the host region (the city of Calgary in their case and the Calgary Stampede *vs.* the 1988 Calgary Winter Olympic Games), there was a decay in that awareness and it was not obvious how image/awareness translated into tourist receipts. However, quite a few researchers are finding that using events (sport tourism) for the sustainable development of a host region is beneficial to that host region (cf. Daniels and Norman, 2003; Gibson et al., 2005; Hall, 1992; Jones, 2001; Lim and Patterson, 2008; Liu, 2006; Ritchie, 1984; Woodside et al., 2002).

Finally, Weed (2005) noted that since the seminal works by Anthony (1966) and Glyptis (1982), the field of sport tourism had suffered from building bricks instead of buildings, that is, from publishing mainly (positivistic) empirical work that did little to truly advance the state of knowledge. This was evidenced by Weed's (2004, 2005) four-year survey (2000–2003) of the sports tourism literature, where he found that 42 per cent of published articles were on sports event tourism (which may explain the trend in defining sport tourism as essentially event tourism), while only 17 per cent examined outdoor/adventure sports tourism. The topics of interest focused mainly on experience/perceptions/profiles and impacts (35 per cent and 32 per cent respectively). Only 6 per cent examined conceptualization/definitional issues. Most (87 per cent) research was positivistic in nature and employed a quantitative methodology. This explained the lack of answers on the how and why. Using other approaches, such as a critical realist approach (see for example Downward, 2005) and qualitative methodologies, would help in this matter.

To understand sport tourism more fully, the reader may refer to the concepts of **sport marketing**, **legacy**, **sport policy** and **mega events** that can be found elsewhere in this book.

FURTHER READING

For some further reading on this concept, we would recommend the following:

Special issue of *Journal of Sport Management* (2003) 17(3), on sport tourism.

Special issue of *European Sport Management Quarterly* (2005) 5(3), on sport tourism theory and method.

Weed, M.E. and Bull, C.J. (2004) *Sports Tourism: Participants, Policy, and Providers*. London: Elsevier.

BIBLIOGRAPHY

Anthony, D. (1966) *Sport and Tourism*. London: CCPR/ICSPE Bureau for Public Relations.

Chalip, L. and Leyns, A. (2002) Local business leveraging of a sport event: managing an event for economic benefit. *Journal of Sport Management*, 16(2): 132–158.

Chalip, L., Green, B.C. and Hill, B. (2003) Effects of sport event media on destination image and intention to visit. *Journal of Sport Management*, 17: 214–234.

Costa, C.A. and Chalip, L. (2005) Adventure sport tourism in rural revitalisation: an ethnographic evaluation. *European Sport Management Quarterly*, 5(3): 257–279.

Crompton, J. (1979) Motivations for pleasure vacation. *Annals of Tourism Research*, 6: 408–424.

Daniels, M.J. and Norman, W.C. (2003) Estimating the economic impacts of seven regular sport tourism events. *Journal of Sport Tourism*, 8: 214–222.

Deery, M., Jago, L. and Fredline, L. (2004) Sport tourism or event tourism: are they one and the same? *Journal of Sport Tourism*, 9(3): 235–245.

Downward, P. (2005) Critical (realist) reflection on policy and management research in sport, tourism and sports tourism. *European Sport Management Quarterly*, 5(3): 303–320.

Fairley, S. (2003) In search of relived social experience: group-based nostalgia sport tourism. *Journal of Sport Management*, 17: 284–304.

Faulkner, B., Tideswell, C. and Weston, A. (1998) Leveraging tourism benefits from the Sydney 2000 Olympics: Keynote presentation. Paper presented at the Fourth Annual Conference of the Sport Management Association of Australia and New Zealand, Gold Coast, Australia.

Gammon, S. and Robinson, T. (2003) Sport and tourism: a conceptual framework. *Journal of Sport Tourism*, 8(1): 21–26.

Getz, D. (1997) *Event Management and Event Tourism*. Elmsford, NY: Cognizant Communication Corp.

Getz, D. (1998) Trends, strategies, and issues in sport-event tourism. *Sport Marketing Quarterly*, 7(2): 8–13.

Getz, D. (2005) *Event Management and Event Tourism* (2nd edition). Elmsford, NY: Cognizant Communication Corp.

Gibson, H. (2003) Sport tourism: an introduction to the special issue. *Journal of Sport Management*, 17: 205–213.

Gibson, H., McIntyre, S., MacKay, S. and Riddington, G. (2005) The economic impact of sports, sporting events, and sports tourism in the UK: the DREAM Model. *European Sport Management Quarterly*, 5(3): 321–332.

Glyptis, S. (1982) *Sport and Tourism in Western Europe*. London: British Travel Education Trust.

Hall, C.M. (1992) *Hallmark Tourist Events: Impacts, Management and Planning*. London: Belhaven.

Higham, J.E.S. and Hinch, T.D. (2003) Sport, space, and time: effects of the Otago Highlanders franchise on tourism. *Journal of Sport Management*, 17: 235–257.

Hinch, T.D. and Higham, J.E.S. (2001) Sport tourism: a framework for research. *International Journal of Tourism Research*, 3: 45–58.

Hinch, T.D. and Higham, J.E.S. (2005) Sport, tourism and authenticity. *European Sport Management Quarterly*, 5(3): 243–256.

Jones, C. (2001) Mega-events and host-region impacts: determining the true worth of the 1999 Rugby World Cup. *International Journal of Tourism Research*, 3: 241–251.

Lim, C.C. and Patterson, I. (2008) Sport tourism on the islands: the impact of an international mega golf event. *Journal of Sport Tourism*, 13(2): 115–133.

Liu, F.-M. (2006) Analysis on influential factors of Olympic tourism development. *Journal of Chengdu Sport University*, 32(2): 15–18.

Preuss, H. (2005) The economic impact of visitors at major multi-sport events. *European Sport Management Quarterly*, 5(3): 281–301.

Ritchie, J.R.B. (1984) Assessing the impact of hallmark events: conceptual and research issues. *Journal of Travel Research*, 23(1): 2–11.

Ritchie, J.R.B. and Smith, B.H. (1991) The impact of a mega-event on host region awareness: a longitudinal study. *Journal of Travel Research*, 30(1): 3–10.

Weed, M.E. (2003) Why the two won't tango! Explaining the lack of integrated policies for sport and tourism in the UK. *Journal of Sport Management*, 17: 258–283.

Weed, M.E. (2004) Sports tourism research 2000–2003: a systematic review of knowledge and a meta-evaluation of method. Paper presented at the Twelfth European Association of Sports Tourism, Sheffield, UK.

Weed, M.E. (2005) Sports tourism theory and method: concepts, issues and epistemologies. *European Sport Management Quarterly*, 5(3): 229–242.

Weed, M.E. and Bull, C.J. (2004) *Sports Tourism: Participants, Policy, and Providers*. London: Elsevier.

Woodside, A.G., Spurr, R., March, R. and Clark, H. (2002) The dynamics of traveler destination awareness and search for information associated with hosting the Olympic Games: theory and preliminary test results on the impact of the 2000 Sydney Olympic Games on international tourism behavior. *International Journal of Sports Marketing and Sponsorship*, 4: 127–150.

Yoon, S., Spencer, D.M., Holecek, D.F. and Kim, D.-K. (2000) A profile of Michigan's festival and special event tourism market. *Event Management*, 6: 33–44.

Stakeholders

Stakeholders are the individuals, groups and/or organizations contributing, voluntarily or involuntarily, to a focal organization's activities, and/or who may benefit or bear the risks of these activities.

Stakeholders were first, albeit broadly, defined by Freeman (1984) as all individuals, groups, and/or organizations which can impact or be affected by an organization's actions. They have alternatively been called constituents. Freeman also proposed that stakeholder groups surrounded the organization of interest in a hub-and-spoke model (although Rowley (1997) later argued that theorists should move beyond this dyadic ties approach). Since 1984, stakeholder theory has sought to develop the concept of stakeholders, examine stakeholder characteristics, describe how organizations see and deal with stakeholders, and outline the types of behaviours a stakeholder can exhibit – all in order to enable managers of a given organization reason to be aware of their organization's stakeholders so as to be more **effective**, **efficient**, and successful in its endeavours.

Organizations do not operate in isolation; they have stakeholders that surround them. Various researchers have sought to identify the stakeholders in an organization's environment and classify them. Three main identification and classification frameworks are worth mentioning here. First, Clarkson (1995) argued that an organization's stakeholders should include its employees, shareholders, customers, suppliers, and public stakeholders. Clarkson then offered the following stakeholder classification: primary stakeholders and secondary stakeholders. Stakeholder groups who are essential to the survival of the organization are termed 'primary stakeholders'. Stakeholder groups who can impact or be impacted by an organization's actions, but are not engaged in direct transactions with it and nor are they essential to the survival of the organization, are 'secondary stakeholders'.

While the primary and secondary stakeholder group classification is simple, it does not provide much in the way of stakeholder salience or relative perceived stakeholder importance. A framework which accounts for this is the one by Mitchell et al. (1997). Mitchell and his colleagues argued that stakeholders could be recognized as such by a manager because they would possess one or more of the following characteristics: **power**, legitimacy, and/or urgency.

Power is described as the ability to influence outcomes according to stakeholders' desires, more so than others. Mitchell et al. offered three types of power based on Etzioni's (1964) work: utilitarian power (the use of material resources or financial incentives), normative power (the use of symbolic influences), and coercive power (the use of force or threat). The second characteristic found in Mitchell et al.'s typology is legitimacy, which is apparent when a stakeholder's action or claim is socially acceptable, expected, and/or appropriate, depending on the prevailing standards of the network within which the stakeholders and organization operate (Agle et al., 1999; Mitchell et al., 1997; Scott and Lane, 2000). The third characteristic in Mitchell et al.'s typology is urgency. If the stakeholders' claims on the organization's attention are time sensitive and critical, from the stakeholder's point of view, they are seen as being urgent. Mitchell et al. (1997) then argued that the more characteristics a stakeholder possesses, the more the organization's managers must pay attention to that stakeholder. Agle et al. (1999) in turn verified the statistical significance of the three proposed characteristics for CEOs.

While both Clarkson's (1995) and Mitchell et al.'s (1997) classifications are widely used, a more recent classification has been proposed. Post et al. (2002: 19) argued that 'stakeholders in a corporation are the individuals and constituencies that contribute, either voluntarily or involuntarily, to its wealth-creating capacity and activities, and that are therefore its potential beneficiaries and/or risk bearers.' They then proposed that stakeholders ought to be defined according to the following dimensions: resource base, industry structure, and social-political arena. Post et al. illustrated the stakeholder environment as one of concentric circles. The inner part is of course the organization, while the first circle is the resource-based stakeholders as they interact directly with the organization through resource exchanges, which are a necessity for organizational survival. These stakeholders include customers and users, share-owners/investors and lenders, and employees. The second circle is the industry structure stakeholders, which includes such groups as regulatory authorities, supply chain associates, and joint venture partners and alliances. Finally, the outermost circle is the social–political arena stakeholders, which will include private organizations, governments, and local communities and their citizens.

The previous classifications provide various ways for managers to group stakeholders and classify them. However, stakeholders are typically placed in broad groups (all municipal, state/provincial, and federal governments are placed within the 'government' stakeholder group) and some stakeholder theorists have warned that the various stakeholders within each group will not necessarily behave in the same manner. More precisely, we cannot assume that all stakeholder groups are homogeneous. There is heterogeneity. In their study on institutional investors, Ryan and Schneider (2003) highlighted the heterogeneity (and power) of this stakeholder group by using Mitchell et al.s framework. The authors were encouraging researchers to re-examine corporate governance in light of the power and heterogeneity of investors in corporate governance. Janssens and Seyvaeve (2000) also touched upon heterogeneity, this time in the school system. They showed how a school based its curriculum on heterogeneity.

Studying stakeholders and utilizing stakeholder theory are increasing within the literature on the management of sport. Chalip (1996) argued that proper **policy** methods would help to empower stakeholders in his *Journal of Sport Management* article 'Critical policy analysis: the illustrative case of New Zealand sport policy development'; Mason and Slack (1997) used stakeholder theory in relation to hockey; and Wolfe and Putler (1999) examined the differing perceptions of athletic programmes according to stakeholder groups in their article 'Perceptions of intercollegiate athletic programs: priorities and tradeoffs', and then went on to look at the stakeholder group homogeneity–heterogeneity aspect in greater depth in their (2002) article 'How tight are the ties that bind stakeholder groups?' In a similar vein, Trail and Chelladurai (2000) examined the 'Perceptions of goals and processes of intercollegiate athletics' in the *Journal of Sport Management*, while Friedman and Mason (2004) argued that a stakeholder approach was appropriate for examining public policy decision making related to sports facilities. With Parent they then went on to suggest that stakeholder theory can be a useful framework for issues management in sport in their article 'Building a framework for issues management in sport through stakeholder theory' in the *European Sport Management Quarterly* (Friedman et al., 2004). Future research could utilize stakeholder theory to further examine the issues and strategies faced by organizing committees. Indeed, in their efforts to address issues of **corruption** in **sport organizations**, Mason and colleagues (2006) used agency theory to study the role of IOC members in the bidding process for the Olympic Games. Finally, Wolfe et al. (2005) utilized stakeholders and stakeholder theory as an example when they provided a rationale for using sport as a good research context for management research.

Although there has already been considerable attention paid to stakeholders in the mainstream management literature and in literature concerning the management of sport, there is still some scope for further study on this concept. The behaviour of individual stakeholders and their interaction need to be documented as sports organizations change, in order to further develop our understanding of ways to manage stakeholders in the dynamic sport industry. This demands research that will be able to recognize the changing nature of both stakeholder motives and the situations within the sport industry in which they are apparent.

To understand stakeholders more fully, the reader may refer to the concepts of **effectiveness/efficiency**, **power**, **sport policy**, **corruption** and **sport organization**.

FURTHER READING

For some further reading on this concept, we would recommend the following:

Friedman, M.T., Parent, M.M. and Mason, D.S. (2004) Building a framework for issues management in sport through stakeholder theory. *European Sport Management Quarterly*, 4: 170–190.

Frooman, J. (2010) The issue network: reshaping the stakeholder model. *Canadian Journal of Administrative Sciences*, 27(2): 161–173.

BIBLIOGRAPHY

Agle, B.R., Mitchell, R.K. and Sonnenfeld, J.A. (1999) Who matters to CEOs? An investigation of stakeholder attributes and salience, corporate performance, and CEO values. *Academy of Management Journal*, 42(5): 507–525.

Chalip, L. (1996) Critical policy analysis: the illustrative case of New Zealand sport policy development. *Journal of Sport Management*, 10(3): 310–324.

Clarkson, M.B.E. (1995) A stakeholder framework for analyzing and evaluating corporate social performance. *Academy of Management Review*, 20: 92–117.

Etzioni, A. (1964) *Modern Organizations*. Englewood Cliffs, NJ: Prentice-Hall.

Freeman, R.E. (1984) *Strategic Management: A Stakeholder Approach*. Boston, MA: Pitman.

Friedman, M.T. and Mason, D.S. (2004) A stakeholder approach to understanding economic development decision making: public subsidies for professional sport facilities. *Economic Development Quarterly*, 18: 236–254.

Friedman, M.T., Parent, M.M. and Mason, D.S. (2004) Building a framework for issues management in sport through stakeholder theory. *European Sport Management Quarterly*, 4: 170–190.

Janssens, M. and Seyvaeve, K. (2000) Collaborating to desegregate a 'black' school. *Journal of Applied Behavioral Science*, 36(1): 70–90.

Mason, D.S. and Slack, T. (1997) Appropriate opportunism or bad business practice? Stakeholder theory, ethics, and the franchise relocation. *Marquette Sport Law Review*, 7(2): 399–426.

Mason, D.S., Thibault, L. and Misener, L. (2006) Research and reviews: an agency theory perspective on corruption in sport: the case of the International Olympic Committee. *Journal of Sport Management*, 20: 52.

Mitchell, R.K., Agle, B.R. and Wood, D.J. (1997) Toward a theory of stakeholder identification and salience: defining the principle of who and what really counts. *Academy of Management Review*, 22: 853–886.

Post, J.E., Preston, L.E. and Sachs, S. (2002) *Redefining the Corporation: Stakeholder Management and Organizational Wealth* (1st edition). Stanford, CA: Stanford University Press.

Putler, D.S. and Wolfe, R.A. (1999) Perceptions of intercollegiate athletic programs: priorities and tradeoffs. *Sociology of Sport Journal*, 16(4): 301–325.

Rowley, T.J. (1997) Moving beyond dyadic ties: a network theory of stakeholder influences. *Academy of Management Review*, 22: 887–910.

Ryan, L.V. and Schneider, M. (2003) Institutional investor power and heterogeneity: implications for agency and stakeholder theories. *Business and Society*, 42: 398–429.

stakeholders

Scott, S.G. and Lane, V.R. (2000) A stakeholder approach to organizational identity. *Academy of Management Review*, 25(1): 43–62.

Trail, G. and Chelladurai, P. (2000) Perceptions of goals and processes of intercollegiate athletics: a case study. *Journal of Sport Management*, 14(2): 154–178.

Wolfe, R. and Putler, D.S. (2002) How tight are the ties that bind stakeholder groups? *Organization Science*, 14: 54–80.

Wolfe, R.A., Weick, K.E., Usher, J.M., Terborg, J.R., Poppo, L., Murrell, A.J., et al. (2005) Sport and organizational studies exploring synergy. *Journal of Management Inquiry*, 14(2): 182–210.

Strategy

> *Strategy can be defined, formally or informally,* a priori *or* post hoc, *as a plan, ploy, pattern, position, perspective, tool, or set of goals, which indicate how to use resources and implement courses of action within an organization. However, it can also be seen as a broader field of study which is interested in helping organizations gain a competitive advantage.*

Strategy may be defined in various ways. The first person to truly do so was Alfred Chandler (1962). He defined strategy as the identification of an organization's long-term goals and objectives, as well as the allocation of resources and the implementation of courses of action needed for reaching the stated **goals**. Whereas Chandler presented a very formalized concept of strategy, Andrews (1980) noted that a strategy may not be enacted consciously or formerly planned, yet still be a strategy. Moreover, the absence of strategy is, in fact, a strategy. Chandler also concentrated on large companies, hence his understanding of strategy is biased towards those types of organizations.

Mintzberg (1987) argued that strategy cannot be defined in advance; it only becomes clear when seen as a *post-hoc* analysis. In this light, strategy can be present in various forms. Mintzberg presented his 5 Ps of strategy: strategy can be a plan, but also a ploy, a pattern of action, a position, or a perspective. Regardless of the name or definition placed on the concept of strategy, Porter (1996) has also argued that it is about fit between an organization's various processes. He also pushes his argument further by stating that it is better to talk of tools for gaining a competitive advantage than strategy.

While strategy can be seen as a plan or tool or set of goals, it can also be seen as a broader field. Researchers examining strategy have been interested in how it can improve an organization's outcomes, or more precisely, how it can increase **performance**, competitive advantage and overall organizational **effectiveness** (see Venkatraman and Ramanujam, 1986). To examine these questions, strategy researchers can adopt a variety of perspectives. One of the most popular approaches is industrial organizational (IO) economics, which informed Michael Porter's work on the structure-conduct-performance (SCP) paradigm. Within this paradigm,

key concepts in sport management

Porter (1980) presented his Five Forces Model. This model focuses on an industry's structure, specifically identifying an organization's rivalry, the barriers to new entrants, buyers, suppliers, and the threat of substitution. Another popular approach is the resource-based view of the firm. Wernerfelt (1984) and Barney (1991) presented a view whereby resources would be unequally distributed between organizations, and these organizations' competitive advantages would be rare, valuable, inimitable, immobile, and sustainable resources.

While Stonehouse and colleagues (2007) claimed that the research on strategy was in its infancy, there have been many different approaches in comparison to Porter's competitive positioning school of thought. McKiernan (1997), for example, identified four, while Mintzberg et al. (1998) suggested ten different perspectives from which the research on strategy can and indeed has developed.

One approach currently gaining popularity is transaction-cost economics. Its main idea is that organizations engage in transactions with other organizations; these transactions, however, must be done to minimize production and transactions costs (Williamson, 1979). For example, vertical integration is one form of organizing transactions. Vertical integration can be forward (e.g., buying a distributor) or backward (e.g., buying a supplier). D'Aveni and Ravenscraft (1994) held that such transactions actually decreased costs and created efficiencies. However, they also found only a weak effect of vertical integration on organizational performance.

Within the literature that looks at the management of sport, there have been a growing number of studies focusing on the concept of strategy. This is significant because all sport organizations will have a strategy. Some researchers have examined specific aspects of strategy. For example, Moloney-Smith (1995) explored the idea of geographical differences in strategy in the context of professional ice hockey, while Slack and Parent (2006) discussed two levels of strategies, i.e., corporate-level and business-level. Corporate-level strategies consisted of 'synergies among the business units and with the corporation' (Yavitz and Newman, 1982: 60). For example, a media organization which creates a sports team, such as the Disney Corporation founding the Anaheim Mighty Ducks (a National Hockey League team), is using this acquisition as a strategy to obtain more content for its media organizations to transmit. Acquisitions are thus growth strategies; other types of corporate-level strategies include stability, defensive, and combination. In turn, business-level strategies are found for organizations with multiple divisions where each division operates in a different market. Business-level strategies allow a division to compete, and gain a competitive advantage, in a specific market. Therefore, each division may very well have different business-level strategies but these should all fit with the corporate-level strategies. Porter (1980) provided three basic business-level strategies that a manager can use: cost leadership (lower cost products than the competition), differentiation (the presentation of product or service as being unique in the market), and focus (serving the needs of a specific, targeted market) strategies. When organizations fail to make the right choices or find themselves in the midst of change, they may, as Porter (1980) terms it, end up stuck in the middle.

Amis et al. (1997) used the resourced-based view of the firm, as developed in the strategy literature, to examine sport sponsorship. Sponsorship as a tool for companies to gain a competitive advantage has been utilized with varying degrees of success

(Amis et al., 1997) and the resource-based view was adopted in order to demonstrate that companies' sponsorship investment returns can be anticipated. Thibault and Harvey (1997) examined another strategy, inter-organizational linkages, in their article 'Fostering interorganizational linkages in the Canadian sport delivery system'. In another article entitled 'Urban revitalization: the use of festival time strategies', Hughes (1999) studied festivals as strategies used by cities to help re-image themselves. Likewise Goslin (1996) also argued that human resource management must be part of a sport development strategy within the context of South African communities. And in addition to this, Legg (2003) focused his efforts on determining an appropriate model of strategy formation in his article 'Organizational strategy in amateur sport organizations: a case study'.

Byers and Slack (2001) looked at strategic decision making in small firms in the leisure industry. Their research sought to identify the factors which constrained small firm owners and owner/managers from engaging in strategic decision making and provided evidence from 16 in-depth interviews that a range of factors were responsible for explaining decision making in this context. The key factor which was present in nearly all cases was that owners had started their business as the result of a hobby and this 'hobby motive' meant that individuals often wanted both to continue to engage in their hobby and operate as a business: this in turn presented considerable time constraints on their focusing on strategically developing these businesses.

Other researchers who have looked at the management of sport have examined organizational performance using one or more strategic perspectives. Mauws et al. (2003), for example, use both the SCP paradigm and the resource-based view of the firm to study performance in professional sports teams in their article 'Thinking strategically about professional sports'. Some sport strategy research has taken a broader perspective in regard to strategy. For example, Sutton and Migliore (1988) provided nine steps for the strategic planning of intercollegiate athletics programmes. Using a more theoretical approach, Slack and Hinings (1992) included strategy as one component of organizational **change** (with structure and processes) in their article 'Understanding change in national sport organizations: an integration of theoretical perspectives'. Thibault et al. (1994) in turn examined strategic tendencies in national sport organizations in their article 'Strategic planning for nonprofit sport organizations: empirical verification of a framework'.

Overall, research on strategy most often aims to develop our understanding of the strategy process, whether planned or emergent within an organization. Research has shown that a variety of factors can influence how strategy is formed and implemented within organizations, including the external environment or internal resources. Some research has focused on elements of the strategy process, such as strategic decision making, strategy formulation, strategic planning or strategy implementation, rather than the whole process. In research on the management of sport, scholars have used the mainstream strategy literature to help understand the strategy process in sport organizations. One area of research that requires further investigation is strategy development and implementation in voluntary sport organizations and the role of strategy in managing organizational change.

To understand strategy more fully, the reader may refer to the concepts of **organizational goals, performance management, change** and **effectiveness** that can be found elsewhere in this book.

FURTHER READING

For some further reading on this concept, we would recommend the following:

Mintzberg, H. (1987) The strategy concept I: five Ps for strategy. *California Management Review,* 30(1): 11–24.
Porter, M.E. (1996) What is strategy? *Harvard Business Review,* 74(6): 61–78.
Thibault, L., Slack, T. and Hinings, C.R. (1994) Strategic planning for nonprofit sport organizations: empirical verification of a framework. *Journal of Sport Management,* 8(3): 218–233.

BIBLIOGRAPHY

Amis, J., Pant, N. and Slack, T. (1997) Achieving a sustainable competitive advantage: a resource-based view of sport sponsorship. *Journal of Sport Management,* 11(1): 80–96.
Andrews, K.R. (1980) *The Concept of Corporate Strategy* (revised edition). Homewood, IL: Irwin.
Barney, J.B. (1991) Firm resources and sustained competitive advantage. *Journal of Management,* 17: 99–120.
Byers, T. and Slack, T. (2001) strategic decision-making in small businesses within the leisure industry. *Journal of Leisure Research,* 33(2):121–136.
Chandler, A.D. (1962) *Strategy and Structure.* Cambridge, MA: MIT Press.
D'Aveni, R.A. and Ravenscraft, D.J. (1994) Economies of integration versus bureaucracy costs: does vertical integration improve performance? *Academy of Management Journal,* 37(5): 1167–1206.
Goslin, A. (1996) Human resource management as a fundamental aspect of a sport development strategy in South African communities. *Journal of Sport Management,* 10(2): 207–217.
Hughes, G. (1999) Urban revitalization: the use of festive time strategies. *Leisure Studies,* 18(2): 119–135.
Legg, D. (2003) Organizational strategy in amateur sport organization: a case study. *International Journal of Sport Management,* 4(3): 205–223.
Mauws, M.K., Mason, D.S. and Foster, W.M. (2003) Thinking strategically about professional sports. *European Sport Management Quarterly,* 3(3): 145–164.
McKiernan, P. (1997) Strategy past, strategy futures. *Long Range Planning,* 30(5): 690–708.
Mintzberg, H. (1987) The strategy concept I: five Ps for strategy. *California Management Review,* 30(1): 11–24.
Mintzberg, H., Ahlstrand, B. and Lampel, J. (1998) *Strategy Safari: A Guided Tour Through the Wilds of Strategic Management.* New York: Free Press.
Moloney-Smith, S. (1995) Meltdown in marketing professional ice hockey: a survey exploring geographical differences in strategy. *Sport Marketing Quarterly,* 4(3): 17–23.
Porter, M.E. (1980) *Competitive Strategy.* New York: Free Press.
Porter, M.E. (1996) What is strategy? *Harvard Business Review,* 74(6): 61–78.
Slack, T. and Hinings, C.R. (1992) Understanding change in national sport organizations: an integration of theoretical perspectives. *Journal of Sport Management,* 6(2): 114–132.
Slack, T. and Parent, M.M. (2006) *Understanding Sport Organizations: The Application of Organization Theory* (2nd edition). Leeds: Human Kinetics Europe.
Stonehouse, G., Snowdon, B. and Porter, M. (2007) Competitive advantage revisited: Michael Porter on strategy and competitiveness. *Journal of International Business Studies,* 37(2): 163–176.

Sutton, W.A. and Migliore, R.H. (1988) Strategic long range planning for intercollegiate athletic programs. *Journal of Applied Research in Coaching and Athletics*, 3(4): 233–261.

Thibault, L. and Harvey, J. (1997) Fostering interorganizational linkages in the Canadian sport delivery system. *Journal of Sport Management*, 11(1): 45–68.

Thibault, L., Slack, T. and Hinings, C.R. (1994) Strategic planning for nonprofit sport organizations: empirical verification of a framework. *Journal of Sport Management*, 8(3): 218–233.

Venkatraman, N. and Ramanujam, V. (1986) Measurement of business performance in strategy research: a comparison of approaches. *Academy of Management Review*, 11: 801–814.

Wernerfelt, B. (1984) A resource-based view of the firm. *Strategic Management Journal*, 5: 171–180.

Williamson, O.E. (1979) Transaction-cost economics: the governance of contractual relations. *Journal of Law and Economics*, 22: 233–261.

Yavitz, B. and Newman, W.H. (1982) *Strategy in Action: The Execution, Politics, and Payoff of Business Planning*. New York: Free Press.

Strategic Alliances

> A strategic alliance is a partnership between two or more organizations, created in response to an environmental threat or opportunity, and resulting in mutual learning.

A strategic alliance is one form of **strategy**, increasingly adopted by firms to gain a competitive advantage. The theory is that it is more advantageous for the firms in the alliance to co-operate rather than compete. Strategic alliances are found when two or more groups/organizations come together to respond to a key opportunity or threat in the external environment, which results in organizational learning. The learning aspect distinguishes strategic alliances (such as joint ventures, collaborations and consortia) from other types of partnerships such as **networks** or virtual corporations, which are based solely on available skills (Child and Faulkner, 1998). Within strategic alliances, learning can take many forms including: forced, imitation/experimentation, blocked, received, integrative, segmented, and non-learning (Child and Markoczy, 1993). Examples of strategic alliances include Adidas and Stella McCartney joining forces to develop fashionable and trendy sportswear (joint venture); a local high school and track and field club coming together to build and manage an indoor sports field (collaboration); and the Disney Corporation with its multitude of sports teams, media and entertainment organizations, and stores (consortium).

The choice of a potential partner is dependent on many factors. First, there must be strategic fit. More precisely, partners' skills and assets must be compatible and complement each other. Second, there must be cultural fit. Partners' **organizational cultures** (such as their organizational stories, symbols, rituals, routines, structures, control mechanisms, employee orientation, and environmental orientation) must also be compatible in order to have a good fit between partners and potential success for the alliance (Child and Faulkner, 1998). Third, partner selection depends on the available information on the potential partners. Information may be freely available such as on television or the internet, or be found in previous relationships with the potential partner (Gulati, 1999). This information should pertain to the various forms of capital an organization/group possesses. The more forms of capital (technical, commercial and social) a potential partner has, the more attractive it is as a strategic alliance partner (Ahuja, 2000). Li and Rowley (2002) caution, though, that there is a tendency here to choose with whom the organization has had previous partnerships and doing so can result in inertia and a lack of innovation.

Faulkner (1995) presented strategic alliances as having three separate dimensions: a scope, a legal nature, and a number of partners. A strategic alliance's scope refers to its degree of complexity, which can range from highly focused to highly complex and broad. A strategic alliance's legal form refers to whether there is the creation of a legally separate organization, as in the case of joint ventures, when the strategic alliance is created. A strategic alliance's number of partners refers to the size of the alliance, from two partners (the most common) to a multitude.

Once the alliance has been negotiated, it must be managed and controlled. To do so, Child and Faulkner (1998) argue that a good alliance manager must be chosen. This manager must be able to be a decision maker, an internal integrator, an external integrator, and an information manager, all at the same time. The alliance manager must have a vision; be able to inspire trust, foster communication, and plan; and also be able to operationalize, all at the same time. To help in these tasks, **control** mechanisms must be put in place from the outset, including dispute-resolution mechanisms, authority (hierarchical and lateral) **structures**, information dissemination mechanisms, control over inputs, control over behaviours, control over outputs, the socialization of common values and adaptation, personal involvement, and a clear termination formula.

Research on alliances has presented varying models of alliance evolution. For example, Murray and Mahon (1993) presented a lifecycle model composed of a courtship phase, a negotiation phase, an alliance start-up phase, a maintenance phase, and finally three possible end phases (divorce, an amicable separation, or an extension of the alliance). Yet Ring and Van de Ven (1994) also argued for a repeating cycle of negotiation, commitment, and execution phases, underscoring the importance of continually revisiting the alliance's **organizational goals** and structure. In contrast, Bleeke and Ernst (1995) presented six different patterns of alliance evolution: inherently unstable alliances which are an alliance disaster; stable and long-lasting alliances showing the complementarity of the partners; two or more weak organizations hoping to become stronger by joining forces; bootstrap alliances with the stronger organization eventually buying the weaker organization; short-term alliances with usually the same end as the bootstrap alliance; and strong compatible partners creating a successful alliance but where one partner must sell out to the other because of lingering competitive tensions between the partners.

Current studies within the management literature typically fall within one of four areas of strategic alliances:

- *Partner choice* (e.g., Ahuja, 2000; Gulati, 1999; Podolny, 1993; Stuart, 2000): studies indicate, for example, that firms will enter into strategic alliances because of the need to access certain resources (physical or information). In addition here, researchers are interested in the benefits of choosing certain partners, especially those held to be 'better'; in such cases, a firm's choices of alliance partners can allow the firm to gain legitimacy and status.

- *Alliance manager characteristics and roles* (e.g., Child and Faulkner, 1998): some of the focus has been geared to understanding the characteristics that the key individual (whether from one of the alliance partners or someone from the outside) should possess in order to manage the alliance well enough for that alliance not only to perform but also to avoid or resolve potential conflicts between partners. For example, Child and Faulkner suggest that a successful alliance manager will be an internal and external integrator, a decision maker, and an information manager.
- *Alliance control* (e.g., Child and Faulkner, 1998; Geringer and Hébert, 1989; Kogut, 2000): some researchers examined the degree to which (and how) a partner within an alliance could control the other partner. Geringer and Hébert (1989) argued that this control could be described following three dimensions: the extent of the control (the range of activities and decisions), the focus of the control (which specific aspects were controlled by a given partner), and the control mechanisms (e.g., personal involvement, socialization and adaptation, hierarchical, and lateral).
- *Strength of the partnership ties* (e.g., Burt, 2000): more closely associated with the concept of networks, this area of study is interested in how weak or how strong the relationship between the partners is; while strong relationships may intuitively be thought of as better, a weak tie can be a source of competitive advantage if it forms a bridge between two different groups/cliques/worlds' that no other organization fills.

Strategic alliances have been examined in the sport management literature. For example, Stevens and Watkins-Mathys (2006) studied the world of five-a-side football and the strategic alliances formed by the Football Association (FA) with relevant stakeholders, both public and private. They developed a framework which they suggested could be used by other sport governing bodies to examine their own strategic alliances. This framework included primary and secondary factors. The primary factors involved questions about the strategic alliance's objectives, including customer and competition assessments, a facilities' geographic location review, and sport product development opportunities. Primary factors also included questions about the resources to be used, such as identifying intangible assets which would provide added value, undertaking a physical resources inventory, reviewing requirements in terms of personnel and their roles, and determining funding requirements. Secondary factors included the degree of integration between alliance partners, the direction of resource flow between partners, the size of the alliance (number of partners), and the duration of that alliance.

In turn, Parent and Séguin (2009) suggested that strategic alliances could be formed in order to bid for and host major sporting events. They provided a model by which such strategic alliances could be evaluated over the course of their lifecycle.

According to Parent and Séguin, an initial key evaluation point was the compatibility between the organizations, such as between an event promoter and the local/national rights holder (the sport organization). This compatibility could notably include resource, knowledge, social capital, cultural, and strategic/intention aspects. If the potential partners were deemed compatible, Parent and Séguin proposed that a formal contract should be drawn up that would lay out the parameters of the alliance, as well as its legal form and clear objectives, any financial issues, conflict and consequences/penalties and alliance termination clauses, and details about the board of directors or other governance structures for the event. Compatibility and contract signing make up the gestation period of the strategic alliance. The alliance then enters into the transition period where the contractual obligations are operationalized. At this point, the alliance has then entered the maturation phase where it is actually being managed. Here, Parent and Séguin suggest that trust, communication, power, learning, and entrainment (defined as the pace, rhythm and cycle of the alliance partnership process) become apparent. Finally, in the infiltration phase, we are able to evaluate the outcomes of the alliance. Parent and Séguin used this strategic alliances evolution model to evaluate the performance of the FINA 2005 World Aquatics Championships bid and organizing committees and explain some of the difficulties encountered in the planning of this event.

The broader examination of linkages and partnerships is increasingly popular in research on the management of sport. For example, Cousens and Slack (1996) provided antecedents, rationales, and impacts for the formation of interorganizational relationships in their *European Journal for Sport Management* article entitled 'Emerging patterns of inter-organizational relations: a network perspective of North American professional sport leagues', while Thibault and Harvey (1997) examined the nature and extent of partnerships and linkages in the Canadian sport system in their *Journal of Sport Management* article 'Fostering interorganizational linkages in the Canadian sport delivery system'. Meanwhile Glover (1999) offered guidelines for partner selection, contract preparation, and partnership management for parks and recreation agencies in an article entitled 'Municipal park and recreation agencies unite!'.

Research on strategic alliances has focused on understanding how alliances are formed and the components of successful alliances. Many aspects of alliances are important including when they are formed, why they are formed, and how they are managed sustainably over time. Culpan (2009) produced a review of the strategic alliance literature and provided a more comprehensive analysis of current literature than we can offer here. He also made some suggestions for future research based on his analysis. This work provided some thought-provoking discussions which are useful for moving research on strategic alliances forward. For a further viewpoint, the reader may wish to look at Parkhe's (2010) 'response' to Culpan's analysis in which he addresses the main concerns Culpan presents about the literature on strategic alliances. Much of the current understanding of this concept has been generated through case study research and there has been little comparative data produced to validate case studies or provide generalizable findings.

To understand strategic alliances more fully, the reader may refer to the concepts of **organizational culture**, **organizational goals**, **control**, **structure** and **networks** that can be found elsewhere in this book.

FURTHER READING

For some further reading on this concept, we would recommend the following:

Child, J. and Faulkner, D. (1998) *Strategies of Cooperation: Managing Alliances, Networks, and Joint Ventures*. New York: Oxford University Press.

Inkpen, A.C. (2002) Learning, knowledge management, and strategic alliances: so many studies, so many unanswered questions. *Cooperative Strategies and Alliances*: 267–289.

Stevens, A. and Watkins-Mathys, L. (2006) The FA's role in developing five-a-side football: strategic alliances with stakeholders. *Managing Leisure*, 11(3): 186–202.

BIBLIOGRAPHY

Ahuja, G. (2000) The duality of collaboration: inducements and opportunities in the formation of interfirm linkages. *Strategic Management Journal*, 21: 317–343.

Bleeke, J. and Ernst, D. (1995) Is your strategic alliance really a sale? *Harvard Business Review*, Jan.-Feb.: 97–105.

Burt, R.S. (2000) The network structure of social capital. *Research in Organizational Behaviour*, 22: 345–423.

Child, J. and Faulkner, D. (1998) *Strategies of Cooperation: Managing Alliances, Networks, and Joint Ventures*. New York: Oxford University Press.

Child, J. and Markoczy, L. (1993) Host-country managerial behaviour and learning in Chinese and Hungarian joint ventures. *Journal of Management Studies*, 30: 611–631.

Cousens, L. and Slack, T. (1996) Emerging patterns of inter-organizational relations: a network perspective of North American professional sport leagues. *European Journal for Sport Management*, 3(1): 48–69.

Culpan, R. (2009) A fresh look at strategic alliances: research issues and future directions. *International Journal of Strategic Business Alliances*, 1: 4–23.

Faulkner, D.O. (1995) *International Strategic Alliances: Cooperating to Compete*. Maidenhead: McGraw-Hill.

Geringer, J.M. and Hébert, L. (1989) Control and performance of international joint ventures. *Journal of International Business Studies*, 20: 235–254.

Glover, T.D. (1999) Municipal park and recreation agencies unite! A single case analysis of an intermunicipal partnership. *Journal of Park and Recreation Administration*, 17: 73–90.

Gulati, R. (1999) Network location and learning: the influence of network resources and firm capabilities on alliance formation. *Strategic Management Journal*, 20: 397–420.

Kogut, B. (2000) The network as knowledge: generative rules and the emergence of structure. *Strategic Management Journal*, 21: 405–425.

Li, S.X. and Rowley, T.J. (2002) Inertia and evaluation mechanisms in interorganizational partner selection: syndicate formations among U.S. investment banks. *Academy of Management Journal*, 45: 1104–1119.

Murray, E.A. and Mahon, J.F. (1993) Strategic alliances: gateway to the new Europe? *Long Range Planning*, 26: 102–111.

Parent, M.M. and Séguin, B. (2009, June 6–9) *Un modèle pour des alliances stratégiques dans le cadre de la gestion d'événements sportifs au Canada*. Paper presented at the Administrative Sciences Association of Canada Conference, Niagara Falls, Ontario, Canada.

Parkhe, A. (2010) Research issues and future directions in strategic alliances: a reply to Prof. Culpan (2009). *International Journal of Strategic Business Alliances*, 1(4): 392–296.

Podolny, J.M. (1993) A status-based model of market competition. *American Journal of Sociology*, 98(4): 829–872.

Ring, P.S. and Van de Ven, A.H. (1994) Developmental processes of cooperative interorganizational relationships. *Academy of Management Review*, 19: 90–118.

Stevens, A. and Watkins-Mathys, L. (2006) The FA's role in developing five-a-side football: strategic alliances with stakeholders. *Managing Leisure*, 11(3): 186–202.

Stuart, T.E. (2000) Interorganizational alliances and the performance of firms: a study of growth and innovation rates in a high-technology industry. *Strategic Management Journal*, 21: 791–811.

Thibault, L. and Harvey, J. (1997) Fostering interorganizational linkages in the Canadian sport delivery system. *Journal of Sport Management*, 11(1): 45–68.

Strategic Planning

> *Strategic planning is the formal or informal process that managers engage in to define their organization strategy, set long-term goals, and allocate resources to achieve the organization's strategic objectives.*

Strategic planning emerged in the mid-1960s as the most effective process for implementing strategies to make businesses more competitive and improve performance (Mintzberg, 1994). The notion that strategic planning is related to the **performance** of an organization has been both supported (Andersen, 2000; Brews and Hunt, 1999; Delmar and Shane, 2003; Miller and Cardinal, 1994; Rhyne, 1986) and refuted by research (Pearce et al., 1987; Shrader et al., 1984). Rudd and colleagues (2008) extended this debate on the relationship between strategic planning and performance by investigating the mediating effect of four types of flexibility on the relationship. Their results suggested that two types of flexibility had some influence on financial performance and two types of flexibility had influence on non-financial performance. There are many different ways by which authors have presented the process that is strategic planning. For example, Nutt and Backoff (1992) suggested an organization must move through six stages: it would need to describe the historical context, provide an assessment of the situation, draw up an agenda of the criticality of identified issues, describe the strategic options, assess the feasibility of these, and then implement the best option.

In turn, Goodstein et al. (1992) described a three-stage/three-phase process for strategic planning. More precisely, the organization must first set the stage for this by planning to plan, scanning its values, and formulating its mission. The second stage is setting the strategic directions. This is done by modelling the strategic business, auditing its performance, and performing a gap analysis. The final stage is implementation where the organization must first integrate the action plans, then plan for contingencies, and finally implement these. Mintzberg (1994), being somewhat critical of the increasing number of ways to go through the strategic planning process, proposed conceptualizing strategic planning as a black box drawn within a network of the following activities: strategic analysis and formation, translating strategies into a plan, and external and internal communication and control of the plan.

Slack (1997) was the first to suggest a strategic planning process specifically for sport organizations. He presented two phases for strategic planning: strategy formulation and strategy implementation. The **strategy** formulation phase includes describing the mission, vision and philosophy (values) of the organization, analysing the internal and external environment, and identifying and making choices about appropriate strategies. An organization's mission answers the question 'why are we here?', an organization's vision answers the question 'what do we hope to accomplish?', and an organization's philosophy or values answers the question 'who are we/what are we about?' Answering these questions provides the foundations for strategic planning. The next step according to Slack is to analyse the internal and external environments of the organization. This is done using a Strengths, Weaknesses, Opportunities, and Threats (SWOT) analysis. This must determine organizational strengths (what it is good at) and weaknesses (what needs to be improved) in terms of the organization's capabilities, resources, skills, and so on. It must also look externally to determine the sorts of potential opportunities and threats that exist in the surrounding environment. Once the internal and external environments have been understood, the appropriate corporate and/or business strategy must be identified and chosen. Next comes the strategy implementation phase, which includes choosing an appropriate organizational **structure**, as well as appropriate **control** and integration mechanisms. As Chandler (1962) noted, there is a relationship between structure and strategy. He argued that structure must follow strategy, although others (e.g., Mintzberg, 1990) have held that this is a mutual relationship where structure follows strategy which then follows structure and so on, just as the left foot follows the right foot when walking. Finally, managers must design ways to put the strategic plan in place and monitor its progress.

One of the best-known works linking strategy and structure to classify organizations in relation to their strategic planning process is that by Miles and Snow (1978). They presented four possibilities: defenders, prospectors, analysers, and reactors. 'Defenders' are organizations that have a narrow range of products or services, which are offered to a narrow (but often very healthy) range of the market segment to carve out a niche for themselves. These organizations pay scant attention to the external environment. 'Prospectors' are organizations that are actively seeking new products/services and/or markets and as such they are innovators. Because of this these organizations will constantly scan their environment for opportunities. 'Analysers' are organizations that situate themselves between defenders and prospectors in order to maximize profits but minimize risks. For such organizations all aspects of the strategic planning process are especially important and will need to be constantly revisited. Finally, 'reactors' are organizations that are doing poorly in the strategic planning process, for example they will have difficulty articulating a strategy or their strategy and structure relationship is not appropriate.

Where Slack (1997) provided a more theoretically-based approach to strategic planning, Chappelet's (2005) approach was based on various Olympic sport organizations' processes. More precisely, Chappelet (2005: 8) argued for a four-step cyclical process to strategic planning: analysis, vision, action, and control. The analysis step is similar to Slack's (1997) initial stages, as an organization's top managers must answer the question 'where are we now?' by doing an internal and external analysis (SWOT). After doing so they must answer the question 'where do we want to be?' so as to establish a new vision, a new mission, and new objectives. They must then determine 'how to get there' by developing strategies and specific tactics for reaching the vision, mission, and objectives. Finally, performance indicators and benchmarks must be established in order to respond to 'are we getting there?'

Research about strategic planning in sport organizations is sparse. Thibault et al. (1994), when looking at the strategic activities of national sport organizations as regards domestic sport, found six strategic factors that needed to be considered when going through a strategic planning process and formulating specific strategies:

- *Fundability:* the capacity of a sport organization to secure financial resources from external sources.
- *Size of client base:* the number of clients the sport organization serves.
- *Volunteer appeal:* the organization's ability to attract human (volunteer) resources.
- *Support group appeal:* the level of visibility and appeal of the organization's programmes to those stakeholders who are able to provide current or future support.
- *Equipment costs:* how much money is required for equipment at the beginner levels of the sport.
- *Affiliation fees:* the amount of money required to participate in the sport.

Thibault et al. (1994) then grouped the factors into two categories: programme attractiveness (fundability, size of client base, volunteer appeal, and support group appeal) and competitive position (equipment costs and affiliation fees). They then created a 2x2 framework based on the relative levels of these two categories, which resulted in the following strategy framework for Canadian national sport organizations: *enhancers* (high programme attractiveness; strong competitive position) such as soccer; *refiners* (high programme attractiveness; weak competitive position) such as ice hockey; *explorers* (low programme attractiveness; weak competitive position) such as equestrian sports; and *innovators* (low programme attractiveness; strong competitive position) such as diving.

More recently, Cunningham (2002) examined NCAA Division I athletic departments to study the relationship between Miles and Snow's strategic types (prospectors, defenders, analysers and reactors) and organizational performance. He found that most NCAA Division I athletic departments were analysers. However, it was the prospectors who had the best organizational performance, thereby indicating that, at least for NCAA Division I athletic departments, being innovative is rewarding. While examining **quality** management in Flemish sports clubs, De Knop and colleagues

(2004) found that one of the main weaknesses of these clubs was the lack of a strategic planning process. In a study on United States Olympic sport organizations, Olberding (2004) found a positive relationship between the size of the organization and the presence of a formal strategic planning process. Only larger sport organizations tended to have a strategic planning process.

Sport management scholars have made good use of the mainstream strategic planning literature to investigate and think about the strategic planning process in sport organizations. There is, however, little verification of the theories generated to articulate the strategic planning process in sport organizations and there is only a small extension of theory to take account of different contexts such as small firms or variations between voluntary and private sectors. It is certainly not conclusive whether strategic planning is positively related to performance in all organizational settings and therefore this is one research area that still needs further evidence from case studies or larger quantitative surveys of various sport organizations.

To understand strategic planning more fully, the reader may refer to the concepts of **control**, **strategy**, **quality**, **performance management** and **structure**.

FURTHER READING

For some further reading on this concept, we would recommend the following:

Chappelet, J.-L. (2005) The process of strategic management and its practical tools. In J.-L. Chappelet and E. Bayle (eds), *Strategic and Performance Management of Olympic Sport Organizations*. Champaign, IL: Human Kinetics. pp. 7–15.

Rudd, J.M., Greenley, G.E., Beatson, A.T. and Lings, I.N. (2008) Strategic planning and performance: extending the debate. *Journal of Business Research*, 61: 99–108.

Thibault, L., Slack, T. and Hinings, C.R. (1994) Strategic planning for nonprofit sport organizations: empirical verification of a framework. *Journal of Sport Management*, 8(3): 218–233.

BIBLIOGRAPHY

Andersen, T.J. (2000) Strategic planning, autonomous actions and corporate performance. *Long Range Planning*, 33: 184–200.

Brews, P.J. and Hunt, M.R. (1999) Learning to plan and planning to learn. *Strategic Management Journal*, 20: 889–913.

Chandler, A.D. (1962) *Strategy and Structure*. Cambridge, MA: MIT Press.

Chappelet, J.-L. (2005) The process of strategic management and its practical tools. In J.-L. Chappelet and E. Bayle (eds), *Strategic and Performance Management of Olympic Sport Organizations*. Champaign, IL: Human Kinetics. pp. 7–15.

Cunningham, G.B. (2002) Examining the relationship among Miles and Snow's strategic types and measures of organizational effectiveness in NCAA Division I athletic departments. *International Review for the Sociology of Sport*, 37(2): 159–175.

De Knop, P., Van Hoecke, J. and De Bosscher, V. (2004) Quality management in sports clubs. *Sport Management Review*, 7(1): 57–77.

Delmar, F. and Shane, S. (2003) Does business planning facilitate the development of new ventures? *Strategic Management Journal*, 24: 1165–1185.

Goodstein, L., Nolan, T. and Pfeiffer, J. (1992) *Applied Strategic Planning: An Introduction*. San Francisco, CA: John Wiley & Sons.

Miles, R.E. and Snow, C.C. (1978) *Organizational Strategy, Structure, and Process*. New York: McGraw-Hill.

Miller, C.C. and Cardinal, L.B. (1994) Strategic planning and firm performance: a synthesis of more than two decades of research. *Academy of Management Journal*, 37: 1649–1665.

Mintzberg, H. (1990) The design school: reconsidering the basic premises of strategic management. *Strategic Management Journal*, 11: 171–195.

Mintzberg, H. (1994) *The Rise and Fall of Strategic Planning*. New York: Prentice-Hall.

Nutt, P.C. and Backoff, R.W. (1992) *Strategic Management of Public and Third Sector Organizations*. San Francisco, CA: Jossey-Bass.

Olberding, D.J. (2004) Measuring planning process formality in U.S. Olympic sport organizations. *International Journal of Sport Management*, 5(2): 91–110.

Pearce, J.A.I., Freeman, E.B. and Robinson, R.B. (Jr) (1987) The tenuous link between formalized strategic planning and financial performance. *Academy of Management Review*, 12: 658–675.

Rhyne, L.C. (1986) The relationship of strategic planning to financial performance. *Strategic Management Journal*, 7(5): 423–436.

Rudd, J.M., Greenley, G.E., Beatson, A.T. and Lings, I.N. (2008) Strategic planning and performance: extending the debate. *Journal of Business Research*, 61: 99–108.

Shrader, C.B., Taylor, L. and Dalton, D.R. (1984) Strategic planning and organisational performance: a critical appraisal. *Journal of Management*, 10(2): 149–171.

Slack, T. (1997) *Understanding Sport Organizations: The Application of Organization Theory* (1st edition). Champaign, IL: Human Kinetics.

Thibault, L., Slack, T. and Hinings, C.R. (1994) Strategic planning for nonprofit sport organizations: empirical verification of a framework. *Journal of Sport Management*, 8(3): 218–233.

Structure

> *Structure is the complexity (how diverse the organization is), formalization (the extent to which there are formal rules) and centralization (locus of decision making) of an organization.*

Structure is a vital concept within organization theory and for understanding how organizations operate. As the reader will have realized when examining the other concepts, structure is related to, affects, and is affected by many aspects of organizations, such as **goals, conflict, control** and **strategy**. As a concept we often think of structure as the 'hierarchy' of an organization. However, this is but a single component of structure. In all there are three components that organization theorists have identified as comprising the structure of an organization, and these are complexity, formalization, and centralization.

Complexity is the extent to which an organization is differentiated, either horizontally (through a specialization of labour or the division of work into simple, repetitive tasks) or vertically (the number of levels of hierarchy in an organization). Robbins (1990) suggested that the specialization of individuals (rather than work tasks) was 'social specialization' and that this created greater challenges for those trying to coordinate or manage these employee activities. Specialization can also occur in organizations in the form of departmentalization (the way in which management divides work groups and organizational sub-units).

Formalization is the extent to which an organization adopts formal rules and procedures. These may be in the form of job descriptions, operating manuals, policies, and procedures for strategy, health and safety, or grievances. Highly formalized organizations are often referred to as 'bureaucratic', but may also be recognized as highly complex and therefore in need of extensive formalized procedures to ensure effective coordination and the achievement of organizational goals.

Centralization is the third component of structure and the most difficult to understand. It refers to the extent to which decision making occurs at the top of the organization. Therefore, a decentralized organization is one where this decision making is delegated to lower levels or throughout the organization, and a centralized structure is one where decisions are taken at the top of the organization. However, decision making in organizations is rarely so straightforward. Some decisions may be delegated while others are not and in some instances decisions can be 'overruled' by hierarchical superiors, bringing into question where decision-making authority actually resides in an organization.

Two concepts we have not discussed yet which are intricately linked to structure are 'environment' and 'agents'. These concepts are vital to understanding how structure operates and also of significant interest to academics and practitioners in understanding how organizations change. All organizations will have an internal (staff, structure, systems, culture, etc.) and an external (socio-cultural, political, economic, competitive, etc.) environment in which they will operate. The relationship between structure and environment is a key one for managers to understand, as the external environment (and changes within it) can affect how businesseses operate but the internal environment (including structure, strategy and agent behaviour) can work to influence and control for uncertainty in the changing external environment. Thus we can see that this relationship is a dynamic one that requires careful observation in order to develop any meaningful understanding. It has been, and continues to be, a focus for researchers (see for example Moye, 1993; Selsky et al., 2007; Ward et al., 1996).

Organization environments have been classified in a number of ways (see, for example Daft, 2004; Starbuck, 1976; Thompson, 1967). Researchers have also provided crucial insights into how environments operate in relation to structure. For example, Burns and Stalker (1961) viewed 'organic' organization structures as those which have low formalization, flexible working practices and decentralized decision making. It was suggested that these organizations tended to operate most effectively in dynamic and fast-changing or demanding environments. On the other hand, 'mechanistic' organizations had more formal structures with clearly defined roles and tasks, primarily vertical communication and high specialization. These organizations were unlikely to be able to respond rapidly enough in a dynamic environment and so were more successful in environments that were stable. The main lesson from this research was that organization structures and environments must 'fit' in order for effective realization of organizational goals. Lawrence and

Lorsch (1967) extended the work of Burns and Stalker (1961) by examining external environmental 'certainty' and complexity (one component of structure), finding that the greater the external environment uncertainty (e.g., rapid changes in technology and/or customer demand), the more differentiated an organization would have to be to cope with such uncertainty. Duncan (1972), concerned with environment uncertainty, sought to further define the term to include the extent to which the environment was 'simple or complex' and the extent to which it was 'stable or dynamic'.

The three studies above have paved the way for researchers to consider many other aspects of the relationship between structure and environment (see for example Dess and Beard, 1984) and the role of agents (see Llewellyn, 2007, regarding understanding agents). In fact, the structure/organization-environment relationship can be examined utilizing the stakeholder perspective, institutional theory, resource dependence theory and population ecology to name but a few. Some more recent work has also looked at strategy and competitive advantage in relation to structure and environment (Llewellyn, 2007), strategic choice (Child, 1997; Moye, 1993) and organization performance (Pertusa-Ortega et al., 2009).

Although all sport organizations are unique in their structure (no two are exactly the same), there are some commonalities which have been observed which allow them to be classified into 'design types' (also known as configurations, gestalts, or design archetypes). Classification is important to developing theory in a field because it provides generalized principles by which managers, event organizers, or students can understand organization function and hence more effectively perform or facilitate within that organization. We discuss this further by examining the key methods for creating organization classifications (design types) as key concepts. These are **typologies** and **taxonomies** and are discussed later on.

For a comprehensive review of the concepts of structure and environment in relation to sport organizations, the reader can refer to Slack and Parent (2006). However, it is worth noting that the three elements of structure have been studied to some extent by researchers interested in sport organizations. Slack and Hinings (1992) examined specialization in Canadian national sport organizations, demonstrating how professional staff were more committed to changes introduced by the government than were the voluntary staff, making interaction among the two groups difficult to manage. Frisby (1986) and Kikulus et al. (1989) also examined horizontal complexity in sport organizations, with Frisby focusing on structure and **effectiveness** and Kikulus et al. utilizing a wide variety of sport-specific measures of specialization in order to understand **change** in national sport organizations. Formalization has been used in studies by Slack and Hinings (1987) and Thibault et al. (1991), although they both used the term 'standardization' to refer to written documentation and procedures.

More recently, Augestad and colleagues (2006) used neo-institutional theory to examine how nations develop structures for elite-level sport. Adopting a more critical and sociological approach to studying sport organizations, Long et al. (2005) examined the relationship between racial equality and structures, while Foster and Washington (2009) used a cross-sectional research design including analysis of nine years' worth of data from Major League Baseball and eight years of data from the National Hockey League to conclude that organizational structure (specifically, task interdependence) did indeed have a significant impact on the performance of a sport team. These authors also noted the implications their findings would have to managing leagues and sport organizations, suggesting that structure needs careful consideration when making adjustments to leagues that may in turn affect competitive balance.

Taylor and O'Sullivan (2009) explored the most appropriate board structure for the UK's national sport governing bodies in their study of 22 senior administrators involved in sport in the United Kingdom. Four key findings reported include: '(1) NGBs should reform the composition of their boards to better reflect business demands; (2) board size should be in the range of five to twelve members; (3) NGBs should have different individuals occupying the positions of CEO and chairman; and (4) boards of NGBs should possess more non-executive directors' (2009: 681). The implications of board structure are primarily discussed in relation to effective **governance** and **decision making** for national sport governing bodies.

The role and function of structure in organizations was of much concern to organization theory researchers in the 1960s and 1970s, with many attempts to verify the theories that were produced by seminal researchers such as Pugh, Hickson, Hinings and Turner (1968). One important result of this attempt to replicate and verify the theories of structure was the continuous refinement of our understanding of structure and the realization that the function of structure can vary in different contexts. Researchers interested in the management of sport have used their understanding of structure developed over several decades to help make sense of the operation of sport organizations. This provides a fairly secure knowledge base of how structure is important to the function of sport organizations, but it could still be challenged and extended by researchers through utilizing new theoretical perspectives/methods or by examining organizations within different contexts.

To understand structure more fully, the reader may refer to the concepts of **strategy, control, decision making, governance, conflict, typologies and taxonomies, effectiveness, change** and **organizational goals** that can be found elsewhere in this book.

FURTHER READING

For some further reading on this concept, we would recommend the following:

Bonacin, D., Rado, I. and Bonacin, D. (2008) Optimization of traditionally designed structure of sports organization. *Acta Kinesiologica*, 2: 75–84.

Child, J. (1997) Strategic choice in the analysis of action, structure, organizations and environment: retrospect and prospect. *Organization Studies*, 18(1): 43–76.

Thibault, L., Slack, T. and Hinings, C.R. (1991) Professionalism, structures and systems: the impact of professional staff on voluntary sport organizations. *International Review for the Sociology of Sport*, 26: 83–99.

BIBLIOGRAPHY

Augestad, P., Bergsgard, N.A. and Hansen, A.O. (2006) The institutionalizations of an elite sport organization in Norway: the case of 'Olympiatoppen'. *Sociology of Sport Journal*, 23: 293–313.

Burns, T. and Stalker, G.M. (1961) *The Management of Innovation*. London: Tavistock.

Child, J. (1997) Strategic choice in the analysis of action, structure, organizations and environment: retrospect and prospect. *Organization Studies*, 18(1): 43–76.

Daft, R.L. (2004) *Organization Theory and Design* (8th edn). Mason, OH: Thomson/South-Western.

Dess, G.G. and Beard, D.W (1984) Dimensions of organisational task environments. *Administrative Science Quarterly*, 29: 52–73.

Duncan, R.B. (1972) Characteristics of organizational environments and perceived environmental uncertainty. *Administrative Science Quarterly*, 17: 313–327.

Foster, W.M. and Washington, M. (2009) Organizational structure and home team performance. *Team Performance Management*, 15(3/4): 158–171.

Frisby, W. (1986) The organizational structure and effectiveness of voluntary organizations: the case of Canadian national sport governing bodies. *Journal of Park and Recreation Management*, 4: 61–74.

Kikulus, L., Slack, T., Hinings, C.R. and Zimmerman, A. (1989) A structural taxonomy of amateur sport organizations. *Journal of Sport Management*, 3: 129–150.

Lawrence, P.R. and Lorsch, J. (1967) *Organization and Environment*. Boston: Harvard Graduate School of Business Administration.

Llewellyn, A. (2007) Introducing the agents … . *Organization Studies*, 29(2): 133–153.

Long, J., Robinson, P. and Spracklen, K. (2005) Promoting racial equality within sports organizations. *Journal of Sport and Social Issues*, 29(1): 41–59.

Moye, A.M. (1993) Mondragon: adapting co-operative structures to meet the demands of a changing environment. *Economic and Industrial Democracy*, 14: 251–276.

Pertusa-Ortega, E.M., Molina-Azorín J. F. and Claver-Corte, E. (2009) Competitive strategies and firm performance: a comparative analysis of pure, hybrid and 'stuck-in-the-middle' strategies in Spanish firms. *British Journal of Management* 20: 508–523.

Pugh, D.S., Hickson, D.J., Hinings, C.R. and Turner, C. (1968) Dimensions of organization structure. *Administrative Science Quarterly*, 13: 65–105.

Robbins, S.P. (1990) *Organization Theory: Structure, Design and Applications* (3rd edition). Englewood Cliffs, NJ: Prentice-Hall.

Selsky, J.G., Goes, J. and Baburoglu, O. (2007) Contrasting perspectives of strategy making: applications in 'hyper' environments. *Organization Studies*, 28(1): 71–94.

Slack, T. and Hinings, C.R. (1987) Planning and organizational change: a conceptual framework for the analysis of amateur sport organizations. *Canadian Journal of Sport Sciences*, 12: 185–193.

Slack, T. and Hinings, C.R. (1992) Understanding change in national sport organizations: an integration of theoretical perspectives. *Journal of Sport Management*, 6: 114–132.

Slack, T. and Parent, M.M. (2006) *Understanding Sport Organizations*. Leeds: Human Kinetics Europe.

Starbuck, W.H. (1976) Organizations and their environments. In M.D. Dunnette (ed.), *Handbook of Industrial Organizational Psychology*. Chicago, IL: Rand McNally. pp. 1069–1123.

Taylor, M. and O'Sullivan, N. (2009) How should national governing bodies of sport be governed in the UK ? an exploratory study of board structure. *Corporate Governance: An International Review*, 17(6): 681–693.

Thibault, L., Slack, T. and Hinings, C.R. (1991) Professionalism, structures and systems: the impact of professional staff on voluntary sport organizations. *International Review for the Sociology of Sport*, 26: 83–99.

Thompson, J.D. (1967) *Organizations in Action*. New York: McGraw-Hill.

Ward, P.T., Bickford, D.J. and Leong, G.K. (1996) Configurations of manufacturing strategy, business strategy, environment and structure. *Journal of Management*, 22(4): 597–626.

structure

Technology

> Technology refers to any system or method which enables the production of some good or service.

The concept of technology can be defined and conceptualized in a variety of ways. However, from an organization theory perspective, we are interested in the effect technology has on an organization's structure and therefore on its management and/or operations. Although many researchers have proposed various definitions of technology, it can be viewed broadly as the techniques used to transform 'inputs' (materials, labour, equipment, systems/processes) into 'outputs' (product or service) (see for example Perrow, 1967). This should not be confused with the broader process of transforming 'inputs' into 'outputs', which is known as the operations function of an organization (see Byers, 2004, for a discussion of the operations function in sport organizations).

Research on technology began with Woodward (1958, 1965), who examined technological complexity and organization **structure**, demonstrating that the technology employed in manufacturing processes had significant implications for all aspects of organization structure and that the most successful firms also shared some similar structural characteristics. Perrow (1967) investigated the group-level impact of technology in organizations, developing a classification consisting of four different types of technology (craft, non-routine, routine, and engineering) that were each associated with a different type of organization structure. This work emphasized that a number of technologies can exist in an organization and that the group level of analysis is important in demonstrating how this difference influences the effectiveness of different groups. Finally, Thompson (1967) developed an understanding of technology in organizations based on the interdependence of departmental groups. Different types of interdependence (pooled, sequential, reciprocal) required different technologies to **effectively** coordinate and communicate between work groups.

While providing key contributions to our understanding of the relationship between technology and organizational structure, the work mentioned above has since been extended and criticized by numerous scholars (for a full review of these criticisms see Slack, 1997). The concept of technology has not been the subject of research from sport management scholars using the organization theory perspective. Rather the impact and effects of technology have been discussed more generally, such as by Turner (2007) who examined the relationship between technology and the supply of sport **broadcasting** and Foxall and Johnston (1991) who discussed the evolution of technology and strategy as regards Grand Prix motor racing. These studies provided interesting dialogue and detail about their subjects but did little to consider how their analysis might benefit from existing knowledge and frameworks from organization theory and indeed how the work may help to advance understanding in organization studies generally and managing sport specifically.

Technology and sport have been examined from an engineering perspective (Fuss et al., 2007) and a performance perspective (Magdalinski, 2009), but the management implications have received scant attention. One exception to this has been a related body of literature which focuses on the ethical/moral implication of technology in sport. In Tamburrini and Tännsjö (2000), Tamburrini and Tännsjö (2005) and Miah (2004) interesting debates were presented on current and future uses for genetic technology in enhancing athletic performance and the management of doping in sport. Houlihan (2002) also examined doping in sport but focused on the **policy** issues rather than moral or management debates.

Technology has undoubtedly and increasingly become important in the management of sport yet few academic studies have attempted to track, document, or analyse the effects and/or consequences of the adoption of new technologies. The management implications or best practice in introducing new technologies have also not been the focus of academic enquiry. This is understandable given the wide ranging settings in which technology can be seen to impact on the management of sport. Technology is increasingly being used by national sport governing bodies in the assessment, prediction and management of athletic training and performance. UK Sport (2009), the Australian Sports Commission (2008, 2009), and less developed countries such as South Africa (2009) are all embracing the use of technology.

Media and **broadcasting** technologies have also featured prominently in the financing and management of sport clubs and professional teams. The importance of media technology to sport managers and marketers has been suggested by O'Reilly and Rahinel (2006) who reviewed the various media technologies used in Canadian ice hockey with the purpose of informing the decision-making process for media technology selection decisions.

The use of technology to distribute sport products and services, to manage sport organizations, to assess athletic performance, and to study its inclusion in governing sporting contests, as well as technologies for the enhancement of athletic performance, have allowed considerable scope for research into these situations to understand the impacts, management processes and critical issues related to the use of technology in sport. Contemporary research in mainstream business and management has moved beyond descriptive accounts of technology use and/or abuse and researchers interested in the management of sport technology may refer to this wider body of literature for direction when formulating research questions. The foci for current thinking include issues such as the institutionalization of technology and its effects on governance, policy and control in organizations (Baptista, 2009) and managing the adoption of technology in organizations (Engl and Stewart, 2007).

To understand technology more fully, the reader may refer to the concepts of **structure**, **effectiveness**, **media/broadcasting** and **sport policy** that can be found elsewhere in this book.

FURTHER READING

For some further reading on this concept, we would recommend the following:

Baptista, J. (2009) Institutionalization as a process of interplay between technology and its organizational context of use. *Journal of Information Technology*, 24(4): 305–319.

O'Reilly, N. and Rahinel, R. (2006) Forecasting the importance of media technology in sport: the case of the televised ice hockey product in Canada. *International Journal of Sports Marketing and Sponsorship*, 8(1): 82–97.

Turner, P. (2007) The impact of technology on the supply of sport broadcasting. *European Sport Management Quarterly*, 7(4): 337–360.

BIBLIOGRAPHY

Australian Sports Commission (2008) Available at http://www.zdnet.com.au/news/hardware/soa/Technology-one-of-the-good-sports-for-ASC/0,130061702,339285372,00.htm (last accessed 21/12/09).

Australian Sports Commission (2009) Australian Institute of Sport – Technology and Innovation. Available at http://www.ausport.gov.au/ais/innovation (last accessed 21/12/09).

Baptista, J. (2009) Institutionalization as a process of interplay between technology and its organizational context of use. *Journal of Information Technology*, 24(4): 305–319.

Byers, T. (2004) Managing operations, quality and performance. In J. Beech and S. Chadwick (eds) (2004) *The Business of Sport Management*. Harlow: Pearson.

Department of Sport and Recreation South Africa (2009) Technology and Sport. Available at http://www.srsa.gov.za/KnowledgePage.asp?id=17 (last accessed 21/09/12).

Engl, I. and Stewart, D. (2007) Executive management and IT innovation in health: identifying the barriers to adoption. *Health Informatics Journal*, 13: 75–87.

Foxall, G.R. and Johnston, B.R. (1991) Innovation in Grand Prix motor racing: the evolution of technology, organization and strategy. *Technovation*, 11(7): 387–402.

Fuss, F.K., Subic, A. and Ujihashi, J. (2007) *The Impact of Technology on Sport, II*. London: Taylor and Francis.

Houlihan, B. (2002). *Dying to Win: Doping in Sport and the Development of Anti-doping Policy*. Strasbourg: Council of Europe Publishing.

Liebermann, D.G. Katz, L. Hughes, M.D. Bartlett, R.M. McClements, J. and Franks, I.M. (2002) Advances in the application of technology to sports performance. *Journal of Sport Sciences*, 20(10): 755–769.

Magdalinski, T. (2009) *Sport, Technology and the Body: The Nature of Performance*. Abingdon: Routledge.

Miah, A. (2004) *Genetically Modified Athletes*. Abingdon: Routledge.

O'Reilly, N. and Rahinel, R. (2006) Forecasting the importance of media technology in sport: the case of the televised ice hockey product in Canada. *International Journal of Sports Marketing and Sponsorship*, 8(1): 82–97.

Perrow, C. (1967) A framework for the comparative analysis of organizations. *American Sociological Review*, 32: 194–208.

Slack, T. (1997) *Understanding Sport Organizations*. Champaign, IL: Human Kinetics.

Tamburrini, C. M. and Tännsjö, T. (eds) (2005) *Genetic Technology and Sport: Ethical Questions*. London: Routledge.

Tännsjö, T. and Tamburrini, C. M. (eds) (2000) *Values in Sport: Elitism, Nationalism, Gender Equality and the Scientific Manufacture of Winners*. London: Routledge.

Thompson, J.D. (1967) *Organizations in Action*. New York: McGraw-Hill.

Turner, P. (2007) The impact of technology on the supply of sport broadcasting. *European Sport Management Quarterly*, 7(4): 337–360.

UK Sport (2009) Military precision keeps British cyclists on track for success. Available at www. uksport.gov.uk (last accessed 21/12/09).

Woodward, J. (1958) *Management and Technology*. London: Her Majesty's Stationery Office.

Woodward, J. (1965) *Industrial Organization. Theory and Practice*. Oxford: Oxford University Press.

Typologies and Taxonomies

> *Typologies are classifications of things based on* a priori *knowledge (independent of experience or empirical data).*
>
> *Taxonomies are classifications of things generated based on analysis of empirical (usually statistical) data.*

Typologies are, in a sense, of an *a priori* nature; they are generated mentally and *not* by any replicable empirical analysis. Taxonomies are derived from multivariate analyses of empirical data on organizations. Typically organizations or aspects of their structure, strategies, environments, and processes are described along a number of variables. Attempts are then made to identify natural clusters in the data, and these clusters, rather than any *a priori* conceptions, serve as the basis for the configurations. Typologies and taxonomies are important because they help to give order to, and some understanding of, diverse and complex phenomena. They identify how something varies which enables us to study the importance of that variability. For example, organizations will vary considerably in their size, structure, purpose, and management. A typology or taxonomy of organizations can help identify groups or types of organizations which can then be studied to understand how management of a type of organization can most effectively be performed.

The first attempt to classify organizations into types can be found in Weber's (1947) writings on social domination and the attendant patrimonial, feudal, and bureaucratic forms of organization. Weber demonstrated how each type of organization could be characterized by a number of mutually complementary or at least simultaneously occurring attributes. In the 1950s, Parsons followed Weber and created a typology based on the **goals** or functions of the organization. He identified organizations that had economic goals, political goals, integrative functions, or pattern maintenance functions.

Burns and Stalker (1961) used the approach of a typology and suggested two types of organizational design: organic and mechanistic. The *organic* type of organization was found in changing conditions where new and unfamiliar problems had to be dealt with; it contained no rigid **control** systems and employees showed high levels of commitment to the organization. By contrast, *mechanistic* organizations were found in stable conditions; tasks were narrowly defined, and there was a clear hierarchy of control, insistence on loyalty to the organization, and obedience to superiors. This form of organization was very much like Weber's legal–rational bureaucracy. These two types of design were viewed as polar opposites, with organizations described according to their position on a continuum between them.

Blau and Scott (1962) produced a typology based on the principle of *cui bono* or 'who benefits?' from the organization. Four types of **structure** were identified: *mutual benefit organizations*, where the prime beneficiary is the membership; *business concerns*, where the prime beneficiary is the owner(s) of the business; *service organizations*, where the clients benefit; and *commonwealth organizations*, where the prime beneficiary is the public at large. Several typologies have focused on the organization's technology as the criterion variable for classification. Woodward (1965) distinguished between organizations based on whether they used unit or small batch, large batch or mass, or continuous-process types of **technology**, while Perrow (1967) focused on whether technology was craft, routine, non-routine, or engineering. Thompson (1967) chose to utilize core technologies, which he described as either long-linked, mediated, or intensive, as his basis for classification.

Another typology is Gordon and Babchuk's (1959) tripartite classification of organizations as instrumental, expressive, or instrumental-expressive. *Instrumental organizations* are designed to maintain or create some normative condition or change. *Expressive organizations* are designed to satisfy the interests of their members. *Instrumental-expressive organizations* show elements of both functions. In a study of the members of badminton and judo clubs, Jacoby (1965) found a very high expressive and very low instrumental orientation. Henry et al. (2005) developed a typology related to **sport policy** and identified four approaches to sport policy. These were termed 'seeking similarities', 'describing differences', 'theorizing the transnational', and 'defining discourse'. Each has a different ontological and epistemological basis.

Taxonomies are empirically constructed classifications which identify clustering among organizational variables that is statistically significant and reduces the variety of organizations to a small number of types. The first empirical taxonomy of organizations was developed by Haas and colleagues (1966). Using a sample of 75 organizations they produced ten design types; the number of organizations found in each design type ranged from two to thirty. Meanwhile Pugh, Hickson, and Hinings (the Aston Group) (1963) developed a taxonomy based on structural data obtained from 52 relatively large (i.e., over 250 employees) organizations.

The most sophisticated use of taxonomy can be found in the work of Miller and Friesen (1984). Using a sample of 81 organizations described along 31 variables of strategy, structure, information processing, and environment, they produced ten common organizational design types, or what they termed 'archetypes'. Identifying six of these as successful and four as unsuccessful, Miller and Friesen argued that the notion of taxonomy could be extended to study organizational transitions between these archetypes. Based on 24 variables that described changes in such areas as strategy-making, structure and the environment for each transition, nine 'transition archetypes' were produced. Thus they held that the taxonomic approach would identify common paths in organizational evolution. In the literature on the management of sport there have been only two instances of using a taxonomic approach. Both of these emanated from the work of Slack and Hinings and their students. Using data on the structural arrangements of 36 Canadian national-level sport organizations, Hinings and Slack (1987) developed 11 scales that addressed three aspects of organizational structure: specialization, standardization, and the centralization of decision making. After a factor analysis, two factors were produced: one concerned with the extent of professional structuring in these organizations, and the other with volunteer structuring. By dividing the scores of the 36 organizations at the mean on each factor, Hinings and Slack produced nine organizational types and were able to demonstrate the extent to which these organizations exhibited the characteristics of professional bureaucratic structuring, a design towards which they were being directed.

In a somewhat similar study Kikulis et al. (1989) created a taxonomy using data from 59 provincial-level sport organizations. Using Ward's method of hierarchical agglomerative clustering, Kikulis et al. produced eight structural design types, ranging from sport organizations that were 'implicitly structured' to those that, within this institutional sphere, showed high levels of professional bureaucratic structuring. Kikulis et al. argued the merits of their study in demonstrating the variation in structural design in these sport organizations and as a basis for understanding a range of organizational phenomena. The only attempt thus far to create a typology specifically related to sport organizations has been that developed by Chelladurai. In his (1985) book *Sport Management: Macro Perspectives*, he proposed a 12-cell classification system for sport and physical activity organizations.

Chelladurai (1985) makes no attempt to categorize sport organizations using the various cells of his model; some of these cells may actually describe few if any sport organizations. In extending his work on classification, Chelladurai (1992) does not focus on sport organizations *per se* but on the services they provide. Using two dimensions, 'the type and extent of employee involvement in the production of services' and 'client motives for participation in sport and physical activity', he produced six classes of sport and physical activity services – consumer pleasure, consumer health and fitness, human skills, human excellence, human sustenance, and human curative.

Typologies and taxonomies have been utilized to some extent in the literature on the management of sport. Specifically, we have seen these concepts applied to sport organizations and policy. It is more common however to see categories suggested for concepts within the sport management literature (e.g., types of volunteers, clubs or fans) rather than the more extensive analysis required to create a typology or taxonomy. Categorization is still useful but perhaps provides a less rigorous and intricate analysis. In short, we feel there is still considerable scope to apply these principles to many concepts within sport.

Those interested in typologies, taxonomies or 'configuration research' should refer to Short and colleagues (2008) who provided a thorough review of past research and the challenges for those engaged in research using this approach. The work is also exemplary of the evolution of research focused on organizations and how critical reflection and a clear focus on basic concepts are crucial to advancing our knowledge in any particular field.

To understand typologies and taxonomies more fully, the reader may refer to the concepts of **organizational goals**, **control**, **structure**, **sport policy** and **technology** that can be found elsewhere in this book.

FURTHER READING

For some further reading on this concept, we would recommend the following:

Chelladurai, P. (1985) *Sport Management: Macro Perspectives.* London, ON: Sports Dynamics.
Chelladurai, P. (1992) A classification of sport and physical activity services: implications for sport management. *Journal of Sport Management,* 6: 38–51.
Kikulis, L., Slack, T., Hinings, C.R. and Zimmermann, A. (1989) A taxonomy of provincial sport organizations. *Journal of Sport Management,* 3: 129–150.
Short, J.C., Payne, G.T. and Ketchen, D.J. (Jr) (2008) Research on organizational configurations: past accomplishments and future challenges. *Journal of Management,* 34(6): 1053–1079.

BIBLIOGRAPHY

Blau, P.M. and Scott, W.R. (1962) *Formal Organizations: A Comparative Approach.* San Francisco, CA: Chandler. (Reissued as a Business Classic, Stanford University Press, 2003).
Burns, T. and Stalker, G.M. (1961) *The Management of Innovation.* London: Tavistock.
Chelladurai, P. (1985) *Sport Management: Macro Perspectives.* London, ON: Sports Dynamics.
Chelladurai, P. (1992) A classification of sport and physical activity services: implications for sport management. *Journal of Sport Management,* 6: 38–51.
Gordon, C.W. and Babchuk, N. (1959) A typology of voluntary organizations. *American Sociological Review,* 24: 22–23.
Haas, J.E., Hall, R.H. and Johnson, N.J. (1966) Toward an empirically derived taxonomy of organizations. In R.V. Bowers (ed.), *Studies on Behavior in Organizations.* Athens, GA: University of Georgia Press.
Henry, I., Amara, M., Al-Tauqi, M. and Lee, P.C. (2005) A typology of approaches to comparative analysis of sports policy. *Journal of Sport Management,* 19: 520–35.
Hinings, B. and Slack, T. (1987) The dynamics of quadrennial plan implementation in national sport organizations. In T. Slack and C.R. Hinings (eds), *The Organization and Administration of Sport.* London, Ontario: Sports Dynamics. pp. 127–151.
Jacoby, A. (1965) Some correlates of instrumental and expressive orientations to associational membership. *Sociological Inquiry,* 35: 163–175.
Kikulis, L., Slack, T., Hinings, C.R. and Zimmermann, A. (1989) A taxonomy of provincial sport organizations. *Journal of Sport Management,* 3: 129–150.
Miller, D. and Friesen, P.H. (1984) *Organizations: A Quantum View.* Englewood Cliffs, NJ: Prentice-Hall.
Parsons, T. (1967) *Sociological Theory and Modern Society.* New York: The Free Press.
Perrow, C.A. (1967) A framework for the comparative analysis of organizations. *American Sociological Review,* 32: 194–208.
Pugh, D.S., Hickson, D.J., Hinings, C.R., Macdonald, K.M., Turner, C. and Lupton, T. (1963) A conceptual scheme for organizational analysis. *Administrative Science Quarterly,* 8 (3): 289–315.

Short, J.C., Payne, G.T. and Ketchen, D.J. (Jr) (2008) Research on organizational configurations: past accomplishments and future challenges. *Journal of Management*, 34(6): 1053–1079.

Thompson, J.D. (1967) *Organizations in Action*. Maidenhead: McGraw-Hill.

Weber, M. (1947) *The Theory of Social and Economic Organization*. New York: The Free Press.

Woodward, J. (1965) *Industrial Organisation, Theory and Practice*. Oxford: Oxford University Press.

Voluntary

> *Voluntary is a concept that can refer to an individual volunteer, a philosophy, an organization, or an economic/social sector (the 'voluntary sector'), and is a legal term used in contract, criminal or tort law. Essentially, 'voluntary' means giving by one's own free will.*

Research focused on the concept of 'voluntary' can be in relation to individuals (Dhebar and Stokes, 2008), organizations (Guo and Musso, 2007) or the broader 'voluntary sector' (Kendall, 2003). Research on the voluntary sector has generally been concerned with documenting the size of this sector (normally by country) and its development and changing nature (including factors enabling or constraining its development). Clark et al. (2010) reviewed trends, facts and information from research conducted by the National Council for Voluntary Organizations as well as government and academic research. It is within the **context** of 'the sector', voluntary organizations and volunteering that researchers have discussed the legal and philosophical issues related to voluntarism. The literature related to understanding the voluntary sector, organizations or the individual act of volunteering is therefore extensive and the issues which arise are considerably diverse and dependent on geographical orientation.

The concept of 'voluntary' appears throughout the literature on the management of sport, including research on the voluntary sector (Davies, 2004; Nichols et al., 2005), voluntary **sport organizations** (Seippel, 2004; Skille, 2008), and of course the volunteers themselves (Coleman, 2002; Cuskelly, 2004). Research on the voluntary sector has mainly attempted to demonstrate its economic value (Sport England, 2007; Sports Council for Wales, 2008) and the pressures which exist for voluntary sport in the UK (Nichols et al., 2005).

Sport England (2003, 2007) demonstrated the breadth and depth of volunteer support in sport and active recreational activity in England. This research, conducted for Sport England by the Leisure Industries Research Centre, suggested that nearly 15 per cent of the population (5,821,400 people) were volunteering in the administration of sport and the staging of sports events. The report also estimated that volunteers contributed 1.2 billion hours per year to sport, representing a value of over £14 billion. With in excess of 106,400 affiliated clubs in England containing over 8 million members, voluntary sports clubs represent a large portion of the sports community. According to Davis Smith (1998), at 26 per cent, sports (and exercise) volunteering represents the largest type of all voluntary activity in the UK.

Houlihan (1997) and Green and Oakley (2001) indicated the crucial role of voluntary sport clubs in the sport development system, especially given the importance of sporting excellence in many developed countries. Garrett (2004) highlighted the active role of voluntary sport clubs in partnerships to deliver publicly funded sport development programmes aimed at community regeneration, i.e., less social exclusion through sports participation. In short, it is thought that voluntary sport clubs provide important services to individuals and society and contribute to the wider goals of government through partnerships with public and commercial sector organizations.

Research focused on the volunteers themselves has included measuring the demographic composition of this population (Coleman, 2002; Shibli et al., 1999). Research from Denmark (Pfister, 2006), Norway (Seippel, 2004, 2005), Canada (Inglis, 1997) and the United Kingdom (Nichols and Padmore, 2005; Shibli et al., 1999) suggested that there was a higher proportion of male volunteers in sport clubs, particularly in leadership positions. Slack and Thibault (1988), in their study of national sport governing bodies, focus more on the impact of volunteers on the operation of (national) sport organizations. Their work demonstrated that the structures and practices within these organizations were heavily influenced by the individual values of the voluntary staff involved. Other work by Kirk and MacPhail (2003) and Pearce (1993) tended to support this notion in small voluntary sports clubs as well by highlighting that (a) some committee members could be founding members and therefore will have demonstrated a significant dedication to the club operations over a long period of time, and (b) there is a tendency in small clubs for the majority of work to be performed by a small group made up of a few individuals, and hence these same individuals would have considerable influence over club operations. Shibli et al. (1999) also noted the disproportionate division of labour within voluntary sport clubs.

Nichols and Shepherd (2006) as well as many others (e.g., Horch and Schutte, 2003; Nichols et al., 2005; Papadimitriou, 2002) have noted that a key external pressure on voluntary sport clubs is to professionalize their operations and focus on improving their service delivery, in line with standards experienced in the private sector. Indeed, the research by Nichols and Shepherd (2006) showed that members of sport clubs exerted some pressure for a more service-oriented club rather than joining because of any shared collective values they may hold with that club.

Some research on voluntary sport organizations and sport volunteers is making greater use of the mainstream literature and theory to understand the sports context. Nichols and Ojala (2009) used psychological contract theory in a case study of event managers and sport event volunteers. Their results suggested that sport volunteers could offer some unique attributes to events but that there were also a number of significant challenges for managers to recognize in managing this population. The use of psychological contract theory highlights the expectations of volunteers and how they differ from those of paid staff and managers. The result is an interesting discussion of this relationship through the use of qualitative methods, which is a unique approach in research using psychological contract theory.

Byers and colleagues (2007) examined **control** in voluntary sport clubs and drew on theories of power and control in order to present a new conceptualization of the control concept which is contextualized and holistic. With this new conceptualization, their empirical data revealed a complex array of control mechanisms operating simultaneously within voluntary sport clubs. These mechanisms ranged from formal administrative mechanisms through to social mechanisms such as capital and emotion, as well as self-control mechanisms emanating from each individual's motivation for action.

Voluntary sport organizations, sport volunteers and the wider voluntary sport sector have been the subject of increasing attention by researchers, partly due to the growth of a need for volunteers in sport and events and therefore a greater need to understand existing practices. Research on sport clubs is growing as these organizations have been and are currently experiencing considerable pressures to change, become more professional, engage with national government policy and formalize their contribution to **sport development** systems. Byers (2009) presented an overview of research on voluntary sport organizations in more detail, highlighting the diversity of studies conducted. She discussed this research using three categories:

- volunteer characteristics;
- limitations and a lack of resources;
- functional aspects of voluntary sport.

In her work, the reader will find reference to many of the concepts presented in this book including **decision making**, **change** and **policy**. In addition, there are some suggestions for areas requiring future research and comment on the appropriate methodology required in the field. Given the size and importance of the voluntary sector and the growth in research devoted to volunteering, voluntary organizations and the wider voluntary sector, we would suggest that one fruitful endeavour for future research would be more systematic analysis of the current literature in order to gauge the current knowledge that exists, where theory requires further verification, and where new theory is needed.

To understand voluntary more fully, the reader may refer to the concepts of **context**, **sport development**, **change**, **sport policy**, **sport organizations** and **control** that can be found elsewhere in this book.

FURTHER READING

For some further reading on this concept, we would recommend the following:

Byers, T. (2009) Research on voluntary sport organizations: established themes and emerging opportunities. *International Journal of Sport Management and Marketing*, 6(2): 215–228.

Clark, J., Kane, D., Wilding, K. and Wilton, J. (2010) *UK Civil Society Almanac 2010.* London: NCVO.

Nichols, G. and Ojala, E. (2009) Understanding the management of sports events volunteers through psychological contract theory. *VOLUNTAS: International Journal of Voluntary and Nonprofit Organizations,* 20(4): 369–387.

Skille, E.A. (2008) Understanding sport clubs as sport policy implementers: a theoretical framework for the analysis of implementation of central sport policy through local and voluntary sport organizations. *International Review for the Sociology of Sport,* 43(2): 181–200.

BIBLIOGRAPHY

Byers, T. (2009) Research on voluntary sport organizations: established themes and emerging opportunities. *International Journal of Sport Management and Marketing,* 6(2): 215–228.

Byers, T., Henry, I. and Slack, T. (2007) Understanding control in voluntary sport organisations. In M.M. Parent and T. Slack (eds), *International Perspectives on the Management of Sport.* London: Elsevier.

Clark, J., Kane, D., Wilding, K. and Wilton, J. (2010) *UK Civil Society Almanac 2010.* London: NCVO.

Coleman, R. (2002) Characteristics of volunteering in UK sport: lessons from cricket. *Managing Leisure,* 7: 220–238.

Commission on the Future of Volunteering (2008) *Manifesto for Change.* Volunteering England, www.volcomm.org.uk

Cuskelly, G. (2004) Volunteer retention in community sport organisations. *European Sport Management Quarterly,* 4: 59–76.

Davies, L. (2004) Valuing the voluntary sector in sport: rethinking economic analysis. *Leisure Studies,* 23(4): 347–364.

Davis Smith, J. (1998) *The 1997 National Survey of Volunteering.* London: Institute of Volunteering Research.

Dhebar, B.B. and Stokes, B. (2008) A nonprofit manager's guide to online volunteering. *Nonprofit Management and Leadership,* 18(4): 497–506.

Garrett, R. (2004) The response of voluntary sport clubs to Sport England's Lottery funding: cases of compliance, change and resistance. *Managing Leisure,* 9: 13–29.

Green, M. and Oakley, M. (2001) Elite sport development systems and playing to win: uniformity and diversity in international approaches. *Leisure Studies,* 20: 247–267.

Guo, C. and Musso, J.A. (2007) Representation in nonprofit and voluntary organizations: a conceptual framework. *Nonprofit and Voluntary Sector Quarterly,* 36(2): 308–326.

Horch, H.D. and Schutte, N. (2003) *Sportmanager in vereinen und verbanden.* Koln: Strauss.

Houlihan, B. (1997) *Sport, Policy and Politics: A Comparative Analysis.* London: Routledge.

Inglis, S. (1997) Roles of the board in amateur sport organizations. *Journal of Sport Management,* 11(2): 160–176.

Kendall, J. (2003) *The Voluntary Sector: Comparative Perspectives in the UK.* London: Routledge.

Kirk, D. and MacPhail, A. (2003) Social positioning and the construction of a youth sport club. *International Review for the Sociology of Sport,* 38(1): 23–24.

Nichols, G. and Ojala, E. (2009) Understanding the management of sports events volunteers through psychological contract theory. *VOLUNTAS: International Journal of Voluntary and Nonprofit Organizations,* 20(4): 369–387.

Nichols, G. and Padmore, J. (2005) Who are the volunteers in sports clubs? Sheffield University Management School, working paper.

Nichols, G. and Shepherd, M. (2006) Volunteering in sport: the use of ratio analysis to analyse volunteering and participation. *Managing Leisure,* 11: 205–216.

Nichols, G., Taylor, P., James, M., Holmes, K., King, L. and Garnett, R. (2005) Pressures on UK voluntary sport sector. *VOLUNTAS: International Journal of Voluntary and Nonprofit Organizations*, 16(1): 33–50.

Papadimitriou, D. (2002) Amateur structures and their effect on performance: the case of Greek voluntary sport clubs. *Managing Leisure*, 7(4): 205–219.

Pearce, J. (1993) *Volunteers: The Organizational Behavior of Unpaid Workers*. London: Routledge.

Pfister, G. (2006) Gender issues in Danish sports organizations: experiences, attitudes and evaluations. *Nordic Journal of Women's Studies*, 14(1): 27–40.

Seippel, Ø. (2004) The world according to voluntary sport organizations: voluntarism, economy and facilities. *International Review for the Sociology of Sport*, 39(2): 223–232.

Seippel, Ø. (2005) Sport, civil society and social integration. *Journal of Civil Society*, 1(3): 65–78.

Shibli, S., Taylor, P., Nichols, G., Gratton, C. and Kokolakakis, T. (1999) The characteristics of volunteers in UK sports clubs. *European Journal for Sport Management*, 6 (Special Issue): 10–27.

Skille, E.A. (2008) Understanding sport clubs as sport policy implementers: a theoretical framework for the analysis of implementation of central sport policy through local and voluntary sport organizations. *International Review for the Sociology of Sport*, 43(2): 181–200.

Slack, T. and Thibault, L. (1988) Values and beliefs: their role in the structuring of national sport organizations. *ARENA Review*, 12: 140–155.

Sport England (2003) *Sports Volunteering in England in 2002: A Summary Report*. London: Sport England.

Sport England (2007) *The Economic Importance of Sport in England 1985–2005*. London: Sport England.

Sports Council for Wales (2008) *The Economic Importance of Sport in Wales*. Cardiff: Sports Council for Wales.

Key concepts are important to identify in any field of study, for students or academics undertaking research. They are also useful for sport practitioners trying to solve problems or improve their working practices. This book offers students, academics and practitioners some useful ideas on concepts which have been identified in both the organization theory literature and in the wider literature on managing sport organizations as key to organizations generally and to the management of sport specifically. For students and researchers, the information provided on each concept provides a variety of references as a starting point for developing appropriate research questions and constructing a literature review.

The concepts presented in this book are those that are found in the organization theory literature and the broader fields of study within research on the management of sport (e.g., sport marketing, sports law, sponsorship) are present both implicitly and at times explicitly in research on the management of sport. This is not necessarily a criticism but something of note that anyone doing research needs to be conscious of; i.e., which key concept is the focus of their study and which related concepts (and literature) may need to be considered in order to answer their research aims. We have demonstrated the *interrelatedness* of the concepts included in this book and while we could not provide an extensive review of the literature for every concept, we have tried to give the reader a good selection of the research that currently exists in the field of management/organization studies generally and in the management of sport specifically.

As time passes, however, research ideas and directions will change and thus it is necessary to seek current sources of information on the concepts we have presented. To assist the reader in this task we now turn to summarize some of the sources which are most useful for this purpose. Once again, while this is not an exhaustive list it does identify many of the key sources that the reader may find useful when they begin their search.

Keeping up to Date: Journals

As can be seen with each concept there are a wide variety of journals which publish research on sport organizations and an even greater variety of journals which focus on organizations generally. However, we consider the key journals that publish organization theory and topics on the management of sport to include the *Journal of Sport Management* (a publication of the North American Society for Sport Management – NASSM) and the *European Sport Management Quarterly* (the journal of the European Association of Sport Management – EASM). Alternatively the reader may be interested in looking at *Sport Management*

Review (the journal of the Sport Management Association of Australia and New Zealand – SMAANZ), the *International Journal of Sport Management and Marketing* (IJSMM), or the *International Journal of Sport Management*. A relatively new journal launched by the publishers Emerald is *Sport, Business and Management*.

There is also the *International Review of the Sociology of Sport* which we have often cited in this book. Of course we would recognize here that these sport-specific journals contain research other than organization standard theory-focused issues. A small amount of sport management and sport policy-related literature can be found in the *European Journal of Sport Science* and the *Journal of Sport Sciences*. Other journals that publish articles on specific aspects of the management of sport include the following:

- *Managing Leisure*
- *International Journal of Sport Policy*
- *International Journal of Sport Marketing and Sponsorship*
- *International Journal of Sport Finance*
- *Journal of Sport Economics.*

We have also mentioned a few journals published in languages other than English and increasingly, as the academic discipline and industry of sport management expand globally, publications are appearing in a variety of foreign languages. Although it is beyond the scope of this book and the authors' language skills to include all the languages which publish relevant literature related to the management of sport, we would wish to make the reader aware of the fact that publications do occur in languages other than English. Some examples include:

- *Revue Économique*
- *Revue Européenne de Management du Sport*
- *International Journal of Sport and Recreation Management* (Greek)
- *Economy and Sport* (Greek).

In addition to these, we would recommend examining the contents of generic management journals such as *Organization Studies, Journal of Management Studies, Administrative Science Quarterly, Organization, Human Relations, Organizational Science, The Academy of Management Review, Journal of Business Ethics, International Journal of Management Reviews, Corporate Governance, An International Review* and *Academy of Management Journal.*

The reader should also be aware that journals can be 'ranked' by various organizations and systems to indicate their quality and therefore the quality of the material published within a particular journal. This is not an absolute measure of the strength and reliability of a journal but it can give some indication of its developmental stage. One such ranking system is the Association of Business Schools' (ABS) 'star system'. The ABS is an independent organization representing over 100 business schools in the United Kingdom and produces a journal quality guide, suggesting:

The ABS Academic Journal Quality Guide is a hybrid based partly on peer review, partly on statistical information relating to citation, and partly upon editorial judgements following on from the detailed evaluation of many hundreds of publications over a long period.

It provides guides to the range, subject matter and relative quality of journals in which business and management and economics academics might publish the results of their research – empirical and theoretical. The journals included cover a wide range of disciplines, fields and sub-fields within the social sciences, representing an inclusive approach to what constitutes business and management research.

(http://www.the-abs.org.uk/?id=257)

Another measure of journal quality is to examine its 'impact factor'. This is a measure of the frequency with which a journal has been cited within a particular year. The system was developed by the Institute for Scientific Information (ISI) which is now part of Thomson Reuters. Impact factors can be found in the *Journal Citation Reports* (http://thomsonreuters.com/products_services/science/science_products/a-z/journal_citation_reports).

However, the reader should also evaluate journal articles individually and examine the theory and methods applied within articles rather than relying solely on ranking systems. Many sport-related journals produce relevant and good quality research in the field of sport management but have yet to be recognized or even to fully engage with the ranking systems. One exception is the *Journal of Sport Management* which is listed in the ABS guide. The *European Journal of Sport Science, European Sport Management Quarterly* and the *Journal of Sport Science* are also listed in the ISI *Journal Citation Reports* along with the relevant impact factors.

In addition there are also a number of periodicals and trade publications which are either devoted to issues and concepts related to the management of sport or publish articles on sport management-related issues. These include:

- *Advertising Age*
- *Forbes*
- *Business Week*
- *Hollis Sponsorship* (www.hollis-sponsorship.com)
- *Sport Business International*
- *Sport Business Newsline* (http://www.sportbusiness.com/get-newslines).

Other journals that publish articles which would be of interest to people who study sport management include:

- *Quest*
- *Culture, Sport, Society*
- *Soccer and Society.*

index

index